Unfinished Business

Closing the Racial Achievement Gap in Our Schools

Pedro A. Noguera

Jean Yonemura Wing

EDITORS

JOSSEY-BASS
A Wiley Imprint
www.josseybass.com

Published by Jossey-Bass
A Wiley Imprint
989 Market Street, San Francisco, CA 94103-1741   www.josseybass.com

Jossey-Bass books and products are available through most bookstores. To contact Jossey-Bass directly call our Customer Care Department within the U.S. at 800-956-7739, outside the U.S. at 317-572-3986, or fax 317-572-4002.

Jossey-Bass also publishes its books in a variety of electronic formats. Some content that appears in print may not be available in electronic books.

Library of Congress Cataloging-in-Publication Data

Unfinished business : closing the racial achievement gap in our schools / Pedro Noguera & Jean Yonemura Wing, editors.— 1st ed.
    p. cm. — (Jossey-Bass education series)
  Includes bibliographical references and index.
  ISBN-13: 978-0-4703-8444-2 (paperback)
  ISBN-13: 978-0-7879-7275-2 (alk. paper)
  1. Educational equalization—United States. 2. Academic achievement—United States. 3. Minorities—Education—United States. I. Noguera, Pedro. II. Wing, Jean Yonemura, 1949- III. Series.
  LC213.2.U49 2006
  379.2'6—dc22

                                    2005032614

Printed in the United States of America
FIRST EDITION
PB Printing   10 9 8 7 6 5 4 3 2
HB Printing   10 9 8 7 6 5 4 3 2 1

Contents

Acknowledgments

When we began the Berkeley High School Diversity Project with our goal of closing the racial achievement gap, our hope was that one day, we would become so integral to the school community that it would be difficult to tell who was officially a part of the project and who was not. Over our years of work, we came very close to reaching this goal. We gratefully acknowledge all of the students, teachers, staff, and parents of Berkeley High School, especially the students of the graduating class of 2000 and the teachers, parents, and staff who volunteered their time and opened their classroom doors, and who opened their hearts and minds to the possibility that age-old patterns of segregation and inequity were neither normal nor unchangeable.

We acknowledge the hard work and commitment of those who served on the Diversity Project Core Team over the years: vice principal James Williams; teachers Susan Groves, Dick LeBlanc, Julia González Luna, Dana Moran, Leslie Plettner, LaShawn Routé Chatmon, and Miriam Stahl; University of California at Berkeley graduate students Tamara Friedman, Emma Fuentes, Anne Gregory, Susan Rebecca Malberg, Lance McCready, Pharmicia Mosely, Anne Okahara, Cheryl Roberts, Anthony Rojo, Beth Rubin, Elena Silva, and Jean Yonemura Wing; and university faculty members Ronald Glass, Jabari Mahiri, and Pedro Noguera.

Special thanks go to those who were a part of the Diversity Project Extended Team: students Siobhan Acosta, Leticia Brown, Joey Christiano, Annie Duong, Eleanor Mayer, Jamie McMaryion, and Santiago Rizzo; administrator Doris Wallace Tanner; teachers

Rick Ayers, Judith Bodenhausen, Terry Doran, John Fike, Amy Hansen, Annie Johnston, John Nigro, Marie Roberts, Dave Stevens, and Louis Thomas; college adviser Rory Bled; counselor Regina Segura; classified staff members Barbara Mellion, Isabel Parra, and Betty Spillman; parents Julina Bastidas-Bonilla, Matica Manuel-Barkin, Robin Ortiz-Young, Peggy Newgarden Seals, and Juana Villegas; Berkeley School Board members Pamela Doolan, Ted Schultz, and Miriam Topel; associate superintendent Nancy Spaeth; University of California at Berkeley undergraduate student Vajra Watson; graduate students Antwi Akom, Colette Cann, Kysa Nygreen, and Maika Watanabe; graduate student research committee members Andrea Dyrness, Soo Ah Kwan, Patricia Sanchez, and Amanda Lashaw; office managers Ann Lee and Alexandria Thornton; volunteers Shane Adler, Samantha Broun, Tony deJesus, Lila Jacobs, and Alicia P. Rodriguez, and Dafney Dabach; and ex officio members, superintendent Jack McLaughlin and principals Lawrence Lee and Theresa Saunders.

We also acknowledge the work of the members of the Diversity Project's Parent Outreach Committee, including Amanda Alarcon, Lattice Banks, Linda DeLane, Sharon Finley, Yolanda Gaitan, Maria Guerrero, Clementina Gutierrez, Henrietta Hansen, Kuaji Hill, Denise James, Altheria "Liz" Jinks, Euloiza Jorge, Matica Manuel-Barkin, Denise McCoy, Karen McKie, Beth Montaño, Barbara Morita, Maria Padilla, Rita Perez, Nohemi Rodriguez, Patricia Vattuone, and other staff and parents from the Diversity Project's Core Team and Extended Team.

Thanks to all of the members of the Diversity Project's Student Outreach Committee, including Bianca Bonilla, Danielle Cameron, Juan Castillo, Mia Gittlin, Joseph Graly, Shanique Griffin, Marc Hand-Wright, Adrian Hill, Freddy James, Nabilah Lester, Vanessa Nelson, Nikitra Newell, Chantip Phongkhamsavath, Shabnam Piryaei, Vanessa Reed, Stacey Reid, Sara Rutherford, Valentino Salgado, Sadiyah Seraaj, Stefen, Jundid Sykes, Daniel Timnit, Rubert Trujillo, Kalsang Tsesel, Jacob Zim, and other students, staff, and graduate students from the Diversity Project's Core Team and Extended Team.

We extend our appreciation to the teachers who participated in the 1998 Summer Institute and in the Diversity Project's Action Research for Teachers, including Leorah Abouav-Zilberman, Rick Ayers, Susanna Bell, Stefani Black, Ellen Bracken, Donatella Carta, José Colon, Amy Crawford, Hodari Davis, James Dopman, Debolina Dutta, Rebekka Ford, Natasha Fuksman, Ken Gonzales, Rodrigo Gutierrez, Joel Hildebrandt, Leah Katz, Jonathan Maier, Crystal McClendon, Nancy McDonald, Alan Miller, Josephine Noah, Kamala Parks, Anne Peacock, Bill Pratt, Marisol Ruiz, Flora Russ, Wyn Skeels, Marcela Taylor, and aforementioned teachers from the Core Team and Extended Team.

We are also grateful to those in the Berkeley High School and larger Berkeley community who supported the work of the Diversity Project in so many different ways: Irma Parker, Katrina Scott-George, Michael D. Miller, and the Parents of Children of African Descent; Father George Crespin and Berkeley Organizing Congregations for Action; staff members Charlene Calvert, Antonio Castro, Daniel Liou, Robert McKnight, and Ernestine Troutman; parents Terry and Peter Bloomsburgh, Fredda Cassidy, and David Watanabe; the East Bay Asian Youth Center's RISE program; and Eugene Garcia, dean of the University of California at Berkeley's Graduate School of Education.

And finally, the Diversity Project would not have existed without the generosity and support of our funders, including Eleanor Clement Glass and the San Francisco Foundation; Nina Moore and Hardy Frye of the University of California Office of the President; Phyllis Friedman of the Howard and Phyllis Friedman Philanthropic Fund of the Jewish Community Endowment Fund; Mary Friedman and the Berkeley Public Education Foundation; Anita Madrid and the Berkeley Pledge of the Chancellor's Office of the University of California at Berkeley; the Bay Area School Reform Collaborative's School-University Partnership; Ray Bachetti and the William and Flora Hewlett Foundation; the University of California at Berkeley Academic Senate Faculty Research Grants; and the Vanguard Public Foundation.

This book is dedicated to all of the teachers, administrators, school board members, parents, and students who have the courage and conviction to stand up to ensure that all children receive an education that expands opportunities and cultivates their talent and potential.

Courage and conviction are necessary because the forces of inequity are powerful. Too many schools and too many educators in the United States have grown accustomed to seeing their students drop out, lose interest in learning, and give up on education. For those who realize that public education continues to be the best—and in some cases the only—hope for poor children, and for those who understand that the struggle to create just and equitable schools that succeed in educating all children is the most important civil rights issue of the twenty-first century, we offer this book as a source of insight and inspiration on what can be done to further your efforts.

During those moments when you feel isolated for speaking up for students who are being treated unfairly, when you are attacked for exposing injustice, and when you are exhausted from putting in long hours to help students in need, know that others share your commitment and are your allies. This is not a struggle that lends itself to easy victories or simple solutions. But because so much is at stake, we hope that you will never regard your efforts as being in vain.

Preface

This book is about unfinished business—the nation's as yet unfulfilled commitment to equality and justice for all. Our focus is on the possibilities for achieving these lofty goals through public education, arguably our nation's most equitable and democratic institution.

Public schools occupy a special place in American society. They are the only institutions that have an obligation to serve all children, regardless of race, gender, ability, national origin, religion, or status. Increasingly, our public schools are also all that remains of the nation's safety net for the poor. They are the only places where children can be guaranteed a meal (often two), adult supervision, a relative degree of safety, heat in the winter, and even some minimal provision of health care. Those who know schools also know that these services are largely inadequate; there are too many poor children in America whose most basic needs—food, shelter, and health care—are largely unmet. Given that public schools are the only institutions that take on the responsibility of serving all children, the role they play should not be dismissed or taken for granted.

Of course, too often we do take these aspects for granted because we expect more of schools. Serving warm lunches and doling out Band-Aids when needed may be laudable, but the American public wants more. We want schools that will enable the United States to maintain its economic and technological dominance in the world. We want schools that will provide students with the knowledge, understanding, and habits of mind to participate intelligently in our democracy. And we also look to our schools to solve a wide variety of our nation's problems: global warming, sexually transmitted diseases, homelessness, drug abuse, and youth violence, to name just a few. Given our expectations, it is hardly surprising that schools fall miserably short.

National polls indicate that while the public believes in the importance of public education, many are largely unsatisfied with what they receive. Too many students succeed in spite of schools, not because of them. Too many students attend schools that leave them bored, unmotivated, and deeply alienated. Our national dropout rate reflects that large numbers of students do not hold much faith in what our schools have to offer; they vote with their feet, hoping that better opportunities lie elsewhere.

If we are to restore the public's faith, we have to do more than point out the accessibility and reliability of public schools as providers of social services. The public wants more, and part of what a segment of the public wants is some evidence that our schools can serve as the great equalizer of opportunity—the bold vision that Horace Mann once used to mobilize support for public education.

Fulfilling the promise of public education is the reason that so many schools and districts are now working desperately to find ways to close the achievement gap. The persistence of wide disparities in achievement that correspond with the race and class backgrounds of students serves as a reminder that America remains a deeply divided nation, a place where the lines separating the haves and the have-nots are manifest in every facet of our lives. While we may not yet have the wherewithal or commitment as a nation to close the gap in income, health, housing, or criminal justice, many Americans believe that we should be able to do it in education. Whether we succeed may serve as the ultimate test of our nation's proclaimed commitment to equality and justice for all.

Education has historically served as the primary means through which groups that have been excluded have been incorporated. For African Americans and others, obtaining access to education has been at times a life-and-death struggle, as important as any of the other basic rights associated with citizenship. From racial discrimination to gender equity, from language rights to educational opportunities for the disabled, our public schools have been at the forefront of expanding opportunities to the disenfranchised and invigorating the practice of democracy. Those who understand the relationship between civil rights and public education understand that while the U.S. Supreme Court's rulings have conferred these rights, the task of making them real has fallen to activists and educators.

This generation of educators has been called on to reduce racial disparities in achievement—to move beyond equity in opportunities and focus attention on the need for equity in results. It is a tall order, and once again we are demanding more of schools, and too often castigating them when they fail to deliver.

This is why we wrote *Unfinished Business*. We believe the public needs to understand why it is so hard to produce equitable schools in a society premised on inequality. We also believe that the story of the work we engaged in to expand opportunities for disadvantaged students and the obstacles we encountered along the way might be beneficial to others—not because we succeeded in achieving our goal but simply because we hope others might learn from our lessons and mistakes.

About This Book

The work described in this book was carried out by educators, students, and parents, and for that reason we have chosen to incorporate their voices and perspectives. As a result, this book may have a sense of many styles of expression and cadences, and perhaps an uneven feel, but we believe that including these multiple perspectives is important for the story that needs to be told. Who better to describe the difficulties in teaching a heterogeneously grouped class than a teacher who has done it? Who could more accurately describe how it feels to be excluded from important decisions that affect the quality of their education than students, who typically are silenced and shut out of the school reform processes? And who better than parents can articulate the hopes and frustrations of working with schools to ensure that their children receive an education that will prepare them for adulthood?

This book is the collective product of the individuals who worked on and with the Diversity Project at Berkeley High School, in Berkeley, California, from 1996 to 2002. It reflects their experiences and the insights they have gained from years of research and organizing to close the achievement gap at this integrated public high school that is nevertheless so segregated from within that it has been described as "two schools under one roof." This book is put together and written in ways that we hope will be of interest to parents and students, teachers and university educators, school reformers and community organizers, and to all others concerned with public education, racial equality, and democracy.

How This Book Is Organized

The chapters of this book are organized under broad themes of the structure and culture of schooling, and agency in the fight for equity. There are two main parts to the book. Part One contains research data, analyses, and background information regarding Berkeley High School and the Diversity Project. All student, teacher, and staff names in Part One are pseudonyms.

In Part Two we hear the many voices of teachers, parents, and students who participated as full partners in the work of the Diversity Project, along with a description and analyses of the project's parent and student outreach committees and its teacher professional development efforts.

The Introduction by the coeditors situates the Berkeley High School Diversity Project in the context of Berkeley's long-standing reputation for being in the forefront of progressive social change and in a broader national context of efforts to close the racial achievement gap in schools and districts across the United States. It describes Berkeley's voluntary desegregation of public schools in

1968 and the conditions that gave rise to the Diversity Project in 1996, nearly thirty years later. Finally, it provides the theory of change and the organizational structure of the Diversity Project, including its action research and outreach committees that provide the data for all of the subsequent chapters in this book.

Chapter One, by Beth C. Rubin, Jean Yonemura Wing, Pedro A. Noguera, Emma Fuentes, Daniel Liou, Alicia P. Rodriguez, and Lance T. McCready, discusses the policies, practices, and organization of the high school that contribute to achievement disparities between white and nonwhite, rich and poor, English speakers and non-English speakers, males and females, and to racial separation throughout the school's academic and extracurricular programs. Rubin and Wing analyze the way that students are tracked, "Berkeley High style," and document the resulting education gap for the students of the high school's class of 2000, using data from the Diversity Project's class of 2000 longitudinal study. Fuentes and Liou, using data from the project's English as a Second Language study, describe the school's English Language Learner program and show that even a hard-working, well-intentioned staff has not been enough to help immigrant students overcome the institutional barriers they face at the school. Rodriguez, drawing from ethnographic data in the school's ninth-grade ethnic studies program, illuminates the unequal opportunities for, treatment of, and responses of girls and boys. Finally, McCready uses data from the project's Taking Stock study to examine the school structures that perpetuate informal racial segregation in extracurricular clubs and activities, as well as cocurricular activities (such as the school newspaper or student leadership class) that carry course credit and athletic teams, some of which could substitute for required physical education classes.

In Chapter Two, Jean Yonemura Wing examines the ways in which social, cultural, and economic capital grease the track to elite colleges for those with the right connections, knowledge, and private supports. Using case studies of individual students in the class of 2000, Wing compares the experiences of a privileged white female student and a Vietnamese male student living below the poverty line—the former relying on a network of friends, tutors, and a private college adviser and the latter relying entirely on the school to guide him toward his college dream.

Anne Gregory, Kysa Nygreen, and Dana Moran draw extensively in Chapter Three from research conducted by the Diversity Project's Discipline Committee and question why a high school in a progressive community such as Berkeley produces the same racialized patterns of discipline as seen in urban schools throughout the country. Referring to the disproportionate punishment meted out to African American male students as the "discipline gap," they demonstrate how these practices mirror the academic achievement gap. They also show how the gross racial inequities in the school disciplinary system parallel those in the larger U.S. criminal justice system and how the differential treatment of black students comes to be seen as "normal," even in Berkeley.

Chapter Four is the initial chapter in Part Two. The author, Pharmicia Mosely, traces the Diversity Project's efforts to use equity-focused professional development and action research by teachers to change teacher practices, improve teacher–student relations, and address the achievement gap inside their own classrooms. This work, led by teachers themselves, was regarded as pivotal to the Diversity Project. We recognized that even if we succeeded in changing inequitable structures and policies at the school, if there was no change in what transpired in the classrooms, the achievement gap would continue to be reproduced. Mosely's introduction is followed by personal accounts of the challenges of teaching to close the achievement gap, written by eight teachers who participated in the Diversity Project or its Action Research for Teachers team: Dana Moran, LaShawn Routé-Chatmon, Miriam K. Stahl, Tamara Friedman, Leslie Plettner, Susannah Bell, Magi Discoe, and James Dopman.

Drawing from the work and data of the Parent Outreach Committee, Chapter Five, by LaShawn Routé-Chatmon, Katrina Scott-George, Anne K. Okahara, Emma Fuentes, Jean Y. Wing, and Pedro A. Noguera describes the Diversity Project's role and evolving strategy to organize, mobilize, and empower parents of color, who had historically been marginalized at Berkeley High School. It also documents the ongoing parent activism for equity that took up where the Diversity Project left off. We have included in this chapter the individual voices and experiences of seven parent leaders and organizers: Isabel Parra, Julina Bastidas Bonilla, Michael D. Miller, Juana Villegas, Vikki Davis, Liz Fuentes, and Valerie B. Yerger.

In Chapter Six, Elena Silva describes the experience of the Diversity Project's Student Outreach Committee, including efforts, or lack thereof, to engage students in action research on issues related to diversity and equity. This chapter documents both the promising practices and the formidable obstacles to organizing a diverse group of students to participate and have a genuine voice in schoolwide equity reform. Following Silva's account are reflections by seven diverse students—Nabila Lester, Joey Christiano, Jimmy Thong Tran, Pranoumphone (Pam) Pradachith, Jamie McMaryion, Shabnam Piryaei, and Niles Xi'an Lichtenstein—who provide seven different windows into the student experience at Berkeley High.

In the Conclusion, volume coeditor Pedro A. Noguera draws lessons from the shortcomings of the Diversity Project's strategy as well as the lasting legacy of its work. Even as he acknowledges the limitations of the project, he also speaks of urgent unfinished business: the ongoing need to work for racial equity in all public schools.

Finally, Jabari Mahiri's Epilogue reflects on the first four years of the Diversity Project, during which most of the major research and organizing took place, and bridges to the final two years during which the Diversity Project participated in schoolwide parent- and teacher-led reform initiatives to address widespread academic failure of students of color and to explore the potential benefits of small schools sharing a single campus. He looks into the advances made and the obstacles encountered, and ponders whether our efforts have succeeded in taking us closer to our goals.

Unfinished Business has been written because we believe that public education is vital for a healthy democracy. We also believe that schools can play a decisive role in making our nation less divided and fractured on the basis of race, class, culture, gender, and language. Our business remains unfinished, but as long as people across America continue to take up this work of making schools more just and equitable, then the business is simply unfinished, not abandoned. That may hardly seem like a victory, but in times like these, it remains a basis for hope.

December 2005

Pedro A. Noguera
Jean Yonemura Wing

Preface to the
Paperback Edition

Since *Unfinished Business* was published in 2006, there have been developments in the ongoing struggle for equity at Berkeley High School (BHS). By all reports, the school feels less chaotic and more stable. Fewer students linger in the hallways and school grounds during class time. Principal Jim Slemp, now entering his sixth year, has ended the revolving door of school leadership that saw five principals come and go over an eight-year period. Perhaps the most promising reform aimed at closing the achievement gap is the creation of four small "schools within a school"—Communication Arts and Sciences (CAS), Community Partnerships Academy (CP Academy), Arts and Humanities Academy (AHA!), and the School of Social Justice and Ecology (SSJE), mentioned in this book's Epilogue by Jabari Mahiri.

In April 2008, the editors convened a roundtable discussion with several former Diversity Project members, including some still at BHS, as well as some teachers who came after the project ended in 2002: Dana Moran, Miriam Stahl, Irma Parker, Flora Russ, Jabari Mahiri, Colette Cann, Tamara Friedman, Susannah Bell, Vajra Watson, Rick Ayers, Jessica Quindel, Kimberley Noel D'Adamo-Muanga, Jaime Knight, Terry Goodman, and Jean Wing. In the following pages we provide excerpts from that conversation as an update to this paperback edition, and as a way of reminding our readers that the efforts to pursue educational equity are ongoing.

Small Schools as Pockets of Hope

Small schools have emerged as pockets of hope. While each small school varies considerably in its organization and focus, we see evidence of unprecedented success with students who were previously not well served by the big high school. At the same time, although they were originally envisioned as a reform to further equity, the small schools serve only about a third of the 3,300 BHS students, and they have primarily attracted students of color through the lottery system. The "big school," serving the remaining two-thirds, offers two academic programs: Academic Choice (AC) and Berkeley International High School (BIHS, or International Baccalaureate). These two programs serve a population that is disproportionately white and significantly more academically prepared and higher achieving than students in the small schools.

The four small schools have different emphases but share an important common quality: all take responsibility for their students in a way that differs from the big school programs. Miriam Stahl, a founder of AHA!, said it best:

> The big change of small schools is in taking responsibility for a cohort of students, and for each student in that cohort. In traditional departments, teachers feel responsible for a curriculum, not for students and their learning.

Flora Russ, founder of CP Academy and its predecessor, Computer Academy, adds the element of small schools opening doors of opportunity:

> It's not enough to be great teachers, because our kids have so many other needs. Each of us must pick up the extra pieces to make sure that our kids have *every* opportunity, whether it means access to scholarships, internships, tutors, experiences, travel—whatever it may be.

Small schools have also found creative ways to raise the level of academic learning and achievement. CAS and CP Academy have simultaneously detracked and accelerated their math program for all of their students. Instead of having ninth graders separated into two different levels (equivalent to Algebra I and Geometry), these small schools place every ninth grader into the higher Geometry-equivalent level, thereby making it possible to reach the Math Analysis level by junior year, with the option of taking Calculus in senior year. This change also increases the likelihood that students will complete the minimum math courses required for eligibility to the state universities. Jessica Quindel, a CAS math teacher, explains:

> Every ninth grader who has skills issues in mathematics has an additional math class, about fifteen to twenty students. We've had a tremendous amount of students of color making it all the way to [Math Analysis level]. Yet when I walk into Math Analysis classes in the big school, I don't see Black and Latino students.

Despite the significance of small victories like these, teachers readily admit that such changes have not moved the larger high school in a direction of equity. In fact, some believe that the creation of these small schools, which are willing to serve students with greater academic needs, may have inadvertently absolved the larger school of its responsibility to serve such students. Still, efforts are being made to further greater equity and student support in the big school. Miriam Stahl describes one such effort, the proposed implementation of an advisory system throughout the high school. She says:

> There was a very bright light, a hope that Advisories were going to happen, but it was shot down because of pressure on the School Board. The best hope that I personally had for an Advisory program was that it would attach every teacher in the school to either a small school or a program in the big school. Inevitably, they would have a cohort of kids, and could have that collegiality that

small schools have around coming up with strategies that best serve our kids. I saw this as the way that the department structure was going to be broken down into really being about a group of kids.

Flora Russ sees it differently, commenting that

Advisories are not happening, but they are not gone—they are still there on the parking lot. But what happened during the last couple of years, we went from people saying advisories are awful, we don't want them, to people accepting that it was going to happen.

Jabari Mahiri, the Diversity Project's principal investigator during its final two years, observes an unintended consequence of the plan to convert only part of the school into small schools. He asks:

To what extent will small schools actually change the culture of the larger school? What we didn't anticipate is that the alterations might actually be further shields for the real structural issues that were complicating the problems of equity and achievement in the first place. This is not to denigrate the small schools, because they're doing good work for a number of students. But there are still twice as many students in the big school than in all the small schools combined.

Rick Ayers, a founder of CAS, adds:

From the beginning, we knew it was a false claim to say we could narrow the achievement gap if we did not deeply change the way we were assessing students and the content of our teaching. Without autonomy and a chance to stretch out in creative curriculum development, with a general discourse and "body of knowledge" that is locked in the white middle class discourse of American schools, we will not change that. So we see pockets of this turnaround, success for all students, but it is difficult to institutionalize.

Tracking and Segregation

Unfinished Business documents what the achievement gap looked like from 1996 to 2000, and the Diversity Project recommended that the district and high school use our findings as a baseline to evaluate its progress in closing the gap over time. However, since the project ended in 2002, there has been no systematic reporting on the achievement gap.

The four small schools are predominantly made up of students of color, and the academic proficiency gap between students in the small schools and the big school programs is vast. One estimate is that fewer than one in five students in the small schools enters ninth grade at proficiency based on state test scores, compared to three out of four in the big school. As Rick Ayers points out:

> The key contribution of small schools is that we created some successful, untracked classes. But the reality is that these small schools exist within a larger school that is heavily tracked, with an ever-increasing number of AP [Advanced Placement] classes offered to those at the top.

Jessica Quindel adds:

> They're tracked before they even walk in the door. When you start talking about a parent in eighth grade choosing between four small schools and a program called Academic Choice or International Baccalaureate, most parents are going to think: These are the academic ones, and these are not.

Meanwhile, the big school International Baccalaureate program also faces tracking issues. The program is entering its third year and will have students in grades 9–11 next year. Lead teacher Kimberley D'Adamo-Muanga talks about efforts to keep the program untracked:

We've worked really hard to say that all students can succeed in a classroom with really high expectations if teachers work hard enough at it. So for us, in the junior and senior year, all of our kids are going to be taking the highest level of English and History classes offered, no matter what their skill level is. It's about putting in the supports to make that possible. It also means looking at the underlying, invisible beliefs that teachers are bringing into their classrooms. So that's been a struggle.

Meanwhile, the former alternative school, now called Berkeley Technology Academy (B-Tech), continues to serve as a "dumping ground" for students of color who are involuntarily transferred from BHS. Jabari Mahiri reports that during the last academic year

> 95 percent of the students were African American and the other 5 percent were Latino—there were no white students; 65 percent were male, 100 percent qualified for free lunch, and 34 percent were designated as needing special education services.

One AHA! student leader is a case in point. AHA! teachers and the counselor had to intervene to prevent this student, an African American male who happened to get into a couple of minor fights, from being sent to B-Tech. AHA! counselor Terry Goodman states:

> This was a student who in every respect was being served well at Berkeley High, but he "looked like" he belonged at B-Tech. So therefore when something happened that in our minds was actually pretty minor, the administration was very quick to say, well, he looks like a B-Tech student, let's send him there. That mind-set continues at Berkeley High.

Give More to Those Who Need More

As the Diversity Project used to say, equity does not mean equal. To achieve equity necessitates giving more resources to those students who need more. It calls for a reorientation of the teaching profession and the union contract structure to enable students with the greatest needs to have access to the better teachers, who will work the hardest and get paid the most. However, teachers in the small schools experience inequity in workload and pay.

Dana Moran, CAS teacher and co-founder of the Diversity Project, suggests that equity cannot be achieved with the highest-performing students getting the same resources from the school as the lowest-performing students, when some are getting so much more at home. She suggests an alternative:

> For example, AP classes should have forty to forty-five students so that Spanish I or Algebra I classes can have fifteen to twenty students. That would be a more honestly equal workload for those teachers. The AP teacher grades more papers, while the lower-track teacher makes more home phone calls, talks to more counselors—safety officers, social workers, mentors, case managers, probation officers—and so on.

Confronting Privilege

There is a feeling of progress in some expanding pockets of the school. At the same time, transformational change has given way to compromise with those who are accustomed to getting what they want within the status quo. The question was posed: If it can't happen in Berkeley, known for its progressive stance on everything from recycling to voluntary school integration, perhaps it can't happen anywhere.

Vajra Watson, a former BHS student and Diversity Project member, reflects:

> Looking back on the Diversity Project, I think it got really good at engaging certain teachers and parents, which is what the Parent Resource Center is about, and which is phenomenal and powerful. But are those parents on the hill really engaged in the conversation? What does it look like to engage a parent who's coming to Berkeley High because there are more AP classes, to get them on that same page of equity? If it's possible, then how?

Rick Ayers responds:

> Vajra asks, can we win the privileged parents? I think we do, in
> some cases, but the story of BHS is one of privileged parents block-
> ing every reform, patrolling the school to make sure that tracking
> was intact. Do we win them over? Or struggle against them? Defi-
> nitely, the problem is there.

Jessica Quindel adds her thoughts about parents and privilege:

> To me, Berkeley's like any other city. People care about their own
> children differently than they care about other people's children.
> You can care about the environment and global warming and things
> like that, but when it comes to race and class and your kid's educa-
> tion, you might not be, as a parent in the hills, somebody who's will-
> ing to make some sacrifices because you have more.

Perhaps this means that parents of privilege need a different
way of thinking about what's best for their children. Kimberley
D'Adamo-Muanga talks about changing the minds of parents and
students alike:

> It's slow work. It's really changing a lot of paradigms about not only
> race and class, but about what does it mean to be an educated person,
> and what does it mean to be successful. So [in our program] there's
> really a lot of effort in the freshman and sophomore classes to change
> the paradigm of "it's every kid for themselves" and "it matters how
> highly you achieve" more to "how are you helping your classmates?"
> and using some of that to temper the rush for the IB [diploma].

Creating the Demand from Parents and Community

From this discussion about the current state of efforts at Berkeley
High to ensure that all students receive the education they deserve,
it should be obvious why we titled this book *Unfinished Business*.

The BHS experience shows that despite sustained efforts of educators, parents, and students to find ways to close the achievement gap and eliminate the ways in which race and class continue to predict student achievement, the forces that work to maintain inequity are even more powerful. Over and over again, we have found that with every step forward there is clear and undisputable evidence of trends taking the school in the opposite direction.

Yet, the unevenness of progress toward change does not mean that change cannot be achieved. We know this because there are other schools that have made greater progress in closing the achievement gap. In such schools—Ossining High School in New York and Abington High School in Pennsylvania, to cite just two examples—strong leadership is crucial. Strong leadership is needed because the factors that undermine efforts to promote equity are largely political, tied directly to the politics of protecting privilege and to the misperception that any effort to support and further the education of disadvantaged students of color must come at the expense of affluent white students. Without leaders who can organize their staff and community around a vision that reconciles the pursuit of academic excellence with the pursuit of educational equity, the pressures to maintain inequity will almost always prove to be more powerful.

This is why the Diversity Project invested so much effort in organizing African American and Latino parents. In the absence of leadership at the district and site level, we knew that external pressure from parents was the only way to ensure that equity issues were not swept under the rug. We knew that, armed with data and supported by teachers within BHS, parents were the only constituency that could hold the school accountable. Pressure from affluent white parents who seek to ensure that their children receive an education that they deserve is unfortunately one of the major forces responsible for inequity. Too often, such parents fight any effort to reduce tracking, to promote fairness in the allocation of resources, or to make changes in the structure of schools to facilitate improvements in outcomes for all students.

Irma Parker, founder of the BHS Parent Resource Center, put it this way:

> I think that we're going to really have to get back to what we did in the year 2001 when we did the REBOUND! program. We're going to have to reach out and work with the parents. This ray of hope that I see is that we will be able to pin down the new superintendent [William Huyett] and actually get him to start looking at some of these things from the community's standpoint. Because if we work within the realm of the school, I already know that doesn't work. It's some kind of way that one side offsets the other. But when you bring the pressure in from the community, things actually happen.

We are confident that while the business of promoting educational equity and closing the achievement gap may remain unfinished, it is far from over. As long as parents and educators remain vigilant and refuse to accept the injustice of the status quo, the possibility that we will be able to create better and more equitable schools remains alive.

May 2008

Pedro A. Noguera
Jean Yonemura Wing

The Editors

Pedro A. Noguera, Ph.D., is professor in the Steinhardt School of Education at New York University, executive director of the Metropolitan Center for Urban Education, and co-director of the Institute for the Study of Globalization and Education in Metropolitan Settings (IGEMS). An urban sociologist, Noguera's scholarship and research focus on the ways in which schools are influenced by social and economic conditions in the urban environment. He has published over one hundred and fifty research articles, monographs, and research reports on topics such as urban school reform, conditions that promote student achievement, youth violence, the potential impact of school choice and vouchers on urban public schools, and race and ethnic relations in American society. His work has appeared in several major research journals, and many are available online at www.inmotionmagazine.com. He is co-editor of *Beyond Resistance: Youth Activism and Community Change* (with Shawn Ginwright and Julio Camarota; Routledge, 2006) and author of *The Imperatives of Power: Political Change and the Social Basis of Regime Support in Grenada* (Peter Lang Publishers, 1997) and *City Schools and the American Dream* (Teachers College Press, 2003; winner of Foreward Magazine Gold Award). His most recent book is *The Trouble with Black Boys: And Other Reflections on Race, Equity, and the Future of Public Education* (Jossey-Bass, 2008).

Jean Yonemura Wing currently works as a researcher in the Oakland Unified School District. She previously coordinated research and best practices for the district's New School Development Group, supporting the design and creation of new small schools throughout the most underserved communities of Oakland, California. A founding member of the Diversity Project as both a parent and graduate student, her doctoral research drew from a wealth of project data, particularly the Class of 2000 study, which she guided for four years. Her dissertation, *An Uneven Playing Field: Behind the Racial Disparities in Student Achievement at an Integrated Urban High School,* received the outstanding dissertation award from the University of California, Berkeley, Graduate School of Education and was supported by a fellowship from UC ACCORD (University of California All Campus Consortium on Research for Diversity). She has worked as an Asian American community organizer, teacher, community journalist and editor, educational policy writer and editor, adjunct faculty at the University of San Francisco, and research associate for the Educational Testing Service Center for Performance Assessment. She has adapted her ongoing scholarship and research to address various policy issues related to racial and class equity in K–12 public education, college access, and urban school and district reform.

Part One

THE STRUCTURE AND CULTURE OF INEQUALITY IN SCHOOLS

Introduction

CLOSING THE ACHIEVEMENT GAP AT BERKELEY HIGH SCHOOL

Pedro A. Noguera, Jean Yonemura Wing

If ever there were a need to identify a school district that could vividly illustrate the phenomenon now commonly referred to as the achievement gap, Berkeley, California, would be an excellent choice. Academic achievement in Berkeley as measured by grades and tests scores has historically followed a distinct pattern. In *every school* in this district of nearly nine thousand students, most white and Asian students perform at or well above national averages on norm-referenced exams, while many African American and Latino students (and some Asians) perform well below the average. Berkeley High School, which the *New York Times* has called "the most integrated high school in America" (Goodman, 1994, p. A1), has a student population that fluctuated during the life of the Diversity Project from a low of twenty-eight hundred to a high of thirty-two hundred: approximately 38 percent are white, 35 percent African American, 11 percent Asian/Pacific Islander, 10 percent Latino, and 6 percent multiracial/"other." Similar patterns can be seen through other indicators of educational progress, including high school graduation and dropout rates, college attendance and completion patterns, as well as enrollment in Advanced Placement (AP) courses, gifted programs, and special education and remedial courses. In nearly every category associated with positive academic outcomes, students of color typically are underrepresented, and in categories associated with negative outcomes, they are overrepresented.

There are exceptions. Some African American and Latino students achieve high academic honors and excel. They stand out among their peers and are held up as role models. And there are a few white students who barely manage to graduate. Some of these students use drugs, cut school, and show through their academic performance and behavior that every stereotype has its exceptions. Then there are the Asian American students at Berkeley High School, who, despite the prevalence of the so-called model minority stereotype, demonstrate perhaps the widest range of variability in academic performance. They are well represented among the most successful and can also be found among the academically at-risk students, but unlike the others, they are the group most likely to be ignored by adults in the school and in discussions about race and student achievement (Wing, 2002). In a school where racial conflicts have historically been framed through a white versus black prism, Asians, and to a lesser degree Latinos, have often been rendered invisible, even though together they comprise over 20 percent of the district population. The experience of these students and others who defy well-established academic patterns shows that the exceptions do not challenge existing stereotypes; rather, they serve to reinforce them, precisely because they are seen as individual exceptions.

Many observers of academic trends have argued that the achievement gap in communities like Berkeley is less about race than class (Gordon, Piana, and Keleher, 2000; Maran, 2000). After all, the vast majority of those who fail, are suspended or expelled, or are labeled educationally deficient and siphoned off into remedial courses are poor and often come from families headed by parents or guardians who lack a college education. In contrast, the vast majority of academically successful white students come from affluent families, and they generally have parents with high levels of education. In Berkeley, even white students who are not affluent—the children of white- and blue-collar workers, small businesspersons, artists, freelance writers—generally outperform their minority peers. Although their families may be technically middle or even lower middle income, these students nevertheless possess the valued "cultural capital" inherited from their typically well-educated parents (Bourdieu and Passeron, 1977). They also benefit from prevailing assumptions about the relationship between race and academic ability. In a district where race and class are highly correlated, even white students who are not high achievers tend to benefit from sorting practices that treat race as an unofficial proxy for academic ability. In other words, they may be given the benefit of a doubt and be placed in more advanced classes than their grades or test scores might support.

Hence, though some in Berkeley like to argue that the achievement gap is not a racial phenomenon but one rooted in socioeconomic inequality, there is little they can say to counter the reality that this is how the issue generally is perceived. As is often the case, perception has a way of creating its own reality.

Those who prefer to place greater emphasis on class than race in their analysis of achievement patterns often do so because they find comfort in the idea that the cause of such pronounced differences in academic outcomes is not some form of inherent racial difference or racism. Innate racial differences rooted in biology have historically served as the favorite explanation for disparities in intellectual performance, while racism has tended to receive considerably less attention (Ladson-Billings, 1994). Unlike many other regions of America where innate or even cultural differences are more likely to be accepted as the cause of group differences in academic achievement, sophisticated liberals in Berkeley tend to shun such explanations. However, they are equally squeamish about the possibility that racism might somehow be implicated in these well-established patterns.

The charge of racism is particularly inflammatory in a liberal community like Berkeley. This is a community that has historically taken great pride in its commitment to racial justice and equality. If racism were indeed the culprit behind persistent disparities in achievement, then surely a community with a well-deserved reputation for its liberalism would be mobilized to take action to address the problem. Of course, that would work only if it were racism of the old sort—the blatant, in-your-face, "we hate black people" variety. If instead it were a more subtle form of institutional racism that worked through seemingly neutral policies and procedures to reward the privileged while covertly limiting opportunities for the disadvantaged, then what could be done?

Those who hope to avoid the thorny issue of race and racism can find solace in knowing that there is no proof that racism of the old type is the cause of the achievement gap in Berkeley, certainly not the racism of bigots wearing white sheets. That perception makes it possible for earnest liberals to shake their heads in disappointment when they hear statistics about the large numbers of black and Latino students who fail. If they care enough, they can call for something to be done—more tutoring perhaps—without having to incur any sense of guilt or culpability for the problem.

For this reason, Berkeleyans, like many other Americans, prefer to attribute the causes of the achievement gap to the effects of poverty and the unfortunate influences of family background—that is, parents who are presumed to have less education and know-how when it comes to raising their children. Such explanations are eminently more palatable than ascribing the cause to some form of discrimination or racial injustice. By attributing the cause of minority student underachievement to a lack of student effort or deficient family background, we can comfortably dismiss the problem as sad and disturbing, and reject the possibility that something more pernicious might be at work. It is undoubtedly at least partially for this reason that conversations in Berkeley about the achievement of students of color have been characterized by a high degree of avoidance or, worse, resignation and acceptance. Like homelessness and air pollution, the achievement gap is regarded as one of those unfortunate conditions that the members of this idealistic community have learned to live with.

Placing Berkeley in a National Context

Berkeley is hardly alone. The racial achievement gap is now widely recognized as an educational challenge confronting school districts throughout the United States (Jencks and Phillips, 1998). The issue is receiving more attention now in part because of the federal No Child Left Behind (NCLB) law, which requires that students be tested annually and that their test results by racial subgroup be released to the public. Yet as greater attention has been focused on the issue, relatively little has been done to provide schools with guidance on how to address the problem. Public reports that certain subgroups are not making adequate yearly progress have helped to expose race and class disparities in school districts, but it has done little to help them figure out what to do to remedy the problem.

The existence of stable and fairly predictable disparities in academic performance that correspond to race and class differences among students is by no means a new phenomenon. Such differences on standardized tests and other measures of "intelligence" and academic ability have been present since the beginning of testing (Lemann, 1999). What is new and different today is that such patterns are increasingly regarded as a problem that must be addressed rather than as a manifestation of the natural order of things. Even the fiercest critics of the Bush administration must acknowledge that despite its many flaws, No Child Left Behind has, in an odd way, moved the national conversation about race and education forward, because for the first time in our nation's history, schools are required to produce evidence that they can serve all students.

Berkeley, like other school districts across the country, has never served all students, at least not equally—but arguably, it has made more effort than most other places. Long before it was fashionable to decry the achievement gap, Berkeley had numerous programs and initiatives designed to assist struggling minority students. That most of these efforts showed little evidence of success is hardly a reason to single out Berkeley for condemnation. The achievement gap is, after all, a national phenomenon (Elmore, 1996), and few communities have demonstrated the same kind of willingness as Berkeley to invest resources to address the problem.

As recently as 1999, Berkeley joined together with fourteen other school districts to create the Minority Student Achievement Network (MSAN). The consortium comprises districts that bear a striking resemblance to Berkeley, including Ann Arbor, Michigan; Cambridge, Massachusetts; Chapel Hill, North Carolina; Shaker Heights, Ohio; and Evanston and Skokie, Illinois. Each MSAN district shared an interesting combination of attributes: liberal, affluent, and possessing a long track record of serving their most privileged students well, while consistently failing to meet the educational needs of poor children of color. To be fair, the challenges confronting schools in MSAN districts did not lend themselves to easy explanations. Unlike most large, urban school districts where a lack of resources often contributes to academic failure, these systems have more resources than most others. Similarly, in contrast to many affluent white suburban communities where racial integration has to varying degrees been tolerated, there is a greater sense that diversity is embraced and there is no widespread overt hostility toward students of color in these liberal communities. Yet despite these apparent advantages, all of these districts have struggled to elevate the academic performance of students of color. They formed MSAN with the expectation that together, they might be able to address their common challenges, and in the hope that there might be wisdom, if not strength, in numbers.

Six years later, MSAN has yet to show that by meeting together on a regular basis the districts could help each other to find ways to close the achievement gap. Like Berkeley, MSAN districts remain largely paralyzed by the persistence of wide racial disparities in achievement and stymied in their efforts to find solutions. They have sponsored research and studied the issue in minute detail, but the search for greater educational equity remains beyond their reach.

Cynics might argue that if the districts in MSAN are unable to find ways to reduce the achievement gap, then perhaps it cannot be done. Such resignation is increasingly common in many suburban districts across the United States that have recently experienced dramatic changes in the demographic makeup of their schools and communities (Orfield and Kurlaender, 2001). As people of color leave or get pushed out of gentrifying cities and growing numbers of immigrants who typically do not speak English take up residence in inner-ring suburbs, a large number of formerly all-white schools are struggling to respond to the academic needs of students they have little experience in serving.

Because of NCLB, these inner-ring suburban school districts are under pressure to find ways to address the achievement gap, but unlike Berkeley and the districts in MSAN, goodwill and good intentions do not appear to be in abundance. Many of these communities have been significantly less magnanimous in their response. Racial integration was never embraced in many of these white suburban communities, some of which were created as a result of white flight from the inner city in the 1960s (Gans, 1993). Now required by law to demonstrate progress in their efforts to close the achievement gap, many of these school districts are complaining loudly that if it were not for the presence of those unwanted "subgroups," their schools would not be labeled as being in need of improvement (Bernstein, 2003).

When placed in the context of the larger national effort to close the achievement gap, Berkeley's efforts to address the problem are laudable. Unlike many other communities, Berkeley continues to take pride in its diversity, and although its commitment to racial inclusion has not helped it in addressing the problem, no one can reasonably question the community's commitment to tolerance. There is a deeply held belief in Berkeley, with its long history of embracing progressive causes, that it is not like other communities and that it should be held to a different standard (Nathan and Scott, 1978). Berkeley is, after all, renowned for its idealism and support of progressive values. It is well known, and widely ridiculed, for its support of outside-the-mainstream social causes and its willingness to adopt cutting-edge social policies. From civil rights to gay rights and from its early commitment to opposing war—in Vietnam, Central America, and Iraq—to its ongoing commitment to providing support to the homeless, the undocumented, and the addicted, Berkeley has long been a community that has nurtured and given birth to movements on behalf of underdogs.

As might be expected, Berkeley's aspirations and attempts to push the boundaries of liberalism have frequently generated resentment and belittlement from conservative critics, and at times the national media. For its detractors, Berkeley's willingness to embrace offbeat and unconventional ideas has been used to justify the derogatory nickname, "Berserkeley." Yet many of those who reside in what is affectionately called the People's Republic of Berkeley take pride in knowing that more than a few policies once seen as avant-garde and wacky have gradually been adopted as sound governmental policy in other parts of the country. This has been true for curbside recycling, sidewalk access for wheelchairs, and domestic partner benefits for gay and lesbian public employees. Berkeleyans feel a degree of pride that they have often been ahead of the curve on national issues, and in more than a few cases, the city has been a leader in progressive social reform.

Berkeley's Approach to Racial Integration in the Public Schools

Not surprisingly, Berkeley also was once at the forefront of change in public education. In 1968, it became one of the first school districts in the nation to integrate its schools voluntarily (Kirp, 1982). Significantly, it did so not through passive acquiescence to a court order but in response to efforts by grassroots organizers.

After several earlier defeats, Berkeley voters approved a plan to desegregate its public schools through a system of shared busing (Noguera, 1995). While white resistance to school integration resulted in violence and boycotts in other communities, integration was largely welcomed in Berkeley. In yet another example of the community's commitment to progressive social values, Berkeley citizens adopted a plan that called for the burden of busing to be shared by the black and white communities. The plan called for largely black children from low-income neighborhoods in the flatlands of Berkeley to be bused from kindergarten through third grade to schools in affluent white neighborhoods in the hills. Students in grades 4 through 6 were bused from the hills to flatland schools in South and West Berkeley. When opponents of desegregation attempted to undo the plan by launching a recall of the members of the school board, Berkeley voters, in a rare display of public support for racial integration, squelched the backlash and resoundingly affirmed their support for the new busing plan (Kirp, 1982).

For many years after 1968, the integration of Berkeley's public schools was cited as one of its greatest achievements. To the city's critics who regarded many of the political causes championed in Berkeley as little more than empty rhetoric that required no sacrifice, its school desegregation plan stood as proof that its commitment to justice and equality was real. In many ways, taking stands against war or global warming was easier than sending white children to school with black children. To its credit, even as white flight steadily undermined school integration in northern cities throughout the 1980s and 1990s (Orfield and Eaton, 1996), Berkeley public schools remained relatively integrated. To this day, it is one of few cities that places its children where its proclaimed values are.

It is largely because of this city's reputation for progressive stances on social issues that the achievement gap in Berkeley has recently generated so much concern. The persistence of disparities in achievement that correspond to the race and class backgrounds of students, patterns that are evident in most school districts throughout the country, indicates that Berkeley may not be the beacon of hope that its reputation suggests. The gap in academic outcomes is a sign that the desegregation was partial; students of various races may attend the same schools, but they receive a very different education within them.

It is for this reason that we have titled this book *Unfinished Business*. Like civil rights activists elsewhere who have called attention to the many areas in American society where racial justice remains unfulfilled (Wolters, 1984), we regard the persistence of the achievement gap in Berkeley and elsewhere as a remnant of the civil rights movement that is far from finished. In the U.S. Supreme Court's 2003 ruling in favor of affirmative action (*Gruter v. Bollinger*), Justice

Sandra Day O'Connor suggested in her majority opinion that there might be no need for such a policy in twenty-five years (Greenhouse, 2003). The implication of her argument was that in the not-too-distant future, public schools would provide all children, regardless of their backgrounds, with an education that would make racial preferences in college admissions unnecessary. Unfortunately, Justice O'Connor did not explain how this feat would be achieved, and so—like the historic *Brown* decision issued nearly fifty years earlier, with its vague call for integration to proceed "with all deliberate speed" (*Brown* v. *Board of Education of Topeka*)—the High Court's *Gruter* ruling provided no guidance on how racial justice in education would be brought about.

The effort to eliminate racial disparities in student achievement is an essential part of the unfinished business of the modern civil rights movement, and it was this recognition that inspired our work at Berkeley High School. To a large degree, our experience as parents, activists, educators, and researchers had convinced us that Berkeley should be a place where it is possible to educate all students. This is, after all, a community that remains committed to the goals of the civil rights movement. However, we believed neither that the conditions necessary for educational change were present in Berkeley, nor that closing the achievement gap would be necessarily easier there than anywhere else. The long history of unequal education in Berkeley and the dogged denial that confronting racial inequality is the responsibility of the schools and community is the clearest evidence to the contrary. Yet our experience has led us to believe that the possibility for change in Berkeley is real because the aspirations for a more just social order are more than lip-service.

Unfortunately, though, this is not a book about Berkeley's triumph over racial disparities in achievement, but about the effort to take on this unfinished work. As this book goes to press, the achievement gap remains firmly entrenched in Berkeley, as it is across the rest of the country. Yet there continues to be considerable energy and commitment to support students and teachers and to close the achievement gap. These efforts have been ongoing since

1968, and for this reason, we believe it would be a mistake to wait until the work was completed to write about the efforts to take on the challenge. Our hope is that other communities and school districts can learn from Berkeley's experience as they pursue their own initiatives to close the achievement gap and contribute to the historical struggle for racial justice.

Taking Up Unfinished Business in Changing Times

In the spirit of taking up the unfinished business of the civil rights movement, it is worth noting that desegregation in Berkeley also preceded an extended period of deindustrialization. The blue-collar jobs that once paid decent union wages are largely gone now, and as the jobs have departed, so too have working-class families. These trends began in the 1970s and accelerated dramatically in the 1980s and 1990s. Berkeley and other East Bay cities have experienced large-scale loss of heavy industry and manufacturing. In the 1980s, three major East Bay auto and truck manufacturing plants (Ford, GM, and Mack Truck), which employed thousands of assembly line workers shut down, and Durkee Foods, Colgate Palmolive, and other big and small manufacturers closed their doors along Berkeley's waterfront during this period. However, unlike the rust belt cities of the Northeast and Midwest, new industries soon replaced the lost manufacturing jobs. Unfortunately, the jobs that have been created are concentrated in the service sector (primarily in health care) and offer lower, largely nonunion pay, or in the high-tech and biotech industries, which typically require postsecondary education, particularly in science and math.

As a result of these economic changes, minority communities in Berkeley have experienced increased unemployment or under-employment, particularly among those with a high school education or less (Wilson, 1989; Gee, Hull, and Lankshear, 1996). As we will show in the pages ahead, these changes to the economic base of Berkeley and the Bay Area have had profound social consequences for students and schools.

In the 1980s and 1990s, housing prices skyrocketed, and Berkeley, like many other parts of the Bay Area, experienced a dramatic gentrification. For example, a section of the industrial zone in West Berkeley has been transformed into a center for high-end home remodeling and boutique shopping. Several pricey restaurants, dress shops, home furnishings, fine produce, and other retail shops are now perched on land once occupied by factories and warehouses. Pockets of poor residents—renters, homeowners, and those who reside in subsidized housing—still remain in the area, but the neighborhood has been transformed. As might be expected, gentrification has contributed to enormous income disparities, and social cleavage and tension have increased among flatlands residents.

In addition to these changes in the character and composition of Berkeley, there have been significant policy changes in California that have had profound ramifications for schools. Perhaps most important among these was the 1996 voter passage of California's Proposition 209 banning affirmative action. In particular, Proposition 209 barred state government and public agencies from using race or gender preferences in hiring, contracting, or college admissions. Even before Prop 209 was adopted, relatively few students of color from Berkeley High School were admitted to the University of California (UC). In the years since the policy was enacted into law, the UC system has become even more out of reach. Out of 8,676 admissions letters for the UC Berkeley freshman class entering in fall 2004, only 211 went to African American students. And although Berkeley High School is located just four blocks to the west of the UC campus, no more than a handful of African American, Latino, Filipino, and Southeast Asian graduates of Berkeley High have gained admission in the past few years.

For all of these reasons, the achievement gap at Berkeley High School is a serious problem, with implications and consequences that extend far beyond the school. With economic, political, and social changes at the national, state, and regional levels creating new barriers and constraints, it has become even more important for the school to figure out how to address long-standing disparities in achievement. Again, Berkeley is not the only school confronted with such formidable obstacles. Because its challenges—both internal and external—are in many ways representative of the kinds of issues confronting schools throughout the nation, our hope is that a close examination of its efforts to address the achievement gap will prove illuminating to others.

A Catalyst for Change: The Diversity Project and Berkeley High School

This book is about the efforts of teachers, staff, students, and parents from Berkeley who collaborated with researchers from the University of California at Berkeley to address the racial disparities in academic performance at Berkeley High School (BHS). Through the Berkeley High School Diversity Project, these individuals sought to find a way to compel the school and community to take on an issue that had been ignored since desegregation. This book is about the strategies and tactics that were used to carry out this work, the accomplishments over the course of six years, and the many things that remain undone. Most of all, it is about the ways in which a school and community has acted in unwitting complicity in the perpetuation of racial inequality and the attempts by members of that community to interrupt its continuance.

We could have chosen any school in the district as the focal point for our work, but we chose Berkeley High School because the issues there were in many ways more visible and intense. Berkeley High is the only public high school in the city, and with over three thousand students, it serves more than a third of the students enrolled in the district. It is the final destination for all students who make it to the ninth grade, and it is the place where future trajectories—to Ivy League colleges, to state and community colleges, to dead-end jobs, or to prison—are determined. With its seventeen-acre campus and its artificial turf football field, public television studio, Olympic-sized swimming pool, and three-thousand-seat theater, it is a prized community resource. And with its reputation for chaos, drug use, and permissive culture, it is the object of anguish and occasionally scorn.

Located at the center of downtown Berkeley, it represents the best and the worst of the city. To understand the paradox that is Berkeley High School, pass by Martin Luther King Jr. Park across the street from the high school on any sunny school day and watch as dozens of its students lounge on the green grass, at all hours of the day, smoking marijuana in full view of city hall, the police department, and the school district headquarters. But before you rush to judgment, keep in mind that many of those students are headed to the best universities in the nation, while others are headed nowhere at all.

With more than its share of National Merit Scholars, a highly acclaimed jazz band, and national award-winning school newspaper, it was easy for many in the community to allow the school's successes to overshadow its glaring failures. All of this changed in 1994 with the airing of *School Colors*. The three-hour documentary on Berkeley High, which the filmmakers hoped would serve as a gauge of the nation's progress in achieving racial integration some forty years after the historic *Brown* decision, jolted the community out of its passive acceptance of the status quo. When the film was broadcast to a national audience on public television, what the public saw was a school mired in deep racial separation and polarization. Based on interviews with students and teachers over the course of a school year, *School Colors* was used as evidence that racial integration in public education had failed. To the shock and dismay of many residents, the spotlight was shining on Berkeley not for its progressive accomplishments but for its utter failure to live up to its ideals.

Interestingly, the airing of *School Colors* had the effect of briefly uniting the diverse elements of the Berkeley community. Although the film was hailed elsewhere as a revealing portrait of racial inequality and resegregation in American high schools, Berkeley citizens uniformly reacted to it with outrage. Many claimed that the film distorted the image of the high school and the community, and they accused the filmmakers of taking advantage of the access to the school that had been so generously provided. When one of the filmmakers dared to return to Berkeley to discuss reactions to the final product, she was met with a rare show of solidarity as large numbers of people turned out to castigate her for misrepresenting the community and the school.

Yet despite the fierceness of their opposition, what the community seemed to forget was that the film footage was authentic, if edited. Although the attitudes of the teachers and students conveyed in the film may have told only part of the story, there was no doubt that the words were theirs and that the sentiments expressed, in their unfettered honesty, were real. Anyone familiar with the school knew that Berkeley High School was a deeply divided place, segregated from within in almost every way that mattered. It was also a school where inequality bred deep resentments and hostility, and occasionally these rose to the surface in frightening ways.

While it was true that the film had not captured all of the complexity that is the whole story of integration at the school, it had captured an important part of the story. So like a fashion model complaining about being photographed on a bad hair day, the reaction to School Colors revealed that BHS and the Berkeley community were engaged in a deep denial.

The Diversity Project was created shortly after the airing of School Colors to help the school and community face up to its denial and to begin to respond honestly to the problems confronting the school. The project was coinitiated by Ronald Glass, a BHS parent and a lecturer at the School of Education at Stanford University, and teacher Dana Moran. Comprising BHS teachers, parents, and students and joined by researchers from UC Berkeley, the Diversity Project commenced its work in the summer of 1996. From the beginning, its purpose was to try to find a way to move the high school beyond the denial that made it possible for long-standing inequities to be accepted.

For years, Berkeley High School's embrace of diversity had disguised the glaring inequities. It was, after all, the only high school in the country that had its own African American Studies Department, offering Afro-Haitian dance, Kiswahili, and black economics, history, drama, and psychology. Berkeley High also offered electives in Chicano studies, Asian American studies, and women's studies, and it required all of its freshmen to take a one semester course in ethnic studies.

Although there was general awareness about the existence of dramatic racial disparities in student achievement at the school, there was no agreement about its causes. There was ample finger-pointing by those who wanted to cast blame on their culprits of choice—"lazy and unmotivated students," "negligent teachers," "parents who don't care"—but there was little evidence of a willingness to take responsibility for finding solutions. Without a clear understanding of the causes, the school could revel in its diversity even as it was unable to make progress in addressing the larger problem.

It was the lack of agreement and clarity about the causes of racial disparity in achievement that prompted the Diversity Project to seize on research as a tool that could be used to figure out what was going on. The project focused on research not because we believed there was any magic in the data and findings that might be generated, but because we believed that it might make it possible to illuminate the problem. Two overarching questions guided our research:

- What are the factors that contribute to the disparity in academic achievement between students of different racial and class backgrounds at the school?
- What are the factors that are responsible for the racial separation of students within the school?

The first question was the obvious big question. We needed to understand what was going on if we hoped to have any chance of making changes at the school. Although data showing wide disparities in academic performance among students from different racial and ethnic backgrounds had been discussed for many years, those data had done little to move the school toward solutions. Instead, various groups argued over how the data should be interpreted and who should be blamed. Our hope was that through our research, we could move the school beyond the paralysis and bitter antagonisms that characterized discussion over issues related to race and achievement.

We posed the second question because we had a hunch that the voluntary and involuntary processes that were used to segregate students at the school had the effect of creating the perception that racial identities were inextricably linked to academic performance. Finding ways to undo that link was one of the central goals of the project. Patterns of racial separation were most evident when one enters the school grounds at the beginning of the school day, and served as a central theme of *School Colors*. Across the sprawling campus, students could be seen gathered in racially distinct groupings. Black students congregated in front of the administration building near a red, black, and green map of Africa painted on the asphalt. White students gathered in the center of the campus quad, on the steps of the Berkeley Community Theater. Along Martin Luther King Way at the periphery of the school, groups of Latino students could generally be found hanging out near a Chicano/Latino mural. Smaller groups of Asian students found their place along a wall adjacent to the Science Building. Each grouping was racially distinct, but those who knew the school well were aware that the boundaries were permeable, because a significant number of students crossed over and maintained close relationships with individuals from other groups.

This form of racial separation is the most noticeable, and because it appears to be voluntary and a matter of choice, there is a sense that this is what students prefer. Yet racial separation is not limited to the clustering that occurs outside the school. It shows up in classrooms and clubs throughout the school, and these forms are not voluntary. Rather, they are products of the school's structure and organization. Although the separations created by tracking— the practice of sorting students into courses based on some measure or estimate of their academic ability (Oakes, 1985)—are less visible, their impact on student outcomes is far more profound. Despite its obvious divergence from Berkeley's long-term commitment to racial integration, racial separation in all its forms, like racial disparities in academic achievement, is a social phenomenon that had come to be accepted as normal at BHS.

The Diversity Project sought to use research to understand what was behind these complex and controversial issues. Like most other research projects, data collection and analysis took up much of our time and energy. However, in a departure from traditional academic research, the strategic dissemination of our findings was always done with an awareness of how we might influence the process of change at the school. We understood from the beginning that even as we sought to find answers to the questions we had posed, the process was as important as the inquiry itself. We purposefully created a team that was representative of the diversity of the school and composed of the various constituencies that made up the broader community, because we wanted to ensure that our work would not be dismissed as a special interest initiative and thereby contribute to further polarization. We deliberately blurred the lines between researcher and subject to avoid the classic division that separates university-based researchers from those whom they study. Most of all, we wanted to be credible to the entire school and community, and for that to happen, there could be no "us" versus "them" in our work.

Our plan was to use findings generated from our research to guide and influence changes at the school. We employed a variety of research strategies, including an annual survey and study of the entire class of 2000 that was maintained over four years; focus groups with all of the core constituencies; analyses of course enrollment patterns; analyses of school discipline patterns; and a review of academic programs, such as the detracked freshman English/history core and the English as a Second Language programs.

We did this to obtain as clear a picture as possible of what was happening in the school. Our hope was that if we relied on research, we could help the school move beyond its preoccupation with searching for blame in order to find genuine solutions. We also hoped that the research would provide the school with a new and different way of perceiving racial disparities that had come to be seen as natural and unchangeable.

From the start, we understood that we would have to do more than merely document the patterns. Our goal was to use research to bring about a change in how people understood the production of student outcomes, and to do this we would have to find ways to change the ways in which people thought about racial patterns at the school (Berkeley High School Diversity Project, 1999).

To accomplish these goals we devised research strategies that were designed to achieve the following objectives:

- *To make the familiar seem strange and problematic*. This is a concept commonly used by anthropologists who seek to uncover the meaning behind practices and beliefs that cultures take for granted (Erickson, 1987). Our hope was that we could use research to enable teachers, students, and parents to question their assumptions about why students do or do not succeed academically. We thought the data and findings our research would generate could provide some degree of detachment from the emotionally charged issues we were investigating. Although we never deluded ourselves into believing that our findings would be treated as politically neutral facts, we did think that by providing an empirical basis for discussion about what was going on, we might make it possible to challenge prevailing beliefs about the relationship between race and achievement.

- *To critically examine the organization and structure of privilege*. For years, discussions about race and achievement in Berkeley had been framed in terms of a search for what was wrong with minority students. Why did so many of them fail, drop out, get into trouble, and not go to college? The experience of high-achieving, white, middle-class, and upper-middle-class students was never subject to similar scrutiny or questioning when it was framed in this way. Our understanding of the school led us to believe that the superior achievement of white students was not merely related to the advantages they inherited from their parents. Rather, our experience with the school led us to suspect that there were formal and informal practices built into the structure and operation of the school that harmed the educational interests of some students while enhancing the opportunities of others. For this reason, we were just as interested in understanding how the school served its most privileged students as we were in the experience of students who were consistently low performers.

• *To empower the disadvantaged and marginalized.* Our experience with Berkeley and its high school led us to recognize that like most other things in this city, education was political. Although the community was renowned for its liberalism, we knew that any effort to challenge the status quo at the high school would be fiercely resisted if it was perceived as undermining the advantages that its most privileged students enjoyed. That segment of the community was active and fully aware of what was happening at the school. While it was unlikely that affluent parents would oppose an effort to help underperforming students, we were certain that they would fight any effort that they regarded as lowering standards or taking resources away from their own children. Hence, we understood that their ability to exert influence on educational leaders in the district and local politicians posed a serious threat to our work and would have to be dealt with.

To offset the influence of these parents, we knew we would have to find a way to make the political playing field more level. We settled on the research process to help parents who had historically been most peripheral to the school (African American and Latino parents) to become informed and organized, so that they too could exert influence over the school. We did this knowing that our efforts might generate conflict within the school, as those who felt their children had not been well served made demands on the school. However, we reasoned that without such a force, the parents of high-achieving white students—parents who were already well organized and benefited from the status quo—might attempt to undermine efforts they perceived as harmful to their interests. We sought to use the research process to create a degree of balance in the school so that parents of students who were not well served could also be heard.

The Structure of the Diversity Project

With a small amount of funding from the University of California and the San Francisco Foundation, the Diversity Project began its work in the fall of 1996. From the start, it was a public process, and our meetings and our work drew attention and scrutiny from the broader community.

Figure I.1 shows the basic structure of the Diversity Project over time, as new research and outreach committees were added each year and as the project became involved in other reform efforts led by the school administration. The Diversity Project began with a simple structure: the Core Team and the Extended Team. The project was led by the Core Team, which was carefully constructed to include equal representation from the university (faculty and graduate students) and from Berkeley High School (teachers and staff) and to include a racially diverse mix. The founding Core Team began with five teachers, three graduate students, one school staff person, and two professors. The larger Extended Team included the Core Team plus over thirty teachers, classified staff, administrators, students, and parents, as well as school board members, and an associate superintendent.

The Core Team met regularly and coordinated the work of the Extended Team and the various research and organizing committees that emerged over time. In order to enable full participation, the Diversity Project paid for 20 percent release time for teachers and paid graduate students as part-time research assistants. The Core Team initially had two university-based codirectors, Pedro Noguera and Ron Glass. But within a matter of months, as the project developed, we chose one codirector from the university,

FIGURE I.1 Creating an Irreversible Momentum for Change

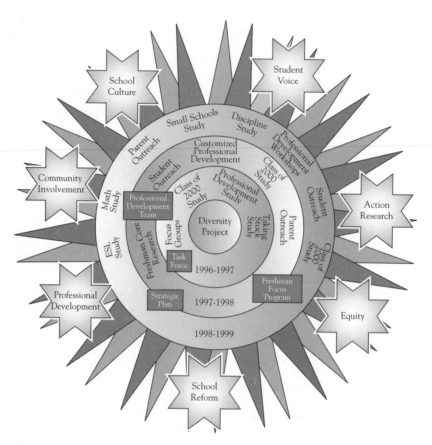

Source: Graphic by Miriam K. Stahl, teacher; computer artwork by Fredda Cassidy, parent.

Pedro Noguera, and one from Berkeley High School, teacher and later vice principal James Williams.

The Core Team initially selected staff, students, and parents to sit on the Extended Team on the basis of their letters of interest and personal interviews indicating a commitment to equity. Extended Team members received a modest stipend and were expected to participate on at least one project research committee.

During the project's first year, four research committees were created:

- *Class of 2000 Committee*. This committee designed and conducted a four-year longitudinal study of the 750 students of the class of 2000 to better understand the factors contributing to the racial achievement gap. The committee analyzed large-scale data on grades, attendance, course-taking patterns, graduation rates, and college-going patterns, disaggregated by race, gender, ZIP Code of residence, home language, and other important markers of inequity. It developed an annual whole-class Internet survey of student backgrounds, perceptions, and experiences of schooling, as well as student access to information and resources pertaining to graduation and college. In the junior and senior years of the class of 2000 students, the committee selected a diverse group of thirty-three case study students to interview in-depth and to shadow for entire school days once each semester.
- *Taking Stock Committee*. This committee investigated patterns of race and gender separation in the high school's abundant extra- and cocurricular clubs, athletic teams, and activities. It organized the entire Extended Team to interview the athletic coaches and club advisers about issues of race and gender separation, diversity, and inclusion.
- *Professional Development Committee*. In the project's first year, this committee conducted a survey of teachers regarding their perceptions of teaching racially diverse students and heterogeneous classes (classes of students with mixed skill levels). In later years, this committee piloted a peer coaching model of professional development and designed a series of professional development workshops, open to all 180 teachers on a voluntary basis, to learn from best practices to address the achievement gap at the classroom level. In the final three years of the Diversity Project (1999–2002), the professional development team facilitated a group called Action Research for Teachers (ART) to expand the number of teachers using cycles of inquiry and various kinds of research data to close the achievement gap within their own classrooms.

- *Focus Groups Committee*. This committee began collecting focus group information from teachers, counselors, clerical staff, campus safety monitors, parents, and students about their perspectives on the factors causing racialized patterns of success and failure and contributing to patterns of racial separation.

In addition, during the first year, the project's graduate student researchers participated in four task forces created by principal Larry Lee to study possible reforms in areas such as school organization and structure and school culture and climate.

In the project's second year, the Focus Groups Committee was disbanded, and focus group research methods were incorporated into the work of some of the other research and outreach committees. The Taking Stock Committee also ended, as it had completed its study. The Class of 2000 Committee continued to survey the entire class and collect data on course-taking patterns, grades, attendance, and discipline. In addition, the project launched a one-year study of the detracked freshman English/history core, and the Professional Development Committee began piloting a peer coaching and customized professional development model to address equity in the classroom. It was also in this second year that we launched two important outreach committees: Parent Outreach and Student Outreach. The Parent Outreach Committee began by organizing eighteen well-attended focus groups to solicit input of marginalized parents of color and to begin mobilizing these parents to have a voice in the school.

In the project's third year (1998–1999), in addition to ongoing committees such as the Class of 2000 Committee, we launched committees to study the prealgebra program, the transition of English learner students in the English as a Second Language department, the possibility of small schools-within-a-school as an equity reform, and the racial disparities in the school disciplinary system. Both Parent and Student Outreach Committees also provided important perspectives and recommendations to principal Theresa Saunders's five-year strategic plan for BHS in the spring of 1999. During this third year, we established the position of site coordinator, a position that also served as a third codirector, and selected LaShawn Routé-Chatmon to fill this post. Her primary responsibility as site coordinator was to integrate the project's research teams with new interventions and changes underway at the high school.

By the project's fourth year, we had begun to reach one of our major goals: weaving the Diversity Project into the fabric of the high school and the placement of the racial achievement gap at the center of every conversation about school change. We still had our Core Team and the Extended Team, but by this time, dozens of parents and students had joined the work of Parent and Student Outreach, and scores of teachers had participated in and supported some aspect of the project's work. By the time the Diversity Project presented its final set of findings to the high school community and the school board in June 2000, the project had truly become a part of the high school to the point that it was difficult to say who was on the Diversity Project and who was not.

In the pages ahead we describe what we learned from our work at the school. We analyze the obstacles we encountered, both those we anticipated and those that were unexpected. We also describe the revelations and insights we gained during the course of our work. Our hope is that full disclosure of the challenges and pitfalls as well as the positive lessons will make this book useful to others who are concerned about making schools more equitable and as committed to carrying on the nation's unfinished business with civil rights and education.

1

STRUCTURING INEQUALITY AT BERKELEY HIGH

Beth C. Rubin, Jean Yonemura Wing, Pedro A. Noguera, Emma Fuentes, Daniel Liou, Alicia P. Rodriguez, Lance T. McCready

Interviewer: You said you chose yourself to be in prealgebra instead of algebra. Do you think you made the right decision?

Chantelle: Yeah, because last year I had prealgebra and this year I'm going to take one semester of prealgebra, and then maybe I'll be ready for algebra, but if I'm not, I'm going to take prealgebra again so I really know what I'm doing. Because, see, my brother, when he came [to Berkeley High], he didn't go to prealgebra. He went to prealgebra in middle school, and then he went to algebra here, and he never went to prealgebra here, so he needed to go to prealgebra this year because it's his last year.

Interviewer: You said you had a hard time with math there [private middle school]. So how is it here at Berkeley High?

Jennifer: Much easier. I'm in geometry, and it's like "Oh, okay. I know how to do that." I have a [private] tutor now, and she's planning to be a math teacher at Berkeley High, and the [geometry] books she's like an expert at going through because her school created them. So she's, like, "I understand how they think about this." So she understands the books . . . and she helps me with that. So I'm getting a lot better, and I'm understanding things a lot better now, but it's only because of her.

This chapter focuses on how the structures of Berkeley High School contribute to the reproduction of racial and social class-based inequality at the school. By *structures* we are referring to operations and procedures such as teacher assignment, course selection and placement, and resource allocation, which profoundly influence student experiences at Berkeley High School (BHS). Our examination of school structures also includes a focus on the organization of the school—the decentralized nature of decision making within departments, the distribution of authority and responsibility among administrators, the accountability (or lack thereof) and function of special programs (such as English as a Second Language, Advanced Placement, and Special Education). We examine how these structures shape and influence the academic outcomes of students. As we will show, these seemingly neutral aspects of the school structure that too often are taken for granted play a central role in reproducing patterns of success and failure and, by extension, in reproducing inequality and privilege.

The achievement gap at Berkeley High is, in some sense, a source of puzzlement. How, in a progressive community like Berkeley and in a high school that appears to revel in its commitment to diversity—with its African American Studies Department and freshman ethnic studies requirement—does the structure of the school lend itself to reproducing the racial achievement gap? Perhaps even more puzzling, why has it been so difficult to confront and transform the features embedded in the school structure that are responsible for facilitating success for some and failure for others?

The words above of Chantelle, an African American ninth grader, and Jennifer, a white ninth grader, give some indication of how a single school procedure—ninth-grade math course selection—serves to reproduce inequality, despite the well-meaning efforts of many school staff. As the comments from these two students show, some students have more information and a clearer sense of how the school works (such as the classes they need to take) than others. In addition, more affluent students like Jennifer can rely on the resources of their parents (private tutors and counselors, the know-how, savvy, and advocacy of their parents), while students like Chantelle who come from poor families have access to fewer resources from home and are more dependent on the school. It is obvious that the backgrounds of students contribute to the unevenness of opportunities for academic success. What is less obvious is the way in which the school structure is also implicated in reinforcing patterns of disadvantage and privilege.

There is relatively little that the school can do to address the inequalities in the backgrounds of students like Jennifer and Chantelle. However, it is possible to address school conditions that contribute to disparities in achievement, such as school size, the student-to-counselor ratio, procedures that are used to track students into higher- and lower-level courses, and processes used to provide academic support to students who are struggling. These aspects of the school structure all contribute to the achievement gap, and unlike the backgrounds of students, they can be easily modified and reformed.

Social scientists have identified significant resources, or forms of capital, that play a role in influencing student academic outcomes. Research has shown that economic capital, that is, the wealth and income of parents, is one of the primary factors influencing student achievement (Coleman and others, 1966; Rothstein, 2004; Farkas, 2004). Student achievement is also influenced by more subtle resources such as social capital—the benefits derived from connections to networks and individuals with power and influence (Coleman, 1988; Stanton-Salazar, 1997, 2001; Noguera, 2003)—and cultural capital (Bourdieu and Wacquant, 1992)—the tastes, styles, habits, language, behaviors, appearance, and customs that serve as indicators of status and privilege. All three forms of capital—economic, social, and cultural—play a role in perpetuating disparate educational experiences and differential access to educational opportunities. However, they do so in interaction with seemingly neutral structures that operate within schools and society.

Chantelle's comments reveal how easily a student who lacks economic, social, and cultural capital can become lost within Berkeley High's large and impersonal bureaucratic structure. She had freely chosen to take prealgebra for her ninth-grade math class, but her reason for making that decision was problematic: she based it on her brother's experience. Even more disturbing, the consequences of her decision are unclear to her. She mistakenly believed that if she became "ready" for algebra after a semester in prealgebra, she then would be able to switch into algebra in the middle of the year—an option not typically available to students at BHS. Based on her brother's own misguided experience, Chantelle believed that if she did not take prealgebra during her first year, she would have to make it up later. Both of these beliefs were based on erroneous information. That she reached the point of enrolling in prealgebra without having these notions corrected is a reflection of the limitations of the school counseling process. However, that her counselor allowed her to make this decision is likely due to his or her assumption that a student like Chantelle—an African American from a low-income family—should be placed in the lowest-level math class, prealgebra, even though she had taken it already.

Chantelle's experience illustrates why students who lack economic, social, and cultural capital are more vulnerable to the impersonal and ineffective structures at the school. Without an adult to encourage her to take algebra, the gateway to college preparatory math and science courses, or to advise her on where she might seek academic support, Chantelle made a decision that is likely to affect her preparation for college and therefore will have bearing in the long term on her opportunities after high school. By taking prealgebra in the ninth grade, Chantelle is all but ensured that she will be unable to meet the admissions requirements to the UC or California State University (CSU) systems. Given that so much is at stake, it must be recognized that a system of course assignment that allows students to choose which classes to take will invariably work better for some than others.

Jennifer's words are equally revealing. Like many of Berkeley High's more affluent, white ninth graders, she did not attend Berkeley's public school system. In fact, according to school records, some 12 percent of Berkeley High School's class of 2000 attended private middle schools, and most of these students were white. This constitutes a particular form of white flight and reentry to the public system at the high school level.

Thus, Jennifer came to the high school from a private middle school with a more rigorous academic program. This may be why Jennifer reports that she found Berkeley High "much easier" than her middle school. Although Jennifer admits that she struggled with math in the past, she elects to enroll in a high-level math class: Honors Geometry. Knowing that the geometry class was a bit of a stretch for her, Jennifer's parents relied on their economic capital to hire a private tutor. It turned out that her tutor also had quite a bit of social capital because this particular tutor was planning to become a math teacher at Berkeley High and was familiar with the textbook and ways of thinking used in the geometry class. Having access to such expert assistance was invaluable for Jennifer, who credited the tutor for her success.

The juxtaposition of Chantelle's and Jennifer's experiences reveals that student resources—economic, social, and cultural capital—interact with the structure of the school to perpetuate disparities in student outcomes and experiences. It is important to note that the structuring of inequality at Berkeley High is subtle, hidden behind taken-for-granted understandings of the way things work. There is no evidence of a conspiracy to favor affluent students and hold back poor students of color. However, the structure of the school is implicated in the stark patterns of inequality that are reproduced year after year—structures that appear neutral on the surface but actually reinforce unequal outcomes.

This chapter explores the ways in which school structure serves to reproduce inequality. It begins with Beth C. Rubin, Jean Yonemura Wing, and Pedro A. Noguera examining tracking "Berkeley High style," probing the means through which racial and class-based inequalities are perpetuated through course placement. In the next part, Emma Fuentes and Daniel Liou present a profile of the English Language Learner Program, demonstrating how and why well-intentioned staff have not been enough to help immigrant students overcome the institutional barriers they face at the school. In the third part, Alicia P. Rodriguez illuminates the ways in which gender is implicated in unequal opportunities, through an examination of the treatment of girls and boys. Finally, Lance T. McCready examines the ways in which students participate in extracurricular activities and shows how their choices reflect and reinforce academic and racial segregation throughout the school.

Tracking Berkeley High Style: Different Pathways to Different Futures

Beth C. Rubin, Jean Yonemura Wing, Pedro A. Noguera

In the broadly disseminated statewide public school rankings released in 2000, Berkeley High School scored a 9 on a scale of 1 to 10, putting it in the top echelon of California public schools. Such a rating suggests that this is an excellent public school, one to which parents should be pleased to send their children. However, a closer look at the academic landscape of this highly ranked school reveals striking disparities in achievement and outcome, which appear tightly linked to race and class.

Tracking on the basis of perceived academic ability is a tradition at many American high schools (Oakes, 1985), but it has changed over the past decades. As awareness has grown about the harmful effects of tracking on some students, there has been a shift away from assigning students to rigid tracks that determine all of their classes throughout high school to a more flexible arrangement in which students can vary in track assignment from class to class (Lucas, 1999). Tracking at Berkeley High blurs the sorting process even further.

At BHS, ninth graders are placed in math classes ranging from Math A to Honors Geometry without any form of assessment. Typically students are allowed to choose which course they want to take in consultation with counselors, who make recommendations based on an examination of their middle school transcripts. As for their foreign language electives, ninth graders can choose to enroll in Kiswahili, French. Spanish, Latin, or German, or in no language whatsoever. Many make their selection without realizing that the most advanced courses are available only in the traditional European languages. A careful examination of students' course assignments reveals troubling patterns with respect to the ways in which choices about math coincide with science and foreign language course placement. This is tracking Berkeley High style, and it has critical consequences for students.

Ninth Grade: An Uneven Start

The class of 2000 entered Berkeley High in fall 1996 with 764 students. This large cohort provides a starting point in tracing the pathways of students through their four years of high school.

In many ways, all ninth graders start off in the same way. All are assigned to detracked English and history core academic classes, in which small cohorts of freshmen—carefully balanced for race, gender, and achievement level—share the same pair of English and history teachers. Most ninth graders also take the required ethnic studies course, as well as physical education. But a close look at the other course assignments of ninth-grade students reveals how differences related to race, class, and language establish patterns that have profound ramifications for students' subsequent opportunities.

Math as a Gatekeeper

Math placement typically serves a benchmark for ninth-grade academic standing, and the disparities in math placement by race are striking. As is true nationally, white, middle-class, or affluent students at BHS tend to receive access to advanced math courses early, and thus start their high school careers with a major advantage (Moses and Cobb, 2001; Perry, Steele, and Hilliard, 2004).

The Diversity Project's class of 2000 research team found that 83 percent of the ninth graders who were placed in Math A, the low-track prealgebra class, were African American. In contrast, 87 percent of students from that same cohort of ninth graders who were placed in Honors Geometry, the advanced-track math class, were white. It also turns out that a disproportionate number of these students had attended private school before entering BHS.

Students like Jennifer who came from private feeder schools are at a distinct advantage. Nearly half (46 percent) of freshmen in the class of 2000 who came from private feeder schools were placed in Honors Geometry, compared to just 18 percent of freshmen from Berkeley public middle schools, all of whom took Honors Algebra in the eighth grade. Meanwhile, virtually all students with an undocumented feeder school (students who entered Berkeley High after the semester had already started, mostly from out-of-district cities such as Oakland), who were predominantly African American, were routinely placed in Math A without any assessment of their math abilities.

Math placement at Berkeley High has far-reaching consequences for students' pathways through the Berkeley High course structure. Figure 1.1 illustrates these different pathways by linking ninth-grade math placement with students' course-taking patterns and electives and indicating their corresponding tenth-grade options for math and science.

Students who entered Berkeley High with advanced math standing were also more likely to be placed in advanced foreign language classes. The research team found that 75 percent of ninth graders in "regular" Geometry and Honors Geometry were taking intermediate or advanced-level foreign language classes, with the remaining 25 percent all in Latin 1, a prestigious language typically taken by college-bound students. In contrast, just 27 percent of students enrolled in Algebra I as ninth graders were in intermediate foreign language classes, with 53 percent enrolled in a first-year language course. It is even more disturbing and telling that the remaining 16 percent of Algebra 1 students were enrolled in no language class at all.

FIGURE 1.1 The Pathways Through Berkeley High School: Class of 2000 Course Options by Ninth-Grade Math Placement

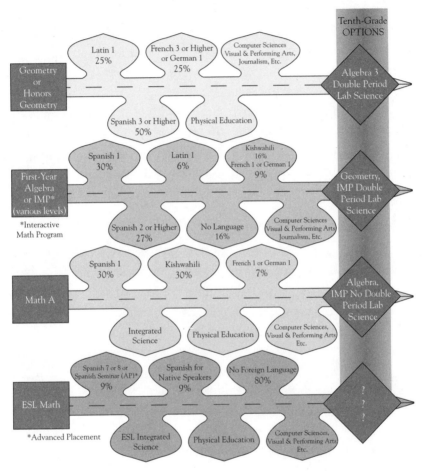

The percentages in Figure 1.1 indicate the percentage of class of 2000 ninth graders with a given math placement who also took particular ninth-grade electives.

Source: Graphic by Julia González Luna, teacher, and Jean Yonemura Wing; computer artwork by Fredda Cassidy, graphic artist and parent.

Still more striking was the comparison with ninth graders enrolled in Math A, the lowest math level. None were taking intermediate language classes, 67 percent were in first-year language classes, and 33 percent were not taking any language class. In addition, almost half of those taking a foreign language were enrolled in Kiswahili, a language offering no Advanced Placement level. No Geometry students and only 8 percent of Algebra students were enrolled in this African language course.

These links between language and math levels also imply a kind of ranking of foreign languages in terms of academic status for college, with Latin at the top, other European languages next, and Kiswahili at the bottom of the language hierarchy.

Quality of Teaching and Learning in Different Tracks

Ninth-grade students noted qualitative differences between their advanced and "regular" courses (Talbert, 1990). In an ethnographic study in which five diverse ninth-grade students were shadowed from their tracked to their detracked classes, there were noticeable differences in both classroom demographics and academic tone. One of these students, an African American student with high grades named Natay, who was placed in Algebra I and Spanish I in her first year, found both classes to be quite undemanding. Her Spanish class, she told an interviewer, was filled with classmates who "don't really want to learn." "People say the stupidest things," she said. "I look at them sometimes and I'm, like, 'How many times have you taken this class!'" Although Natay focuses her criticisms on her classmates, our observations revealed that the students were most likely responding to the low expectations and mediocrity in teaching found in her "regular" grade-level classes (Perry, Steele and Hilliard, 2004).

Natay found her Algebra I class to be similar to her Spanish I class in its lack of both order and rigor. Her math teacher was impressed by her work and had advised her to try to get into Honors Geometry as a sophomore. An Honors Geometry teacher commented, however, that students coming from Algebra I rarely succeeded in Honors Geometry, and he discouraged her from enrolling in the course.

It is noteworthy that Natay had taken both Spanish I and Algebra I in eighth grade, a fact that an examination of her transcript readily would have revealed. However, she was not placed in the higher-level courses as a ninth grader, and she did not challenge her counselor and struggle to be placed more appropriately. "It's okay," she said. "Hey, I'm getting A's." By starting high school in introductory courses, however, this academically oriented student was going to be limited in reaching the highest course levels by her senior year. It is equally distressing that in the lower-level courses, she experienced a lower quality of teaching and learning.

For ninth graders, who are new to the high school, these differences were striking. Natay and other case study students noticed the difference in the racial demographics of their low-level classes as compared to their detracked freshman core classes, which were racially mixed. Mike, a white student, declared that he was the only white student in his Math A class. Leticia, an African American student, noted that the only all-black class she ever attended at Berkeley High was not in African American studies but was Math A. When researchers from the Diversity Project asked members of the Student Outreach Committee to document classroom segregation in photographs, the students picked up their disposable cameras and fanned out across the school, snapping photos of predominantly white AP classes and predominantly black and brown math and English "backup" classes, which provide extra time for homework and tutoring. Wells and Serna (1996) argue that this academic segregation across classrooms discourages higher-achieving students of color from electing higher-tracked classes when given the chance, because they do not want to be isolated as "the only one." It is also likely to act as a deterrent to academically struggling white students enrolling in classes designed to provide remediation and support.

Easy to Jump Down, Hard to Jump Up

It is difficult, though not impossible, to "jump track" upward (Harklau, 1994). Very few students try, and even fewer succeed. In general, students found that retreating to a lower math track was easier and far more common than advancing to the honors track, especially for students of color.

Such was the case for Manuel, a middle-class Chicano student who had been placed in Honors Geometry based on his strong middle school math record but who found the class too difficult in the way it was taught. Unlike many other students who were experiencing difficulty in this class, Manuel did not have, and could not afford, a private tutor. He asked his counselor for a transfer to a "regular" geometry class, but he was instead placed in Algebra I, a class he had taken already in middle school and passed with high marks.

Zion, a middle-class African American/Latino student, was an exception who managed to jump track. Zion was good in math yet found himself placed in an algebra backup class in ninth grade, where he joined a classroom filled with other students of color. Whether it was his flatlands address or his dark complexion and urban style, somehow Zion was misperceived as needing extra help. Fortunately for him, within weeks his algebra backup teacher realized that he did not belong in the class, and the following year, his teacher recommended him for Honors Geometry.

Math Placement Opens the Gate to Advanced Placement

Starting math a year above grade level puts all of the Honors Geometry ninth graders on track to take Advanced Placement (AP) Calculus or AP Statistics in their senior year. It also provides an advantage in gaining admission to AP Biology, AP Chemistry, AP Physics, and Honors Human Anatomy. These AP science classes and other college-preparatory laboratory science classes have math prerequisites, and the AP sciences have entrance exams.

Success in these courses gives students an edge in admission to selective colleges and reinforces the privileges they derive from their access to economic, social, and cultural capital.

Self-Scheduling Camouflages Tracking

Tracking is not the only school structure that supports the success of high-achieving students. Policies such as self-scheduling also do so by perpetuating the myth that students choose their own pathways through high school. The myth of student choice, integral to the culture of personal freedom exercised by students at Berkeley High, further camouflages the effects of tracking.

How does this happen through free choices made by students through self-scheduling? For years, rather than having a standard curriculum for all students or randomly assigning students to teachers, Berkeley High has allowed students to choose their teachers for at least some of their classes. The process is called "self-scheduling" and is done with little or no counselor guidance. Under this system, college-bound students, often under the guidance of their parents, seek out and choose teachers known for interesting and challenging classes. In contrast, poor students from flatland neighborhoods often use the process to choose teachers who are known for being less demanding—teachers who show videos every day and are easy graders. Students who are new to Berkeley High and have no circle of adults or peers to advise them often wind up with the teachers whom few others choose.

Starting with the class of 2000, a computerized self-scheduling system was launched in efforts to alleviate the gross inequities of the old arena scheduling system, under which students went to tables in the gym and pulled class cards for specific teachers and classes. Under the old system, savvy students would converge on teachers who were known to offer popular and demanding courses and take all the class cards before other students had a chance to pick. The computerized system was introduced because it was seen as more fair and impartial. It allowed each student to choose at least one teacher in a class that the student designated as high priority. However, savvy college-bound students also realized that for a class such as AP Physics or Latin 7, with only one or two sections offered, it would be a waste to use one's priority teacher choice on these classes, which were guaranteed to have quality teachers for the few students eligible to take them. Instead, such students would frequently use their priority pick for their English or history classes, for which two dozen sections were offered, or for their math class, to get the teacher they felt was the best. Through careful course selection and planning, combined with judicious use of the priority teacher and class pick, a student might be able to schedule all or most classes with a teacher of choice.

This system privileges students and parents who have a way of knowing who the "best" teachers are and who know exactly which classes they need to take to enhance their college applications. Moran, McCready, and Okahara (2000), in their paper on institutional reproduction of racial inequality at Berkeley High, state that these students "are able to 'hoard' the best teachers while the neediest students end up with the teachers deemed least effective. . . . To underscore this point, there is currently an email tree among parents listing the preferred teachers and warning parents against other teachers, and this has obvious consequences tied to income and the 'digital divide,' which are both tied to race" (p. 4).

For many students of color, however, "freedom of choice" too often has meant freedom to fail or to barely get by. The high school allows students to pick an "easy" teacher or to "choose" to retake a failed class in summer school and fall further and further behind. As our research showed, these "choices" are made by students who typically lack information and insight regarding how course selection will affect the opportunities available to them after graduation. In addition, students who have grown accustomed to taking classes that do not challenge their minds are unlikely to embrace the opportunity to enroll in more rigorous courses. Unless adults on the BHS staff take deliberate steps to influence students' choices, it is highly unlikely that these patterns will change.

The Upper Grades: Widening the Gap

As students move through the Berkeley High system, they become increasingly stratified and segregated by race and class. The racial achievement gap, as measured by course-taking trajectories and grades, does not level off after the ninth grade but grows wider over time. In part, this is because the largely white, middle-class student population, who entered high school at or above grade level in math, spent their ninth-grade year taking care of graduation requirements and prerequisites for advanced science and math classes, and then they took off in tenth grade along a college-bound track. It is also due in part to a cycle of failure among many students of color, who often end up failing Algebra I or Math A and then repeating it in summer school and tenth grade. With each failure and repetition, these students fall further behind.

By the end of the ninth grade, it is clear that while some students are accelerating forward, others are slipping backward. By senior year, the ninth-grade gap of one or two years in math has become equivalent to as many as five years in math courses taken and passed. For the class of 2000, 19 percent of all seniors were able to enroll in calculus: 68 percent of these students were white, 20 percent were Asian, 3 percent were Latino, and only 5 percent were African American. This meant that one out of three white seniors took calculus, while only two out of one hundred African American seniors did so.

Math is in many ways the most striking example of how students become racially stratified over time, but a similar process occurs in other academic classes that become increasingly more segregated as they approach graduation. This segregation represents more than merely a voluntary social separation of students. As seen in the class of 2000 study, racial segregation in classes began in math and spread year by year to nearly every academic subject area. Add to tracking the effects of self-scheduling and teacher choice, and we find a situation in which students who started ninth grade in racially balanced freshman core classes can go through an entire day without any racial diversity in their classrooms.

Thus, while some students build impressive college resumés, filled with AP courses and high grade point averages (GPAs), others fulfill the minimum graduation requirements that actually fall short of meeting admissions criteria for the state universities. Inadequate counseling, institutional barriers, peer influences, and academic difficulties built over years of inferior education before and during high school are some of the forces responsible for this divide.

Ten-Unit Science Courses

Laboratory sciences are required for admission to the state university systems. At Berkeley High, laboratory science classes are double-period and carry double course credits toward graduation (ten units instead of five). Nearly all white and Asian American students in the class of 2000 took at least one ten-unit science course, while only about half of Latino students and less than 60 percent of African American students did so (Figure 1.2).

FIGURE 1.2   Ten-Unit Science Courses Taken by Students in the Class of 2000, by Race

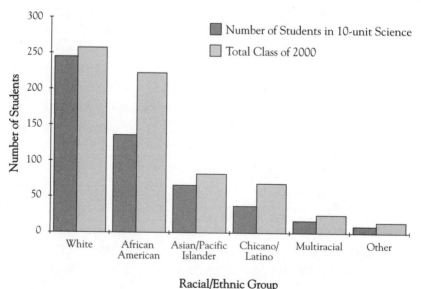

Advanced Placement (AP)

Figure 1.3, based on data from the class of 2000 cohort at the time of their graduation, shows that white students predominate in every AP subject area. Asian American students are generally represented proportionately and are slightly overrepresented in math and science. African American and Latino students are greatly underrepresented across subject areas, with the exception of AP Spanish, in which Latino students are slightly overrepresented.

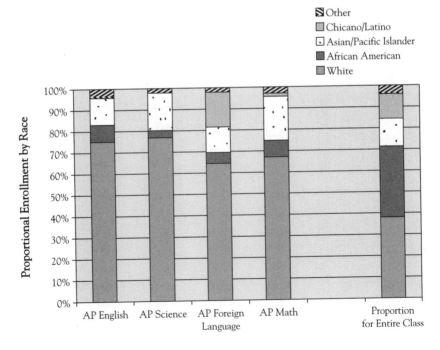

FIGURE 1.3 Proportion of Class of 2000 Students Enrolled in AP Classes, by Subject Area and Race

AP Classes by Subject Area

Grade Point Averages

Grade point averages (GPA), another aspect of student achievement considered in the college admissions process, also reveal distinct racial patterns (Figures 1.4 through 1.6). On a four-point scale, a GPA of 4.0 = A, 3.0 = B, 2.0 = C, 1.0 = D, and 0.0 = F. These patterns start in the ninth grade, and the gap in cumulative GPAs grows wider over time. With the exception of math and foreign language, class of 2000 ninth graders took the same detracked classes in English, world history, and ethnic studies. However, their GPAs at the end of ninth grade, when disaggregated by race, show the beginnings of the achievement gap as measured by grades. Thus, whether they were taking the same heterogeneously grouped classes or more advanced math and foreign language classes, white and Asian American ninth graders significantly outperformed African American and Chicano/Latino ninth graders in terms of overall GPA.

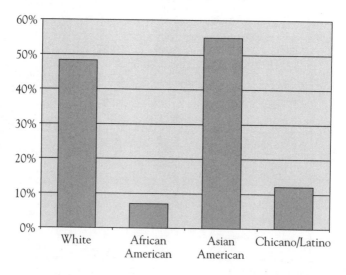

FIGURE 1.4 Class of 2000 Ninth-Grade GPA Above 3.5, by Race

FIGURE 1.5 Class of 2000 Ninth-Grade GPA Below 2.0, by Race

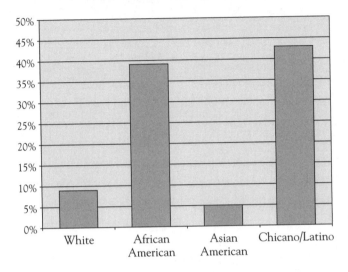

FIGURE 1.6 Percentage of Students in the Class of 2000 with Senior GPA of 3.0 or Higher, by Race

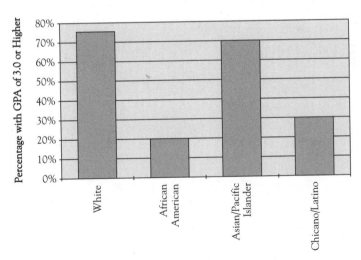

Consequences for the Future:
Graduation and Beyond

Tracking results in a student body with different levels of prepared-ness and eligibility for higher education. The class of 2000 provides a striking example. About 87 percent of white and Asian American graduates were eligible for admission to the UC or CSU system, while only 65.7 percent of African American graduates and 46.3 percent of Latino graduates met eligibility criteria for state university admissions.

The post-high school outcomes for class of 2000 graduates mirror the disparities in their academic pathways through high school, as shown in Figures 1.7, 1.8, and 1.9 (Wing, 2002). In the multitiered system of higher education, middle-class and affluent white students are disproportionately represented in the most selective institutions, whether public or private, just as they were overrepresented in the most advanced high school classes. A mere 5 percent of white students took advantage of the CSU system, whose enrollment draws from the top third of statewide high school graduating classes. Instead, white students tended to choose the more selective of the nine UC campuses or to enroll in prestigious private institutions concentrated in the Northeast, such as Harvard, Brown, and the University of Pennsylvania. Meanwhile, students of color and the poor were disproportion-ately represented in the lower tiers of public higher education—the community colleges and the CSU system. African American students who chose private institutions enrolled overwhelmingly in the historically black colleges of the South, such as Howard, Morehouse, and Xavier. In high school, these students were underrepresented or entirely absent from the AP classes and sometimes started high school in English or algebra backup classes or Math A. And while community college is often portrayed as a sound, economically viable way for disadvantaged students to transfer to a four-year public university, the actual transfer rates are very low.

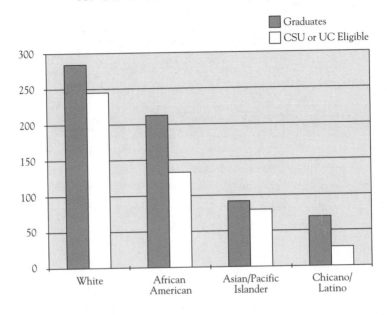

FIGURE 1.7 Numbers and Proportions of Class of 2000 Graduates Eligible for UC or CSU Admission, by Race

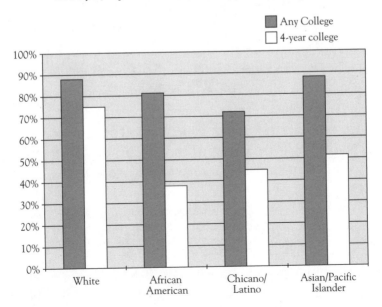

FIGURE 1.8 Class of 2000 College-Going Rates for Racial Groups, by Four-Year College/Any College

FIGURE 1.9 Class of 2000 College Enrollment Rates for Racial Groups, by Type of College

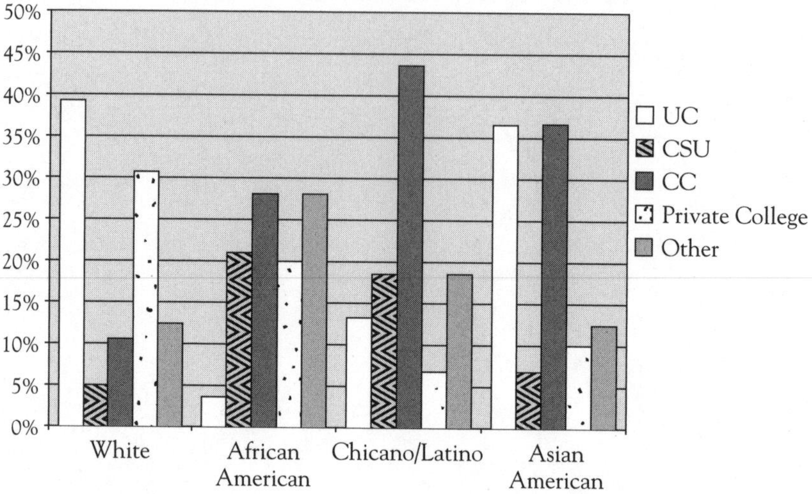

Why the Paths Diverge: Navigating the System

Complex forces underlie the ways in which the institution structures inequality at Berkeley High. The insufficient number of academic counselors—each with a caseload of 550 to 650 students in a school with a highly specialized and complex course structure—certainly plays a role, particularly for the many students without access to private resources or insider knowledge about the pathway to college. The experiences of Chantelle, Natay, Manuel, and Zion are testimony to the ways in which students who lack advocates and private resources, and who tend to be students of color, find themselves placed in inappropriate classes. The counseling system is just one example of how sorting and stratification structures of the school contribute to the achievement gap and disparate pathways after graduation.

What besides economic and social capital explains the differences in how students navigate the difficult institutional structures of Berkeley High? Pierre Bourdieu (1977) argues that cultural knowledge, status, and distinctions mediate the relationship between economic structures, schooling, and people's lives. Students at BHS possess different forms of cultural capital, including social skills, norms of behavior, dress, styles of interaction, and language. These vary by race, class, social status, and one's comfort and relationship to individuals with power. For Bourdieu, schools act as institutional agents that reward the cultural capital of the dominant classes and devalue those of the working classes and the poor. In the Berkeley High context, students who possess the cultural capital associated with wealth and power are offered a high-quality education. Such students, who are mainly white and from middle- and upper-middle-class backgrounds, tend to be perceived as smart, skilled, and highly motivated, and they are generally treated with dignity and respect. This is likely to occur even for white students who cut class, use drugs, and are not doing well academically. In contrast, students of color, who tend to lack the forms of cultural capital that are most highly valued, are generally perceived as less intellectually capable and are less likely to benefit from assumptions about their potential. This form of favoritism is not unique to Berkeley High. As Bourdieu observes, schools in general play a key role in the process of reproducing the social order.

Yet the students themselves also play a role in reproducing privilege and disadvantage. The tracking system is not designed to cheat some students and reward others. It has to be navigated, and students and their parents are the navigators. Throughout their time at BHS, students make choices—about which classes and teachers to take, which clubs to join, and with whom to socialize—that influence this complicated dynamic. In *Jocks and Burnouts* (1989), an ethnographic study of a suburban high school, Penelope Eckert writes:

> There is apparently no end to the subtle and not-so-subtle ways in which schools direct children into their parents' niche in society. But the relation between the individual students and the school does not simply develop through one-on-one interactions between children and adults in and out of school; instead it is mediated by an emerging peer culture that develops both in and out of school, *from common experience with adults and adult institutions* [p. 11, emphasis added].

Different subgroups of students tend to adopt different social norms in relationship to their education and their experience in school. These norms reinforce their position within school and influence their treatment by adults inside and outside school. Although there are exceptions, the social landscape at Berkeley High tends to be racially polarized, with students forming social groups among peers of the same racial/ethnic background. Given the racialized split in academic achievement at the school, these peer groups end up playing a powerful role in reinforcing patterns of school performance.

This section has provided an overarching picture of how tracking and other school policies are part of an institutional structure that results in the reproduction of race- and class-linked inequalities. The following case study of the English Language Learner program provides an in-depth look at the institutional barriers faced by immigrant students.

Language, Culture, and Access

Emma Haydée Fuentes, Daniel D. Liou

My First Day in High School

In December 1996 I came to the United States of America.
I went to BHS.
There were different classes, and it was big.
I didn't know anybody there.
I didn't speak English. I saw different teachers.
I saw different classmates.
I didn't understand what the teacher was saying.
I couldn't find my classes and I had no friends in school.
I felt lonely. It was a new school for me.
Berkeley High School is a new school for me.
Everything is new. But I like this school.

Gene Singh, ESL Level 1, 1996

This poem was written by an English Language Learner (ELL) student. Gene Singh, a recent immigrant from India, describes what it feels like to enter a large school where he did not know other students and was unfamiliar with the rules and norms. It provides a useful snapshot of his first impressions of Berkeley High School: its impersonal nature and a structure that is difficult to navigate, especially for recent immigrant students who do not speak English.

Gene Singh is one of many new faces coming to California. According to a 2004 study by Children Now, 48 percent of California children are from immigrant families. The number of limited-English-proficient students more than tripled in a decade, and the proportion is increasing yearly. Berkeley, like many other school districts throughout the nation, is struggling to serve immigrant students, but as we will show, much of the difficulty is due to an unwillingness to fully integrate these students and treat their needs as a central concern of the school (Olsen, 2000).

Coupled with Gene's feelings of fear about Berkeley High are feelings of comfort in the ELL program. Most ELL students agree with Gene's sentiments about the program, which provides a small, closely knit community where they are known and cared for. They expressed these sentiments during interviews, informal conversations, and focus groups. Throughout the history of the program, the ELL staff has made many attempts to create a nurturing environment for the students. The department has a history of community-building activities, including field trips and its own student yearbook. Teachers make an effort to know their students personally and create classrooms that meet their needs.

Staff efforts to personalize the high school experience for ELL students is partly a response to the ELL program's position within a larger school structure that is not accommodating to the social, cultural, and academic needs of immigrant students and parents. Despite the support that the program provides, ELL students are marginalized in much the same way as many African American, Latino, immigrant, and low-income students at Berkeley High. For a variety of reasons, English Language Learners are often excluded from school activities. They also tend to lack information and access to resources that would empower them to succeed in school and beyond.

Research on the educational experiences of immigrant students in public schools suggests that the experience of English Language Learner students at Berkeley High School is fairly common. For example, in her research on immigrant youth, Laurie Olsen shows that the U.S. educational system is deeply embedded in structural inequalities of the larger society and subject to "the tenacity of those who seek to slot people into places according to skin color, class, or gender with different levels of access, different resources, and different futures" (Olsen, 1997, p.16).

This section examines the educational opportunities of students in the ELL program within Berkeley High. In order to illustrate the various ways that academic outcomes of ELL students are influenced by the structure of opportunity within the school, we describe the makeup of the ELL student body and then analyze both the broader institutional constraints and the academic and social isolation that is fostered by the program. Our intent is to show how the various constraints—from the larger, external barriers created by funding regulations and federal policies, to the more site-specific barriers that affect student educational experience—work together and make it difficult for ELL students to navigate the system.

This study in no way seeks to imply that ELL programs are ineffective or should be dismantled.[1] On the contrary, our research revealed that students need the services this program provides and that many would have been lost without the program's support. However, especially in the wake of such California propositions as Propositions 187, 209, and 227, it is important to stress that this analysis of the program is made with an explicit desire to strengthen it. Proposition 187, passed by California voters in 1994, denied access to public services to undocumented immigrants. Two years later, the U.S. Supreme Court reversed the proposition as unconstitutional. In 1996, California voters passed Proposition 209, which eradicated the state's affirmative action policies. Finally in 1998, in a campaign sparked by billionaire Ron Unz, California passed the "English-only" Proposition 227, which all but eliminates bilingual education programs in California public schools.

Our hope is that research of this kind can help the faculty and staff to find ways to improve the support provided to students acquiring English as a second language. This study attempts to identify the barriers that limit opportunities for ELL students and the gaps in the program as identified by students and staff, with the hope that these issues can be addressed to allow equal learning opportunities for ELL students.

English Language Learners Department

We are like a very small school inside of the bigger school [ELL student, 1999].

The ELL Department at Berkeley High serves from 275 to 300 students per year, roughly 10 percent of the high school population. Of these students, half are enrolled full time in ELL classes, with the other half still designated as ELL but making the transition into mainstream classes under a special status that calls for monitoring of progress. Students in the program come from some forty-five language groups and a wide range of ethnic and socioeconomic backgrounds. Latino students, primarily from Mexico, make up 40 percent of the population, with East Asian/Pacific Islander (Chinese, Vietnamese, Cambodian, Laotian, Hmong, Japanese, Thai, Korean, and Filipino) students at 30 percent, followed by smaller numbers of South Asian (Indian, Pakistani, Sri Lankan, Tibetan), Middle Eastern, African, and European students. Severe economic or wartime conditions in countries of origin cause many students to arrive with interrupted schooling, often rendering them unprepared not only in English but also in content knowledge and basic study skills (Lucas, Henze, and Donato, 1990). On top of these hardships, ELL students typically arrive at BHS unfamiliar with the knowledge needed to navigate this complex school.

As in most other high school ELL programs, students in Berkeley High's program face the dual challenge of simultaneously learning a new language and mastering secondary-level course content. ELL students enter the high school with differing levels of education and at different times of their school careers. Some recent arrivals have never been to school before and are not literate in their native languages. Others, particularly the children of foreign scholars and graduate students, are at or above grade level in some or all subject areas, but simply lack English language and literacy skills. Seventy percent of ELL students are newcomers to the program. Interestingly, 20 percent are designated as ELL but have been in the Berkeley school system their entire academic careers. Another 10 percent of ELL students have transferred to BHS from other districts. Students are placed in the ELL program based on English language proficiency—not by age, grade level, or academic ability in their native languages. Each ELL class is made up of a heterogeneous student body with an array of educational, social, academic, and cultural experiences and needs that differ from students in the larger high school.

Cycle of Funding and Defunding

Berkeley High School's English as a Second Language (ESL) Department (also referred to as the ELL Department) was established in 1987 in response to a pending lawsuit filed against the school district by bilingual parents and community members dedicated to addressing the needs of underresourced communities of the East Bay.

Prior to the lawsuit, the existing ESL Department was in reality a subprogram of the school's English Department. Under this arrangement, parents and community members felt that newcomers and bilingual students were not receiving appropriate services. In an attempt to forestall the lawsuit, the district provided large block funding toward a new ESL program in the late 1980s and created a handful of classes that became the ELL Department. As the department grew and became politically empowered within the larger school, it was able to fund a department chair (actually, only 40 percent of this person's time was dedicated to the program), two bilingual community liaisons, a bilingual clerk, a secretary, and sixteen professional instructional assistants.

Throughout the 1990s, student activities also increased, and the department sponsored eight student organizations. These included the first award-winning ELL speech team, the first ELL yearbook (*In Living Cultures*), and a student government that brought first- and second-generation immigrant students together to collaborate on ethnic and culturally specific issues at Berkeley High. In effect, the ELL program functioned as an autonomous school within a larger school—a fact that has never been acknowledged by school or district officials.

As the lawsuit became a distant memory, the program experienced gradual erosion in funding. With annual and midyear budget reductions up for consideration by the school board, defending the fiscal integrity of the program became an ongoing struggle for teachers, students, and parents. Things took a turn for the worse in 1995, when program funding was switched from per program to per pupil allocation. This had the unintended consequence of creating an incentive for staff to keep a consistently high number of ELL students in the program regardless of their readiness for mainstream classes.

By the year 2000, the department had been reduced to program status, left with only two staff positions to oversee services to students. The declining budget allocation greatly shrank the department in staffing and political power. In an interview, the former program director expressed concern that budget cuts during the 1999–2000 school year would affect the scheduling of the ELL exit exam. As a result of the delay, program staff would not be able to redesignate students for the following school year, based on their increased fluency in English. In a community meeting on June 11, 2001, attended by three hundred people including the principal and three school board members, Latino parents expressed frustration that their children were being kept in the ELL program far too long. One mother poignantly stated, "Many of our youth are making tremendous efforts to advance very little in school. These are the same youth that we know as intelligent, beautiful, and full of possibilities. We understand that the reasons are complex and stem from the school, the community, and especially this society we live in. We no longer accept the lack of success of our children as 'normal.'"

Despite past progress, interviews with teachers, staff, and parents showed that without adequate access to resources, the ELL program has been incapable of fully meeting the needs of its students. As a program dedicated to recent immigrants, who generally lack political power and influence within the school district, the program was subject to regular budget cuts that severely limited the program's ability to serve its students. With decreasing political power within the district and a school administration that had historically allowed the program to function on the margins, its students and their academic needs were made largely invisible within the school.

Rendering Invisibility

In our research on the ELL program, we conducted a survey of ELL students in which they were asked what they liked most about the ELL program. Almost all of the students spoke positively about their experiences and were effusive in their praise for supportive and caring teachers. A sophomore from Peru responded:

> I love Berkeley High School. In [my country] the teachers are not really close to the students. But here, at BHS, when I first came here I don't speak much English, and as [ELL] teachers I really love them. They really take care of me and, like, now I can really speak English. Like when I came to this country . . . in my first year of school, I really cried a lot. I did not understand everything. Like, she used to tell me everything really, really slowly.

Students also indicated that the extracurricular activities organized by ELL staff and teachers increased the feeling of community within the department. These activities included the annual field trips, end-of-year celebrations, and the Language Exchange program through which immigrant students paired up with native English-speaking students as friends and co-mentors, learning from each other's language and culture through informal cultural exchange. Tom, a senior, shared, "When we go to field trip or the [public] library, we can also learn a lot from talking with the teacher and students. Activities do not have to be in class. In conversations, teachers can also learn about your background and native country. I think outdoor activities are very good."

Despite these positive experiences and the obvious good intentions on the part of the ELL staff to create a school-within-a-school, without the support of the larger school to help ELL students make the transition into the mainstream classes, students in the program were effectively denied access to other resources within the larger high school. This included college preparatory courses in academic subjects, electives and AP classes, and several extracurricular activities. The ELL students' isolation in the program, despite the support they received, also rendered them invisible to the rest of the school. The mainstream staff's unwillingness to accommodate ELL students' presence, in fact, reinforced the program's desire to shelter them.

One illustration of how ELL students were not accommodated by the larger high school took place during the self-scheduling process. ELL students faced limitations because their class schedules were predetermined by their ELL courses, making it more difficult to schedule many mainstream classes for which they were eligible. In response to this situation, ELL staff and teachers often took it on themselves to plan ELL students' class schedules—at times overlooking students' desires to take courses outside the ELL Department.

While this advocacy on behalf of ELL faculty may be well intended, it does not ensure their students' access to college preparatory courses or teach students how to advocate for themselves. Ben, an ELL alumnus in his third year at the University of California, Davis, said, "To enroll in difficult classes was the most difficult thing about BHS." In the end, the program's way of caring for students inhibits their attempts at self-sufficiency and exposure to a wide range of classes offered outside the program.

One ELL teacher whom we interviewed stated that she believes that the ELL program's physical location is academically and socially detrimental for language-minority students because they are isolated in one wing of the school or another. When we began our work with the Diversity Project, the ELL Department was located upstairs in the B Building, alongside Special Education, the school library, and a teen parents' program. After a major arson fire that destroyed the building in April 2000, the ELL classrooms were relocated three times—first to various marginal locations. Finally, after parent protest, the program was relocated in 2001 to one of the central classroom buildings. But during the time of our research, the program was housed in the B Building, one of the oldest buildings, with poor ventilation and no heat. Most ELL teachers agreed that the physical proximity of ELL classrooms to each other in the B Building was helpful to students and teachers and helped generate a sense of community. However, this arrangement also led to the larger school's lack of awareness of ELL students' existence.

As a result of the physical isolation of the program and the structural isolation of the students, recent immigrants' daily interactions with the larger student body were limited. This lack of meaningful incorporation of ELL students into the greater school community led to the perception of the ELL program and its students as remedial and subordinate to the rest of the academic departments. Recognizing this problem, the ELL program established transition classes in 1999 in an effort to mix ELL and mainstream students in academic classes taught by teachers trained in techniques designed for students acquiring English proficiency. The following is one junior's reflection of the treatment ELL students felt in the larger school:

It's [transition classes] going to be like mix ELL students and regular classes together. Yeah. Because regular class students, they look down on ELL people. Like you don't know anything. . . . And they, like, ignore us, and they leave us, like, in the back. It's too bad for when we go in class [if we had classes together] they can understand us. More understanding so we can be, like, "We can do that too." And they can be, like, "Oh, okay."

Such perceptions of ELL programs have serious implications for students' success within the program as well as in the larger school. Students within marginalized ELL programs lack a sense of belonging and ownership at the school. This feeling of isolation leads some students to become disenchanted with the educational process as they come to realize how little they matter to the larger school. In a May 2001 issue of the mainstream student newspaper, the *Jacket*, ELL students appeared on the front page with an article entitled, "Forgotten?" in which they documented their sense of academic isolation and neglect:

ELL senior Martin Guerrero . . . feels excluded from the mainstream school in many ways. Guerrero said that the lack of security guards near the portables (where most of the ELL classes are now located) makes him feel as if the school doesn't care as much about the safety of the ELL students. . . . Another discrepancy between the ELL department and other departments that Guerrero noticed is the difference in the classrooms, in his classroom the chairs and desks seem older than those in non-ELL classrooms. "We should be treated equally!"

The article goes on to say that it is easier for the administration at BHS to focus less on the concerns of the ELL students because their families often do not have the English skills to comfortably communicate with the administration, while at the same time the administration does little to nothing to accommodate these parents.

College (In)accessibility

I want to go to UC Berkeley, but I know that I'm an ELL student and it will be hard for me. But, I'll go to a four-year college and transfer to UC Berkeley. Something like this. I am really interested in biology. So, I want to study biological science or biotechnology. And, I want to major in them [ELL student from India].

When looking at the factors that contribute to ELL students' isolation, it is clear that the ELL students are wedged between two extremes: sheltering and neglect. One of the consequences of the positioning of ELL students within the school is that there is no sustainable structure that informs, encourages, and advocates for their college aspirations. Due to a lack of resources, ELL staff have no data on how many ELL students graduate from high school, matriculate to college, or graduate within four years or more. The absence of such basic data on students is stunning in view of how many students are served.

In our formal and informal interactions with ELL students and their families, we found that many expressed clear desires to continue their academic careers after high school. As one ELL student states, "Every parent has great expectations for their child. My parents wish that I would study hard in the U.S. and get a Ph.D." Unfortunately, these desires do not coincide with their immediate reality. The following is an excerpt from field notes written by another member of the Diversity Project's ELL Committee: "Today [the teacher] asked how many of the seniors planned to go to college next year, they all said yes. [The teacher] then asked how many students had taken the SAT and/or even knew what the SAT is. Not one student knew about the test and that it was needed for college."

The reality is that for an ELL student to be admitted to a four-year college, she or he would have to go through the difficult process of completing all of the following: ELL requirements, including the ELL exit exam measuring English fluency; Berkeley

High graduation requirement; and finally the minimum course requirements for state university admissions: two years of history/social science, four years of English, three years of math, two years of laboratory science, two years of foreign language, one year of college preparatory electives, and one year of visual and performing arts, also called the "A through G" course requirement for state university admission. Furthermore, in the case of newcomers who have attended a foreign high school prior to Berkeley High, students' foreign high school transcripts are not typically analyzed to determine the number of earned high school course credits until their senior year, making it impossible for these students to plan for college or prepare applications. Because ELL student assessment is largely based on English ability rather than content knowledge, preparation toward college becomes secondary, even though most ELL courses are regarded as college preparatory. Because there is so much emphasis on students passing the ELL writing proficiency exam, orientations about the PSAT, SAT I, SAT II, and ACT are largely ignored. There is no doubt that students felt they were inadequately informed about postsecondary opportunities.

The following excerpt from Diversity Project classroom observation field notes provides a vivid illustration of the ways in which ELL student needs are often ignored:

> The Daily Bulletin [a page of announcements and news from the BHS administration and college adviser] gets passed around . . . Daily Bulletin gets passed around in second period, not read aloud as it used to be, and today I noticed that several students chose not to read it. I looked at it and noticed that there were many college application announcements from the College Adviser [scholarship and financial-aid deadlines, SAT registration deadlines, free SAT preparatory classes offered at UC Berkeley, and others]. There are several seniors in the class who could benefit from this information, but since the Bulletin is never read, they might never get this stuff.

Efforts to increase college awareness among students is a formidable challenge for students whose parents do not understand the process and therefore are unable to act as advocates for them. Within the ELL program, many teachers and counselors disagree on students' readiness for or capability of handling mainstream classes. While some counselors, teachers, and staff feel that ELL students should focus aspirations on survival and vocational skills due to the hardships they face—undocumented legal status, economic hardship, assumed familial expectations, and lack of English proficiency—others are more likely to encourage students to take academic risks because college preparation would broaden students' chances for social and economic mobility. However, in an environment of ongoing budget cuts, orientation toward college is often viewed as an extracurricular activity. College information is periodically accessible when a college orientation event is organized, and college tours are limited to weekends when most ELL students are working to help support their families (both here and abroad).

According to federal and state bilingual compliance, college preparation is not a mandate. For this reason, ELL students are disproportionately excluded from academic plans that would prepare them for postsecondary education. During the 1999–2000 school year, only 1.5 percent of ELL students were placed in AP courses. Meanwhile, none of the ELL sheltered courses carried AP status, and many students spent their entire four years unaware of the necessary steps to qualify for admission to four-year colleges. As is true in many schools, there is a tendency to assume that ELL students are low skilled and therefore academic offerings should emphasize remediation. Following are two separate field notes excerpts, both reflecting the lack of information ELL students receive:

> The questions students had about the survey were revealing. One of the survey questions was, "Have you taken any Honors or Advanced Placement (AP) courses?" At least two students called us over to ask what that was.

Then I showed her [ELL student] the list of requirements for U.C. admissions. She was shocked to discover that [BHS] graduation requirements were not the same as college entrance requirements and that she might never have known she wasn't getting the courses she needed for college. "¡Que pesado!" [How terrible!] she kept saying.

The few ELL students who are knowledgeable about the college admission process seem to restrict their aspirations to local two-year community colleges. Even students with strong academic records generally do not see themselves as worthy candidates for the UC system. As one ELL student reveals: "I can go to a community college. And then make my transfer to San Francisco State. I have two things that I really like. One of them is medicine and the other one is law. I really like it. I need to wait to see what I'm going to do."

While others felt that counselors and teachers discouraged them from applying to four-year colleges, one Latina senior who had been in the program all four years stated:

I got a 2.9 GPA. I don't want to go to community college. I know I'll drop out. I asked the teacher, "What can I do to go to a four-year college?" And the teacher makes it sound like I wasn't gonna be able to, "It would be better for you to go to community college and find out what you want to do." I already know what I want to do. I want to be a midwife or a trauma nurse. I think [the teacher] just says those things to make me feel like I can't do it.

In one conversation, an ELL staff member expressed her opinion about why ELL students aspire toward community college:

A lot of our kids for financial reasons go on to community college, and simply for reasons of transportation. Most go to Laney or Vista [two local community colleges] and don't even think of going to any others. I also feel that by going to community college, they don't run the risk of ending up in a class with three hundred students.

A close look at the various ways ELL students are limited in their access to four-year colleges reveals obstacles that extend beyond the program. In a counselors' meeting, one bilingual counselor who was not part of the ELL program stated, "ELL students do not need to attend a UC school to be successful, and if they [ELL students] want to go to UC Berkeley, they should go through the community college system." It is ironic that the counselor would express such certainty that this pathway to a four-year college would work for a student, given that research by the Western Association of Educational Opportunity Personnel, a federally funded college outreach association, shows that only 3 percent of community college students in California transfer to four-year schools each year.

The other structural impediment comes from the UC system itself. The acquisition of college preparatory credits in ELL classes leads to the assumption that ELL students will be eligible for UC admission by the time they complete their required courses for redesignation to mainstream classes. However, ELL staff have come to realize that the UC admissions process systematically disqualifies certain ELL courses, even though they are recognized as college preparatory. The 1998–99 *U.C. Reference Guide for Counselors* (University of California Office of the President, 1998) states, "English as a second language courses may be acceptable *for a maximum of one year*, provided they are *advanced* college preparatory ELL courses, with strong emphasis in reading and writing" (p. C3, emphasis added). For this reason, a student like Tom, a senior who was regarded as one of the strongest students ever to be part of the ELL program, chances for attending a four-year college were limited. Despite his tremendous effort and ability, he would not be able to attend a four-year college because he would not receive college credit for many of the courses he had taken. He spent two years in ELL and ELD (English Language Development) levels 4 and 5 (the highest levels), yet received only one year of college preparatory English credit. Moreover, ELL students' participation in the school Forensic Team and ELL yearbook could not be counted as part of the "A through G" state university admissions requirement because these activities' lack of funding prevented them from being considered courses for credit. Compared to their mainstream peers, those who participate in the school newspaper or are on the school yearbook staff garner academic acknowledgment on their transcripts that can be used in applying for college. Examples like these show some of the ways in which students' college aspirations have been systematically deterred by the combined institutional structures of the ELL program, Berkeley High, and the UC system.

Equity, Access, and Integration?

We began our study of the ELL program expecting to conduct an analysis of ELL students' learning experiences within BHS. However, as the voices of students, parents, and staff came together through our interviews and observations, a clear picture of structural inequality began to emerge. The voices of those within the program helped to unravel and expose the obstacles students encounter each day: funding constraints, academic and social isolation, college inaccessibility, and several others. In the light of these challenges, ELL students' mobility is limited not because they lack effort or ability, but simply because of the way the school has been organized to meet their academic and social needs.

Both the ELL program and the larger school fail to collaborate to reduce the barriers students face. BHS treats the ELL program as a separate autonomous school within the larger school, even though it fails to provide it with the resources needed to serve its students. Its autonomy allows the larger school to ignore the needs of the students within the program and overlook the program's weaknesses. The program's isolation allows some of the faculty to serve even though they are not well trained. Some do not share the life experiences of the ELL students, and language and cultural differences prevent these teachers from providing the support students need.

Many of the teachers are quite skilled academically and culturally. They are also deeply committed to their students and go above and beyond what is required of them to help their students. However, despite their efforts to create a viable, self-sufficient community within BHS, the program has not been given the support it needs to ensure that its students will receive the opportunities they deserve. Without recognition from the district and the larger school of the absolute need for quality services in a program like ELL and its potential contribution to the school, issues of equity, quality, and integration will continue to undermine the efforts of students and staff.

In closing, we echo the powerful sentiment of a publication advocating for the needs of new immigrant students: "[We need to] ensure that immigrant students have fair opportunity at school success by restructuring those policies, structures and practices which impede their access to effective instruction and sort them into programs which prepare them for inferior futures" [National Coalition of Advocates for Students, 1988, p. 118].

The Role Gender Plays

Alicia P. Rodriguez

In addition to inequalities based on race, social class, and language, there are more subtle, hidden structures of inequality based on gender, sexuality, and perceptions of gender roles that are often overlooked. In many ways, how Berkeley High appears from a gender perspective is very much the same as in most other schools in American society (Sadker and Sadker, 1994). At a social level, girls are valued more for their dress and sexuality than for their intelligence and academic abilities. For youth who are gay, harassment from peers is a regular part of their school experience, and their mistreatment directly affects their achievement. Schools, whether they wish to admit it or not, promote certain attitudes about gender and sexuality that influence the academic performance of boys and girls.

This section focuses on how gender factors into the structures of inequality from a social and curricular perspective. In this part of the Diversity Project's research, we asked, What are teachers' perceptions of the different academic abilities of boys and girls, and how does that affect student course selection and performance? In what ways do these perceptions limit the educational attainments of girls at Berkeley High? General perceptions of gender-appropriate behavior are discussed in relation to the concept of feminism and sexuality. Despite the dominant rhetoric of equality at Berkeley High—as seen in the course offerings, extracurricular activities, and school ethos—gender often is not considered in the discourse of antidiscrimination.

Youth Acting Out Gender Identities

Mari: Me and my friends also have this little thing, it's kind of a joke, but we always make fun of hoochies.

Interviewer: What are hoochies?

Mari: They are like people who, girls who dress really scanty like—tight shirts, small revealing shirts, and short shorts and tight pants, stuff like that, lots of makeup. They're, like, glued back to your head in a ponytail. And, well, we look down on them because they have no originality. They are the same. They all do the same things, go to the same parties, think the same. Well, probably not think the same, but in a way they're all the same. They all have the same attitudes toward everything. They don't care. They don't care about school, they just care about themselves, mostly.

Interviewer: Are there equivalent terms for male hoochies?

Mari: Yeah, there's not really a term for it. But guys who dress in overly baggy pants and, like, Tommy Hilfiger shorts or Polo Ralph Lauren or something.

What does it mean to be a male or female youth at Berkeley High School? Is it all about image, appearance, dress, posing? Is it the same as in mainstream settings? Is it the same for every youth, whether straight, gay, or bisexual? In a progressive school like Berkeley High, is the equality of the sexes taken for granted? Are there dominant views, or is it a belief that may be operative at a more subtle level that sends the message to a girl that her desire should be to find a mate, get married, and have children? Are the expectations for young men the same as for young women?

It is interesting to note from the interview that Mari connects certain styles of dress, of which she is critical, to attitudes about school and academics. She paints a portrait of girls who care more about their appearance than anything else as conformists and uninterested in academics. Her comments about boys are not nearly as critical, suggesting that she holds girls to a different standard.

Rose, a student from Ethiopia, sees the gender codes in a similar way, but through a foreign lens. She also views the "cool" dress styles as heavily coded with academic interests and behaviors:

> If you're a boy, you wear jeans . . . not put their pants on properly [low-rider style]! And also shave your head like they do and listen to the music all the time. Don't listen to your teacher. And not [be] really smart. If you're really smart, they would talk to you, but just for, like, homework or something. Not for real. And if you're not smart, they would talk to you. For girls, it's wear makeup every time, have a lot of boyfriends, and a lot of guys talk to you. Dress like girls do here. And look like white, or something. Just a lighter skin. Not dark color. And when you're in class, you just talk to all the boys and don't care what they do to you. Give them hug whenever you see them, like, all the crazy things.

As an immigrant student, Rose has already learned how to interpret the meanings associated with gender, social performance, and physical appearance. She notes that wearing the right clothes makes girls (and African Americans) cool, but to appear smart does not. This tension between being cool and therefore socially accepted, and being smart, and how that corresponds to race and gender, is one that several researchers (Fordham, 1996; Davidson, 1996; Phelan, Davidson, and Yu, 1998) have written about. What makes Rose's comments even more disturbing is her belief that complexion, or what she terms "looking white," is clearly related to being seen as more desirable to boys.

Celia has also noticed that girls, including herself, downplay their academic accomplishments in front of boys. In an effort to be desirable to males, they often want to prove that they are not as smart as boys:

> I've seen people who have lied. They do really well in the class and they lie, like, the boy that's next to them who isn't doing as well. I've seen it. I've seen it. I was talking in my women's studies class. I did it in junior high once. I was, like, "Oh, f_! Like, I got an F on my test. . . . F_! the teacher." And he was, like, "What did you get?" And I lied about my grade. This was in junior high. And I see girls do this all of the time.

It is difficult to say how much the self-belittling behavior of girls comes from themselves, from the culture of youth, from home, or from the culture of BHS. Most likely, it is a combination. However, it is clear that youth who are given the message that their identities (or race, gender, class, or some other characteristic) limit what they can achieve are likely to engage in behaviors that will constrain their intellectual and social development (Erickson, 1987).

The messages related to what constitutes acceptable behavior for gay youth are even more pernicious than for straight youth. Christopher, an openly gay junior who has been repeatedly harassed by peers and school personnel because of his sexuality, tells us that he has experienced a school that condones homophobia and heterosexism: "I have made complaints time and time again and nothing's happened about them. I was told by one of the vice principals that it was my fault because the way I dress and because I was open. And, see, that type of administration would do nothing."

That Christopher is African American has further contributed to his marginalization. Like many other gay and African American students, he has not excelled academically, despite his abilities. On top of the racial barriers that he and others like him encounter, he must also contend with continual harassment and hostility. This has affected his self-esteem and caused him to hate school. Christopher paints a fairly circumscribed picture of youth identity, one that is heavily determined by stereotypes related to race, gender, and sexuality:

> I think normal here is just, like, everyone should have a girlfriend—every guy should have a girlfriend, every girl should have a boyfriend. You know, guys should be playing sports and being athletic. Girls should be dumb cheerleaders. You know, if you're white or Asian, you should be in class studying, studying, studying. And if you're Latino you should just, like, you try to kill each other. I think that's what is normal to a lot of people here.

Stereotyping Who Is "Smart" by Gender

While many girls and boys at Berkeley High, as in other high schools around the nation, mark their identities in ways that communicate the different interests and capabilities of girls and boys, many students report that teachers also engage in stereotyping by gender. Students report that white boys are seen as academic and intelligent, and girls are seen as not quite as bright as boys. In other words, young people at BHS are not the only ones who perpetuate stereotypes about what girls can and cannot do; adults also contribute to this. Even in AP classes, where presumably all of the students are high achievers and highly motivated, some girls find that gender stereotyping by teachers prevails. Brooke, a white student who was enrolled in advanced math and physics classes, shared her experiences as a girl in AP classes:

> *Brooke:* Sometimes, I guess, I feel a little bit as a girl, kind of not taken as seriously sometimes. I mean, generally, everyone always sort of tries to be respectful all the time, but I've had before sort of felt, like, my opinion doesn't count as much. . . . Like in math and science, particularly at our school, is kind of, like, "Did you get the right answer?" Then, you go, "You got the right answer." But if you're, like, "Well, maybe we could do it this way, or how about trying this?" people are like, "No, no. I don't think so."

There's two levels of calculus. There's BC and AB. And I started out in BC and there was too much homework and stuff, so I transferred. And now in AB it's not really a problem. But in the BC class, which is supposed to be harder, more people just kind of didn't listen to you.

Interviewer: Was it the students?

Brooke: Yeah, students.

Interviewer: Did the teacher do anything?

Brooke: Well, not in that class, but my physics class, the teacher sort of in the beginning, I think, was like that. But there's a lot of smart girls in that class. And he sort of realized that and changed it a little bit. But at first . . .

Interviewer: So he had some biases about girls?

Brooke: Yeah, I think so.

Brooke's experiences in calculus and physics are common for girls in advanced classes. Her experiences attest to an underlying structure of gender inequality that is especially pernicious for girls in science and math. It is possible that Brooke may have actually transferred to the lower Calculus AB class not because of the amount of homework but because of the message she was given that as a female, she could not compete with the males in the higher-level class. Like many other girls, it could very well be that she accepted stereotyped assumptions about her abilities. Despite being smart, industrious, and sensitive to issues related to feminism, she and her like-minded friends accepted their "inferiority" as being normal: "We've had conversations before about the issue of not being treated as smart as men. . . . They didn't say that those issues were problems. They just said, 'Oh, that sucks that we're not as smart.' They didn't say, 'That sucks that we think that.'"

If academically advanced white girls feel inadequate, it is probable that the less academically inclined girls, such as the girls described as the "hoochies," might feel even deeper levels of academic inadequacy. Unless deliberate efforts are undertaken by school staff to counter the negative effects of race and gender stereotypes, the social identities of students will determine their academic outcomes. Gender becomes part of the self-fulfilling prophecy related to the achievement gap, and it must be recognized that within a school culture where stereotypes are uncontested, girls will perpetuate gender stereotypes by selling themselves short.

Achievement: Who is Responsible?

It behooves a school that is concerned about diversity and equality to examine achievement from a gender perspective as well. Why is it that in a school like Berkeley High, complete with a women's studies program, so many girls succumb to narrowly framed gender roles that limit their academic and social development? Why do so many female students reject feminism—the idea that girls can be as strong and as smart as boys? For a student like Brooke, who had taken the women's studies class and supported women's rights, labeling herself as a feminist was scary: "When people talked about, like, feminism and women's issues, it seemed like I don't want to be part of that. . . . It kind of felt bad to be trying to say that I'm a feminist because it seems kind of looked down on."

To those who know the progressive culture of Berkeley and BHS, such comments may seem surprising. The fact that a girl would be afraid of being ostracized if she were seen as a feminist seems unlikely in this type of community. Yet this is what many of the students told us. How can it be acceptable to have a security staff member, as witnessed by Christopher, "yell to a group of girls, calling them hoochies and telling them to 'get their hoochie asses off campus'"? Why do so many girls feel they have to hide their intelligence? Such behavior might seem to be unacceptable at BHS, yet the students we interviewed described numerous examples in which adults demonstrated blatant forms of bias.

Equally if not more disturbing is the way in which hostility to gay and lesbians students is allowed to go unchecked. How can it be acceptable for a teacher to let students make fun of a gay student in his or her presence, as Christopher experienced on numerous occasions in an English class? Silence in the face of such hostility may be interpreted by students who are being victimized as a form of tolerance. Clearly, the way students dress, the way they express their sexuality, and the values they hold are outside the control of the school. However, building a school culture that protects gay youth and promotes the abilities of females is critical to the realization of creating conditions where all students have an equal opportunity to achieve. Unless adults at the school, starting with those in positions of leadership, clearly and loudly extol the abilities of women and defend the rights of gay and lesbian students, students will continue to care more about how they look than what they learn. They will also conform to stereotypes that limit their chances, because they will have learned that race, gender, and sexuality determine what a person can or cannot do.

Unraveling the Social Dynamics of Racial Segregation in Extracurricular Activities

Lance T. McCready

In spring 1997, Fran Thompson, faculty adviser for Project 10 (the social and support group for lesbian, gay, bisexual, transgender, and questioning students), invited me to speak at an upcoming meeting focused on the Diversity Project. I readily accepted.

On the day of the Project 10 meeting, I walked into Fran's classroom expecting to see a collage of students who reflected the racial and ethnic diversity for which Berkeley High is famous. Instead of diversity I found homogeneity: twelve white, female, lesbian, and bisexual-identified students. The racial composition of the group was somewhat of a shock, in part because my experience as an after-school coordinator and community organizer in urban settings had shown me that large numbers of gay students of color did indeed attend public schools. I left the meeting wondering why students of color did not attend Project 10 meetings at Berkeley High School.

The lack of diversity in Project 10 raises the question: Why are extracurricular programs and activities at Berkeley High segregated along the same lines as academic programs in the school? While much has been written about the ways tracking produces racial segregation in a school's academic program, less is known about informal, peer-driven social pressures that produce and reproduce racial segregation in extracurricular activities. Pedro Noguera (1995) notes that "at-risk," "gifted," and other coded racial language used by parents and teachers during Berkeley school board meetings have contributed to the political paralysis around issues of equity in policymaking at all levels of public discourse. I build on Noguera's premise by exploring how the discourses of faculty advisers for various extracurricular activities contribute to political paralysis in addressing racial segregation in their programs.

Data are based on interviews conducted as part of the Diversity Project's Taking Stock study of extracurricular activities. The interviews show that teachers have a complex understanding of the social dynamics that produce racially defined patterns of participation in extracurricular activities. Most faculty advisers, however, were frustrated with finding ways to challenge racial segregation. Only one, the coach of men's varsity baseball, found a way to diversify his team. By presenting his narrative and those of less successful faculty advisers, I hope to start a dialogue on how teachers can intervene in peer-driven social dynamics that create racial segregation in school programs and activities.

Taking Stock

The Diversity Project's Taking Stock inquiry team was one of the project's first committees. Its origins can be traced to the summer of 1996 when the Core Team spent a lot of time discussing how Berkeley High School's racially segregated environment affects the academic performance of students, particularly low-achieving black and Latino students. The team had a suspicion that segregated patterns of participation created the impression that students' racial identities determined their level of academic success. Understanding how this link was created was seen as a first step toward undoing it. The team also believed that a study of segregation in clubs and teams would be less threatening to school staff than a study of the same segregated patterns in the core academic program, so this was a good place to start.

Interestingly, the school never kept data on the racial composition of extracurricular activities. For this reason, the Taking Stock Committee decided to survey teachers who served as faculty advisers for Berkeley High School's forty athletic teams and forty clubs and activities. Survey questions included the racial and gender breakdown of participating students, target populations, recruitment strategies, and purposes of the activities. We conducted the survey through face-to-face interviews rather than putting paper surveys in teachers' mailboxes to increase the faculty adviser response rate. Direct interviews also provided an opportunity for follow-up questions and elaboration in answers.

In analyzing the survey data, one of the first questions we wanted to answer was whether patterns of participation differed by race. We began by classifying each activity as academic/career, athletic, cultural, visual and performing arts, or social, based on the purpose of the activities as stated by faculty advisers. Academic/career activities such as the *Jacket* (school newspaper), the yearbook, and the Tutoring Center were activities where students could acquire academic or career-related skills. We also considered academic/career activities to be those valued on college applications (Holland and Thomas, 1987).

Athletic activities included freshman, junior varsity, varsity, and club sports for men or women, such as basketball, football, basketball, lacrosse, crew, field hockey, wrestling, and soccer. Cultural activities such as the Black Student Union, Chicano/Latino Graduation, Project 10, and the Vietnamese Student Association were clubs and programs where students could explore, affirm, and celebrate cultural heritage and identity. Visual and performing arts activities such as Dance Projects, the Afro-Haitian Dance Program, Orchestra, and Magic Club were clubs and programs where students could practice visual and performing arts, or stage productions and exhibitions. Social activities were clubs where students could get together for social reasons based on some common interest.

Overall, we surveyed advisers for seventy-three activities: nineteen academic/career, twenty-nine athletic, ten cultural, thirteen visual/performing arts, and two social. Each activity was labeled "mixed," "predominantly students of color," or "predominantly white," based on the racial demographics reported by faculty advisers. Clubs and activities were identified as mixed if the reported demographics mirrored those of the student body (approximately 40 percent white, 60 percent combined students of color). If white students or students of color were disproportionately represented, the clubs or activities were designated "predominantly students of color" or "predominantly white."

What became immediately noticeable was the small number of activities that are mixed. Of the seventy-three activities surveyed, only two were racially mixed. Of the nineteen academic/career activities in our research, only the Key Club, which focuses on community service, was racially mixed. Of the twenty-nine athletic teams surveyed, sixteen were missing demographic information, but the available data showed that they tend to be racially segregated. Five were predominantly students of color, and seven were predominantly white. Only varsity baseball was mixed. Five cultural activities comprised predominantly students of color, three were predominantly white, and two were missing information. Eight performing/visual arts activities were predominantly white, four were predominantly students of color, and one was missing information. Finally, both social activities surveyed were predominantly white.

Peer-Driven Social Dynamics That Lead to Racial Segregation

Several faculty advisers claimed that social dynamics in students' peer groups were to blame for segregation in extracurricular activities. Faculty advisers of academic/career activities reported that a number of these activities that were predominantly students of color served the needs of students who had been excluded from the predominantly white mainstream groups. For example, the faculty adviser for *Ujamaa*, the black student newspaper, said the activity serves as "an alternative to the *Jacket*, the school newspaper whose staff is predominantly white students." The faculty adviser for *In Living Cultures*, the English as a Second Language (ESL) yearbook, said it "was created because already existing publications in the school often exclude ESL student life." These responses raise questions about the subtle ways through which students of color are excluded from predominantly white extracurricular activities.

But how and why does this exclusion occur? One possible explanation is that students' everyday lives occur in racially, linguistically, or culturally separate spaces in the school. The ESL classrooms were located in a physically separate section of the B Building that housed administrative and counseling offices, the library, and the health clinic. Much of the academic and social lives of black students also take place in physically separate spaces in the school, in part as a result of tracking.

In the film *School Colors*, students point out different areas of the school that over time have become racial/ethnic enclaves, most noticeable at lunchtime. This happens not only in physical spaces but in other parts of the school as well. Most of the students and parents in the audience at Afro-Haitian Dance performances are black, while most of the students and parents at Dance Production performances are white. Both clubs engage in dance, which suggests that theoretically it should be possible for students from different backgrounds who enjoy dance to participate in either activity. However, because the clubs have been racially identified, it is unlikely that students will cross these racial boundaries on their own. The overall effect of students of color and immigrant students carrying out their academic and social existence in racially segregated spaces is that the white students who participate in the yearbook, *Jacket*, Literary Magazine, and other mainstream extracurricular activities are also alienated from the everyday lives of students of color.

Why do students separate themselves by race? Some of the faculty members believed the roots of racial segregation are developmental and begin in middle school, when students begin to align their participation in school with same-race peers. The faculty adviser for Jazz Band Lab reported:

> At the junior high level, there is a change beginning: white kids continue [to take music lessons], but there is a lessening of interest by black and Latino kids. Why? It's not economics, it's a social thing. It's a matter of who they want to hang out with. Overall, I just try to keep them interested. As students get to the secondary level, however, the curriculum gets more difficult, more demanding. Student interest veers toward sports, social things, unless there is a passion, a deep commitment.

What the adviser did not add is that students also need to be encouraged and even pushed by adults. Several of the white students in the jazz band received private lessons and strong encouragement from their parents. Most students of color do not receive similar kinds of support. Likewise, the coach of men's and women's cross country observed that although black and Latino students were interested in participating, they were reluctant to join without the support of their same-race peers:

> I have tried to attract people on track who would facilitate diversity, but have not been very successful. The three most successful runners have all been black, but it is difficult to get [black] kids to run because peer recognition is for fastness, not running distance. Plus, this sport is at the same time as football and basketball, which are more popular among blacks. For example, some kids would rather sit on the bench in basketball than compete and do well at cross country. Plus, they want to play with their friends, and basketball is a bigger sport.

As this coach points out, students are drawn to extracurricular activities with status among their peers. It is important to note that the social status of particular activities tends to vary by students' racial identity. Men's soccer, Latino Graduation, and Baile Folklorico are the most popular activities among Latino students; badminton and Asian cultural clubs are most popular among Asian students; men's and women's basketball, football, cheerleading, and Afro-Haitian Dance are most popular among black students. The faculty adviser for Black Gold, an African American performance troupe, commented:

> You'll notice among black students, if they've been in Afro-Haitian Dance for four years, they walk with a certain swagger among other black students. They have a certain swagger, they have a certain, like, "I'm FRESH because I do this and I get out there and people scream for me." Most people at Berkeley High don't go to Afro-Haitian dance performance. Very few people actually go. People in the circle go, but the white students [and] the general population at Berkeley High doesn't go. . . . But they still have that "I'm a good dancer at this school." It's a status thing, a popularity thing.

Incidentally, the yearbook, the *Jacket* newspaper, Literary Magazine, men's and women's crew and lacrosse, women's soccer, swimming, and water polo, all academically and economically elite activities, are some of the highest-profile activities among white students. The clubs and their participants reflect and reinforce racial patterns at the school. They also reinforce racial stereotypes and send the message that a student's racial identity determines what he or she can or cannot do, both inside and outside the classroom.

How and why do particular activities gain currency among students? The faculty adviser for Jazz Band Lab cited popular culture as an influence. The track and field coach thought it was something more intrinsic, which he described as "heart." However, the varsity baseball coach approached the question of status from a purely social standpoint. When he began coaching during the 1995–96 school year, his team had eighteen white participants and one African American. According to the coach, baseball was not a "glamour sport," and many student athletes who might have played baseball instead were attracted to higher-profile sports such as football and basketball. One year later, the team significantly diversified, with eight African American, two Latino, seven white, and three multiracial ballplayers. The coach, who felt "committed to the team based on service to the community and love of sport and youth," did a lot of "informal player relations," such as when he followed up on relationships that his players had with students of color in the network of little leagues, summer leagues, and fall leagues. Over his three years as coach, he was able to increase the number and diversity of students who tried out for varsity baseball. It is important to note that the team's membership changed not because the stereotypes changed but because the coach intervened in the patterns of participation.

At the same time, this coach reported that many Berkeley High students continued to perceive baseball and a host of other athletics, such as lacrosse, golf, crew, and tennis, as "preppy white guy" activities, even though varsity baseball was now over 50 percent nonwhite. Despite this nagging perception, the coach felt good about the close cross-racial sense of brotherhood that he witnessed among the players.

Challenging Racial Segregation Outside the Classroom

Most of the faculty members we interviewed were either reluctant or unsure of how to intervene in peer-driven social dynamics that produced segregated patterns of participation. The one faculty adviser who successfully diversified his activity, the boys' varsity baseball coach, did so by tapping into a lot of informal player relations in the baseball networks of students of color. He knew that many students of color were playing baseball in leagues outside school and understood that he could recruit players to his team if he actively sought them out. This raises the question: To what lengths should faculty advisers go to recruit underrepresented groups of students?

The point that needs to be understood here is that this is not merely a matter of student choice or voluntary segregation. The Taking Stock study indicates that faculty advisers are much less proactive than they could be. The work of faculty advisers often takes place above and beyond the regular hours of teaching, which is why some are reluctant to spend even more time recruiting underrepresented students. However, when they do nothing, they contribute to the mistaken belief that racial segregation is normal, if not inevitable, and that students themselves are responsible for racial segregation, at least outside the classroom walls. Our research showed that if the adults do not challenge racial stereotypes, then they should not expect students to do so on their own.

Conclusion

Although students from diverse backgrounds enter Berkeley High School with the promise of access to a high-quality education, the structure of the school is such that this goal is only selectively achieved. BHS offers a wide array of sports and clubs that are the envy of even many private schools. Yet because of perceived racial barriers to participation, many students fail to take advantage of what the school has to offer. In so doing, they not only limit their opportunity to play an instrument or receive academic support that might be helpful for gaining admission to a selective college, they also limit their opportunities to experience personal growth. While many teachers, administrators, counselors, and other school staff lament the ways in which students segregate themselves, few are committed to evaluating the institutional structures and priorities that allow this segregation to occur. This analysis and reflection needs to happen before significant progress can be made toward educational equity (McCready, 2002).

At Berkeley High, as at most other schools, human and financial resources are bound up in a particular set of school priorities that are often not explicitly expressed. Resources are directed toward maintaining the school's reputation as a public school where middle-class and more affluent students can receive an elite, college-preparatory education and where already well-prepared students can be intellectually challenged and get what they need to be admitted to a good college. Berkeley High maintains a huge number of elective courses and a wide selection of AP and honors classes, and allows its students to express a preference for particular teachers in the course selection process. Yet the diversity of the school, which parents and students often cite as one of its greatest assets, is rarely part of a student's experience, aside from the diversity they observe in the hallways.

School structures such as the master schedule have the effect of reinforcing existing patterns of racial separation and play an important role in reproducing patterns of academic success and failure. Just as we showed how the course selection process, which appears neutral and available to all, is actually difficult to navigate without informed parental support, insider knowledge, and perseverance, so too are other features of the school, such as the extracurricular activities. Adult intervention is needed to ensure that opportunities for academic success and social support are available.

Struggling students often need more than study halls and extra attention from individual teachers, especially when academic expectations are raised. Targeted tutoring and support classes have been shown to be effective in supporting such students (Mehan, Hubbard, and Villanueva, 1994). Institutionalized mechanisms for monitoring the progress of students across academic classes would enable the school to target students for comprehensive support rather than the piecemeal supports that exist currently. The school could also build stronger ties with community organizations that offer support services for students and work to maintain better relationships with families to foster genuine collaboration with parents rather than the often adversarial relationship that currently exists.

Berkeley High's baroque course structure creates conditions under which many students fall through the cracks. Chantelle taking prealgebra twice and Natay not being put in geometry as a ninth grader are but two examples of how students make important decisions based on misinformation, and the lack of safeguards within the system to catch such mistakes. A different set of priorities, structures, and programs could be created to prevent such problems. More counselors and more frequent meetings between students and counselors, dividing the school into smaller units, teacher-led advisories, and respect for the aspirations of all students would help to address the disparities among students with regard to the resources they bring with them to navigate the system.

Finally, the success of equity-geared measures at Berkeley High may be linked to the ability of the school's adults to encourage a change in the social landscape of the school. This could be accomplished through structural reform, creating smaller schools-within-schools or small, autonomous schools sharing a large campus, which should be designed explicitly to foster community and academic excellence among diverse students. Also important is a reconsideration of the social spaces of the school, which in their current starkness (the courtyard) and discomfort (crowded school hallways) encourage defensive huddling rather than friendly mingling. Adult attention to students' social needs and active recruitment of diverse students to the high school's vast array of clubs and athletic teams would be a positive change from the current laissez-faire attitude toward this extracurricular dimension of school life and would facilitate the collaborative interaction of students within and beyond the classroom context.

The point that must be recognized at Berkeley High School and schools like it throughout the United States is that the structure of schooling (tracking, teacher assignment, and so forth) often places low-income students of color at a distinct disadvantage. The structure undermines efforts to provide a consistently high-quality education to all students, regardless of how well intentioned the teachers or how hard working the students. Critical analysis of school priorities and practices, and of racial boundaries, real or imagined, is needed to counter the effects of race and gender stereotypes and the influence of social inequality outside the school (Fine, Weis, Pruitt, and Burns, 1997). Active intervention is needed to support the needs of students who have less support or fewer resources at home, and leadership at multiple levels is required to ensure that excellence in teaching and a rigorous curriculum are available for the lowest-achieving students too. Without such interventions, the achievement gap will never close, Berkeley's dream of becoming a community that lives out its values of equity and justice will never be realized, and students will be denied the education they deserve.

Note

1. Four members of the Diversity Project conducted a study (1999–2000) in the English Language Learner (ELL) Department at Berkeley High School. During the 1999–2000 school year, the team spent 180 hours in participant-observation in eight ELL classrooms over a sixteen-week period from February through May 2000. The classrooms included both sheltered English content courses (using specific methods of modified instruction in English without oversimplifying or watering down the content) and English as a Second Language (ESL) and English Language Development (ELD) courses at different levels, including ESL 1, 3, 4, and a transition class. The major sources of data include field notes; interviews with nine ELL students and ten ELL graduates; one student focus group; two student social events; and numerous informal conversations with students, staff, and community members. The study provides a glimpse of the ELL program's dynamics and cannot serve as representative of the whole program. However, it provides some indication of the types of obstacles students face during their time in the program, whether recently arrived or having been in the Berkeley school system for years.

2

INTEGRATION ACROSS CAMPUS, SEGREGATION ACROSS CLASSROOMS

A Close-up Look at Privilege

Jean Yonemura Wing

Whoever you are, you can always find people that are like you, and it makes it easier to, to, like, get through the day knowing that there are people. And especially if you pick your classes selectively, like my junior year, I was basically then kind of on a track with the same people, because of my math. I mean, it was Latin and Bio, like the AP classes and stuff like that. And so you can really find your place [Pamela, white female, junior-year interview].

When I first came to teach at Berkeley High, a long-time teacher in my department approached me, saying, "You know, we send a lot of students to Harvard—a lot! Can you teach the 'high-end' kids? Can you?" I replied, "Yeah, I taught AP Government at my last school." Then he said, "You need to understand—if you teach a certain way, you can attract the students you want." In other words, I could teach in a way that would intimidate the lower-end kids, and using the teacher choice system, the high-end kids would pick me and fill up my classes. I was stunned [Ms. Lee, Asian female history teacher].

Pamela is one of Berkeley High's academic stars. By her junior year, she was already thinking about which elite university she would attend. Her pathway to a highly selective college had been made possible by her hard work and commitment: she had taken several honors courses and consistently distinguished herself by earning high grades. There is no doubt that students like Pamela are deserving of the academic rewards they earn. Nevertheless, a closer look at her experience at Berkeley High School raises a question: How is it possible that she ended up "on a track with the same people"? That is, how is it possible that in a school as diverse as Berkeley High, a student like Pamela could find herself in multiple Advanced Placement (AP) classes and elective courses with a group of students who shared so much in common with respect to race, class, and social status?

Close examination of the processes used to sort students into academic tracks reveals that there is more going on than simply hard work and talent. Certainly academic stars like Pamela are generally smart and hard-working, but her success is also the product of her family's resources, of the reinforcement and encouragement she receives from her academically ambitious peers, and of her own ability to navigate a large, impersonal, and understaffed high school. Put more simply, the system at Berkeley High School works for students like Pamela. She enjoys several unacknowledged privileges, both inside and outside school, that allow her to "pick [her] classes selectively," tap into resources and social networks, and "really find [her] place" on the top rung of the high school academic ladder. With the backing and support she has received, there is little doubt that she will prevail in the fierce competition for admission to the most prestigious and selective colleges.

This chapter features the experiences and perspectives of two Berkeley High School students in the class of 2000, selected from among the thirty-three diverse case study students whose high school lives were examined in depth by the Diversity Project's Class of 2000 Committee. The two students are Pamela, a white student from an affluent family living in the Berkeley hills, and Kevin, a Vietnamese student living below the poverty line in a Berkeley flatlands apartment. Pamela's story illustrates the types of economic, social, and cultural capital that enable the academic elite students, who at this school are predominantly white and disproportionately female, to gain entrance to prestigious universities, and ultimately, promising futures and careers. In contrast, Kevin's story demonstrates what happens to a college-oriented student who has excellent grades but lacks access to the hidden advantages of social capital (who you know and how you know them) and cultural capital (what you know and what impression you give), which in his case prove more valuable than economic capital (Coleman, 1988; Bourdieu, 1977).

Information about college is one of the main commodities of exchange within the social networks of Berkeley High School's top academic performers. Of particular value are the kinds of information that help students to navigate the large, complex high school bureaucracy and select classes and teachers who will further their chances of admission to a high-status college.

How Capital Exchange Works at Berkeley High

Economic, social, and cultural capital translate into privilege in the day-to-day interactions within school. The components of privilege in the context of Berkeley High School, like so many other aspects of the school, break down along racial lines. For white, middle-class students, privilege means having almost exclusive access to the most advanced classes and most qualified teachers, along with the academic support to succeed in these classes. It means being able to bend school rules regarding attendance, graduation requirements, and classroom behavior, with no negative consequences.

The various forms of capital also form a safety net for Berkeley High students in honors math, as we showed in Chapter One. Although their ninth-grade math placement indicates that the high school considers them to be prepared for the rigors of honors math, in reality, many of these students struggle to pass. Parents of means hire private math tutors for their children, often continuing this practice throughout high school. The regional parent e-tree, a social network that has taken root primarily among upper-middle-class white families, abounds with requests from Berkeley High parents for advice on choosing the best math, science, foreign language, and writing tutors. Advertised at fifteen to ninety dollars an hour, private tutors are available only to those who can afford them (in other words, those with economic capital), and the utilization of the network and the information that is exchanged are examples of social and cultural capital, respectively. As one Berkeley High Diversity Project teacher commented,

> I never realized the extent of this phenomenon, but it is huge at BHS. You have whole AP science classes supported by privately paid tutors. . . . It also means that an AP Chem[istry] teacher, for example, does not have responsibility to get the kids to really understand the material . . . because the tutors will actually teach it after school. Of course, the kid trying to get the education just from what is offered during the day is at a huge disadvantage.

Perhaps even more beneficial than advice about specific tutors is the information about the value of taking honors classes and Latin, or participating in crew or lacrosse, in positioning students for the fierce competition for admission to the Ivy League and other elite private colleges or to the most selective University of California (UC) campuses. This information is so well known and widely disseminated among upper-middle-class, college-educated white parents that they consider it to be common knowledge—something "everyone" knows.

Navigational skills and knowledge cannot be underestimated in terms of gaining access to the most advanced academic classes. From 1996 to 2000, Berkeley High School's academic counselors each carried a student caseload of 550 to 650 students, which meant that each student, on average, could see a counselor (often a different one each time) for a few minutes a year. Students from affluent families have an advantage in this area as well. During the course of our research, we learned that a growing number of these students work with private coaches who assist them in writing college essays and packaging their applications to college. For students to enroll in the most advanced classes that are needed for admission to selective colleges and universities and to obtain their choice of specialized electives, they need navigational skills and some insider knowledge about how the system works—skills and knowledge that their counselors do not have time to provide. Moreover, one college adviser serves the entire student population of twenty-eight hundred to thirty-two hundred students.

Given this situation, middle-class parents play a role in counseling their children or in intervening on behalf of a child to gain access to certain classes or programs (Lareau, 1989). Nicole, a class of 2000 white female student from a nearby city, provides a description of how she, as an out-of-district student, gained admission to Berkeley High through the advantage of social and cultural capital and parental intervention. Nicole especially wanted to go to Berkeley High because, as she put it,

> [Berkeley High] has really high AP scores, generally. And other schools can't necessarily match, especially for a public school. And Del Norte High [the high school in her city] doesn't have the greatest reputation, and there were a lot of changes [underway at Del Norte], like they were going to go to block scheduling and all this weird stuff. And my mom's just like, "Let's forget it. Let's go to Berkeley High."

For this reason, Nicole applied for and received an interdistrict transfer to BHS. Her permit was granted on the basis that she wanted to take Latin, which was not offered at Del Norte High. Nicole and her mother—like many other white, middle-class, out-of-district students and parents—knew that the best way to secure an interdistrict transfer was by requesting specific classes not offered in their own school district and which provide a bonus in college admissions. Nicole's "stay-at-home mom" also immediately sought ways to involve herself as a parent at Berkeley High and secured a parent seat on the influential School Site Council, which provided her with further access to other networks of middle-class parents.

However, peer culture and informal student networks become the most useful form of social capital, as students make friends with those who are in the same classes and have similar interests, backgrounds, and aspirations. They share among each other which classes to take, which teachers to request, which counselor to see in order to more easily change their class schedules, which extracurriculars "look best" on college applications, and which classes to "waive" or take during summer school. Parents of high-achieving students frequently request waivers from classes such as ethnic studies and Social Living, which are one-semester, heterogeneous classes required for graduation. These parents seek waivers by citing objections to the content of the courses, particularly Social Living, which includes sex education. They do so for various reasons, primarily so that their children do not "waste their time" in heterogeneous classes and can instead take more advanced academic electives or pursue enrichment through the performing and visual arts electives—courses that "look better" on student transcripts for elite colleges.

Under these conditions, students' and parents' social and cultural capital, combined with economic resources, can make the difference between a good academic record and a stellar one. However, these kinds of resources remain unacknowledged and camouflaged for three reasons: (1) because they are part of the normalized and racialized landscape of success and failure, so that no one questions why so many white students are so successful; (2) because these nonmaterial resources are not readily visible; and (3) because they operate outside the formal structures and policies of the school. Thus, the high school keeps count of students who use the school-based tutorial and counseling services, yet private sources of assistance remain invisible.

Ironically, credit accrues to Berkeley High School for producing and supporting so many successful students and to its AP program for producing so many students who score a 3 or better on the AP test, which allows the student to receive college credit and advanced placement in college in the subject area tested. The high school measures its success based on students like Pamela, who know how to work the system and are supported by high-quality private tutors and enrichment programs, rather than based on the students like Kevin, whose education depends entirely on the resources available through the public school system.

Figure 2.1 shows the GPAs of ninth-grade students in the class of 2000 and the median household income (1990 Census), by ZIP Code of residence. This illustrates one aspect of the achievement gap between students from affluent families in the Berkeley hills and low-income families in the flatlands—a gap that grew wider over time.

The Cases of Pamela and Kevin: Privilege Versus Disadvantage

Privilege—defined here as the favors and advantage granted by the school to some students, and not to all—is at the crux of the different pathways that Pamela and Kevin took in their quests to reach their college destinations. Pamela's pathway to college was smooth, fast, familiar, and well marked, and it led directly to her destination. Kevin's pathway was bumpy, uphill, unfamiliar, and poorly lit, and

FIGURE 2.1 Ninth-Grade Class of 2000 GPA by ZIP Code of Residence and Median Household Income

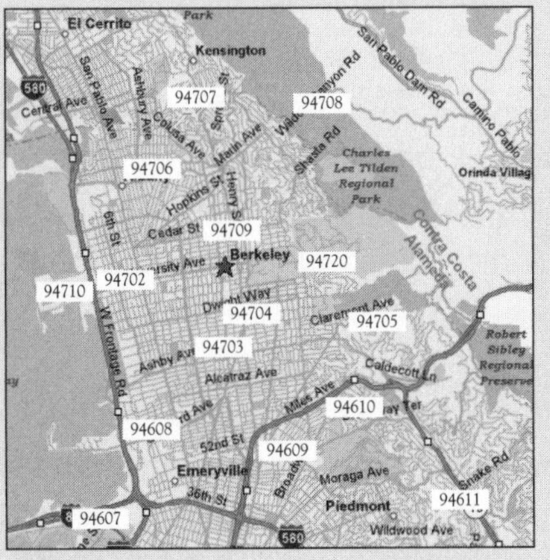

Zip Code	Median Household Income	Mean GPA for 9th graders
94710	$22,866	2.19
94704	$17,930	2.44
94703	$24,499	2.46
94702	$25,389	2.49
94706	$34,522	3.02
94709	$27,105	3.17
94705	$46,689	3.25
94707	$62,567	3.30
94708	$68,911	3.37

any number of accidental wrong turns would have led him off course from his destination, with no one standing by to help him get back on the path.

Pamela grew up in the San Francisco Bay Area and moved after fourth grade to the Berkeley hills, where she lives with her parents, her younger sister, and her dog. Their home is a spacious, Mediterranean-style house with a red tile roof and a terraced, landscaped garden. From kindergarten through middle school, Pamela attended a local private school of just two hundred students and was one of only seventeen students in her eighth-grade graduating class. She traveled for six weeks during one summer to Europe and the Middle East. She drove her own car to school because buses ran infrequently up in the hills. After school, she was a teaching assistant at a private elementary school, an intern in a child psychology office, and a member of a peer counseling group. She aspired to become a child psychologist and someday write a book about her practice. Pamela's cumulative senior-year GPA was 3.69.

Kevin moved to Berkeley from Los Angeles at age four. His father left the household when he was young, so he grew up in Berkeley with his single mother, who worked as a manicurist in his aunt's nail salon. They have always lived below the poverty line. At one point, they were homeless; for about three years, during the time that Kevin was in fifth through seventh grades, they lived in the back of the nail salon and eventually moved to a cramped, one-bedroom apartment. Kevin explains how difficult it was to be a child in this semihomeless situation: "That was like the only secret I kept from my friends. And it was kind of hard, too. I mean I couldn't tell them, and then I, I was always inviting them here . . . and I was like, yeah, we're just kicking it at my nail place, and they're, like, 'Can we go to your house?' I'm like, 'No, we can't go to my house,' you know?"

Kevin has always been a strong and persistent student and a talented visual artist. He has volunteered at various Asian community organizations, sometimes making use of his drawing skills to produce projects such as a cartoon book on prevention of sexually transmitted diseases aimed at Asian youth. Kevin's cumulative senior-year GPA was 3.78.

Although they encounter some gender bias and other obstacles, white female students are the top academic performers in the high school. Pamela's high GPA of 3.69 and her record of nearly straight A's nevertheless places her just above the median of 3.57 for white female students in the class of 2000, or close to average for her race and gender. Asian American male students, on average, also have high GPAs, though somewhat lower than those of white females, with a median of 3.28.

Kevin's GPA of 3.78 puts him well above the median for Asian males and even above Pamela. However, if Pamela's grades are weighted—adding one grade point for every AP course grade so that an A in an AP class is worth 5 points, as is done for the University of California and some private colleges—her GPA comes to 3.88. Figure 2.2 compares the median GPA (represented by the horizontal line within each box) and the GPA range for the middle half (first and third quartiles) of student GPAs for class of 2000 white female and Asian male students. The short horizontal lines at the top and bottom indicate the highest and lowest GPAs earned by students in each of these subgroups.

However, Kevin's and Pamela's comparable GPAs and those of their respective race and gender groups tell only part of the story. Differences in course-taking patterns and informal academic tracks (honors and Advanced Placement versus regular) reveal significant disparities even among higher-achieving students and predict differential outcomes in the competition for college admissions. The following sections detail the ways in which privilege boosts Pamela's already strong chances for admission to a selective college or university, while lack of privilege and exclusive reliance on the high school's services put Kevin at a disadvantage.

**FIGURE 2.2 Comparison of GPA Range and Medians
for Class of 2000 White Female and
Asian Male Seniors**

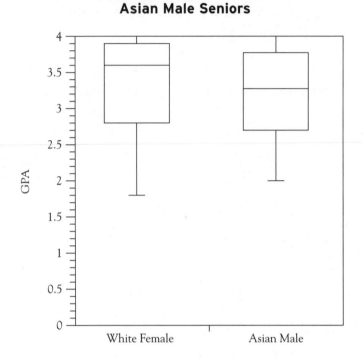

Pamela: Sacrificing Her Present to Craft the
Perfect College Application

Pamela's case illustrates the kind of privilege enjoyed by students
from private school backgrounds, who quickly rise to the top of the
class. At the same time, her case illustrates the way privilege works
in favor of students from public or private school backgrounds who
have access to various resources outside the domain of the high
school. Following Pamela through her four years at Berkeley High
School reveals that her primary focus—like that of many in her
peer group of white, middle-class, and affluent students—was largely
an exercise in crafting the perfect college application. Virtually all
of her sacrifices or trade-offs in high school were made in an effort
to ensure herself a place in the freshman class of an elite university.

Privilege: Choice of School, Choice of Classes

Because her private K-8 school had no high school, Pamela faced a choice of applying to one of several prestigious private high schools or going to Berkeley High. She chose Berkeley High after a brief visit. She said,

> Yeah, I really liked it. I just, I remember when I went there and I vis-ited, I just got this feeling of, um, it felt really, like, comfortable. And I didn't feel, like, intimidated or anything, even though it was, like, really big and there's all these kids around. Like, I kind of got a feel-ing of, like, security, and, like, closeness. So that was my main impression of it.

Part of what Pamela liked about Berkeley High School was its size. She also liked the vast array of course offerings. Powell, Farrar, and Cohen (1985) liken this kind of high school to a shopping mall and called secondary education "another consumption experience in an abundant society" (p. 8). According to this analogy, in an insti-tution such as Berkeley High, students "have wide discretion not only about what to buy, but also about whether to buy" or simply to browse or stay away from the mall altogether (p. 8). The best-served students tend to be those who, like Pamela, already know what brand and style they want and have the currency to purchase it.

As a ninth grader, Pamela was placed in Honors Geometry and chose Latin, a language taken by 25 percent of ninth graders in honors math and reputed to be the most valuable in terms of col-lege admissions. She described teachers in her other classes, partic-ularly her detracked freshman English/history core classes, as "dumbing down the material" to accommodate other students. She felt these classes helped her socially in terms of making friends and being exposed to the racial diversity of the high school. However, she was anxious to take more classes that she felt were taught "at my level" and would allow her to move ahead of students who were not "at her level" (Oakes, 1985). Pamela provided the following ratio-nale for tracking:

I got the feeling that, like, the teachers were, like, really kind of, like, dumbing down material, and stuff like that. . . . They have, like, I guess in their minds, like, a good idea of, like, they wanted to incorporate, like, everyone. But in the process of doing so, like, I mean there's people in my sophomore English class that, like, barely know how to read. So, I mean, like, you know, like, what are you supposed to do about it, you know? It's not like, you don't want to say, like, well, you know, they shouldn't get a chance either, because obviously, you know, like, that's not the point. The point is that, like, it's hard to, like, learn yourself while you're trying to teach people at such a different level. And I think that's the main problem with Berkeley High, is that they kind of forget about the people who are still trying to, like, keep at their own pace, instead of, like, help other people, which is also good. But I mean, in the process you kind of hurt yourself. . . . I mean, I don't personally think that I write at the level I could write, and . . . I think it has a lot to do with, like, the kind of like, Mickey Mouse-ness of the English and history classes.

Pamela seemed to believe that Berkeley High catered to the low-performing students, and "they kind of forget about" students like her, who "are still trying to . . . keep at their own pace." She felt that detracked classes held her back and detrimentally affected her writing abilities.

Thus, as a sophomore, Pamela seized every opportunity to take more advanced classes. She took AP Chemistry for her science elective instead of the regular double-period, college preparatory chemistry class and continued to take Latin and honors math. It is the most advanced students like Pamela who enjoy the greatest degree of choice among the widest range of electives, tracks, and teachers. That same year, Pamela's parents hired an expensive private college adviser to begin the process of determining to which colleges Pamela might apply and to obtain expert advice on her course selection for the remainder of high school.

Privilege: Accumulating AP Credits to Gain Academic Advantage

The choices for Pamela, like her classmates in Berkeley High School's unofficial honors track, were conscious, strategic, and almost single-mindedly aimed toward gaining a college admissions advantage. Pamela did not seek her counselor's assistance in choosing her classes but instead relied on the information network of her friends and her private college adviser. Her statement below demonstrates the extent to which Pamela sacrificed her personal academic interests and curiosity in order to craft her college resumé, based largely on taking multiple AP classes, while allowing herself more freedom to pursue what she enjoyed in her cocurricular classes such as dance, stagecraft, choreography, and yearbook. In total, Pamela took two years of honors math and nine semesters of AP classes—two semesters of AP Calculus, one semester of AP Latin, four semesters of AP Science (Chemistry and Biology), and two semesters of AP English (British Literature and Modern American Literature).

When I shadowed Pamela during her junior year, she told me that her AP Biology class was "the most boring class in the world" and that she "hated" it. She seemed to see no contradiction between taking classes she hated and striving for higher education. It was as if, once in college, she would finally be able to take classes she enjoyed. In a junior-year interview, Pamela elaborated:

> Basically, all the classes that I've taken, it's been in the back of my mind that this will look good in colleges. I don't want to be a scientist, but I took AP Chemistry and AP Biology. And I don't want to be a mathematician, but I took Honors Geometry and Honors Algebra, and now I'm in calculus. So for classes-wise, I probably have limited it to what will look good as opposed to what I really want to study. But in terms of extracurriculars, I think I haven't really done that. In the back of my mind, I'm like, well, I should have some extracurriculars. But I don't take them because, like, "Oh, this will look good." I pick them because I'm interested in them.

. . . Like, it's always good to kind of stand out, especially at Berkeley High. And so I think that in that way, it's been beneficial, because I've—for colleges, I can say, "Look, I just didn't take regular biology. I took AP Biology." But, like, for me personally, the knowledge—I don't think I needed to know it!

When asked whether the sacrifice was worth it, Pamela replied in one senior-year interview:

You don't really think about it at the time. Like at the time, I wasn't thinking that. I was just like, "Oh! This will be interesting." And by the end of the class, you're like, "I don't want to do this anymore. It's not what I'm interested in." But then you console yourself by saying, "Well, at least it will look good for college." . . . I know it's not the best way to live life, like, always looking ahead, but hopefully it'll be better [in college].

. . . Like, junior year was pretty much like a terrible year. I mean, I was, like, so stressed out. I was, like, going insane. But I got into UCLA, and I have a feeling that if I hadn't taken all those AP classes, I probably wouldn't have. And so, then, it was worth it.

Pamela found a good supply of social and cultural capital among her friends, who pursued the same strategy of amassing AP credits. Pamela's peer group preferred their social network as a source of information rather than seeking advice from one of the overburdened school counselors, on whom the rest of Berkeley High's students had to rely. Pamela and her friends visited their counselors only when they wanted to change their schedules at the beginning of a new semester. Otherwise the informal information exchange among the top students was viewed as more valuable, timely, and reliable than the information from the academic counselors. Pamela provided this example:

I switched out of my core class freshman year. You're *not* supposed to switch out of your core class. They, like, make that very clear, and somehow I managed to. So that's the main thing that I see my counselor as. . . . I mean, they come in every semester [to go over self-scheduling procedures]. I guess it was more helpful freshman year when I didn't really know what I was supposed to take. But now . . . you usually just ask people. I mean, I know a bunch of seniors, and you just ask people who've had those teachers before. And they can usually give you pretty good advice.

Pamela further explains the detailed planning that went into choosing her schedule for senior year in order to maximize her college resumé while also minimizing her workload compared to junior year. According to Pamela, junior year "is the year colleges look at most," so she took as many AP classes as possible that year. But for her senior year, she declared,

I'm not taking any PE or AP science. I'm not taking the hardest math. I am not taking Latin—I haven't liked Latin since freshman year. And those were, like, the basic things that give you the most work. And then I *really* want to take AP English, but I'm not sure I'm going to get in. If I don't, I may take AP Stat [Statistics], which would be an additional math class I've heard is kind of easy. And it, it's just like a good way to get another AP class in, 'cause I feel kind of guilty about not taking Latin, which would be AP.

Pamela took AP Calculus A/B, which is equivalent to one semester of college calculus, rather than AP Calculus B/C ("the hardest math"), which is equivalent to a full year of college calculus. Thus, her transcript showed AP math during senior year, but with a fraction of the workload of Calculus B/C.

Pamela enjoyed the privilege of information and choice. She picked freely from the wide range of course offerings, and she had opportunity to learn. She was never made to feel that she did not belong in the more advanced and challenging classes. Rather, she fit in well—socially, culturally, and academically. In fact, during her junior year, her best friend in the school was also in five of her classes.

Privilege: Access to the Most Qualified Teachers

Because the AP classes are supposed to be taught at a college level and prepare students for an AP test that will determine their college placement in a given subject area, Berkeley High first assigns the most subject-matter-qualified teachers to these classes (Finley, 1984). School and district administrators are well aware of Berkeley High's reputation for high scores on AP tests in every subject offered, and they are aware that AP classes play a major role in keeping white student enrollment high.

Pamela commented on teacher quality and remarked that she felt she learned the most in her AP classes

> because the teachers expect us to learn the most. Like, since they don't have low expectations for us, we kind of rise to the occasion. I think . . . you do struggle a little bit, but, like, especially in AP Chem . . . you have to do, like, twice as much work as a normal chemistry class because you're trying to get ready for the AP test in May, and it's supposed to be, um, like a college level. And you're reading from, like, a college textbook and stuff. . . . So they also have good teachers in AP classes, but basically, they just give us a lot of work, and they usually are better at explaining things, and we have more tests, I think, than normal classes.

Privilege: Bending Attendance and Behavior Rules for "Academic" Reasons

Pamela reports that she frequently cuts class, without negative consequences to her grades or her disciplinary record. While many students cut class for social reasons or to avoid a test, Pamela and many of her peers usually cut for academic reasons. Pamela described her class-cutting practice in the following excerpt from my junior-year interview with her:

> *Pamela:* I cut lots of times. Sometimes it's to do homework. Sometimes it's to go home, 'cause I don't feel good. Sometimes it's 'cause I don't like the class.

Interviewer: Does it affect your grades at all?

Pamela: Um, I like to think it doesn't. . . . I have a pretty high GPA, and, um, maybe it, maybe it does, like, to some extent. But usually I know—I mean, I usually don't cut for, like, a test or something like that. . . . Sometimes I won't go to my first and second period. I'll sleep in or I'll do homework, and then I'll go to Bio [AP Biology], 'cause I always feel like it's like a big waste of time to go to my first and second classes when I could be sleeping. . . .

Interviewer: So it's kind of a trade-off? You basically cut one class to do work for another?

Pamela: Yeah. It's usually dance or English, I'll cut to do work for Bio—that, and Latin.

School staff generally treated tardiness and cutting class as acts of truancy for students of color, but many turned a blind eye to white students who skipped class. This is in part because white students were widely perceived to "care about school" (Valenzuela, 1999), so their absence from class or presence in the hallways often went unquestioned. It is also in part because white students who cut class usually left the school grounds, while African American and Latino students often continued to roam the hallways and socialize during class time, and thereby were caught and disciplined (see Chapter Three). Differential perceptions of white and nonwhite students and their respective class-cutting behaviors help to account for the underrepresentation of white students and the overrepresentation of black students in the school disciplinary system.

On one shadow day in the fall semester of Pamela's senior year, as I followed Pamela from class to class, she cut her Dance Projects class so that she could run some errands related to her college applications and then study for calculus. She stopped by a former math teacher's classroom to drop off a special form for his letter of recommendation to a college, and then went to her calculus classroom to work on a problem set with the teacher and other students during an optional study session. She justified cutting her dance class because she was not performing in the dance to be rehearsed that day. She simply gave herself permission to cut. As we walked from building to building during class time without a hall pass, not a single teacher hall monitor or campus security person stopped us or questioned what we were doing.

This particular privilege extended beyond class cutting. Pamela's teachers, especially in Latin and her advanced science and math classes, treated the students as intelligent, responsible young adults. In Pamela's double-period physics class, students used the restroom hall pass whenever they wanted. This stood in marked contrast to many lower-track or regular classes in which students must ask the teacher's permission to use the hall pass, and often permission is denied. The lack of rules and controls regarding the hall pass denoted a sense of trust in the students.

In addition, Pamela and her cohort suffered no penalty for eating in class or indulging in other behaviors forbidden in many regular classes. Pamela and her classmates were allowed to bring soda, water, and coffee latte, as well as candy, gum, and food, to all of her classes. In Latin, two boys sat on top of a table and put their feet on the chairs in front of them, and loudly called out responses to the teacher's question about a passage in the *Aeneid* without ever raising their hands. These behaviors seemed to be the norm, as the teacher conducted a lively, seminar-like discussion about language and literature, culture and politics, with some thirty-five high school students. In many other classrooms throughout the high school, any one of these behaviors could have warranted a disciplinary referral to on-campus suspension (OCS).

Privilege: Access to Extra College Information

Berkeley High School has a single college adviser for the entire student body. She does an extraordinary job in providing information and assistance to students. She issues a daily bulletin with a calendar of college representatives who are visiting Berkeley High and other items regarding SAT dates, scholarships, and other related information. However, in advanced classes with many seniors in them, teachers provided extra information to this top 10 to 20 percent of students.

On one shadow day in the winter of Pamela's senior year, several teachers gave out college-related information or made statements indicating their understanding that students faced looming application deadlines and that they needed to work on their applications and get letters of recommendation from other teachers. Pamela's AP Calculus class teacher made announcements about a special state mathematics exam and provided some information for students who planned to be pre-med in college. In Pamela's physics class, the teacher announced deadlines for requesting transcripts from the registrar and for teacher recommendation letters, and underscored other college application deadlines. Students responded by stating that they were already aware of these deadlines and commented that UC applications do not require teacher letters. That the teacher made a point of reminding students, however, indicated that she saw these students as college bound and therefore focused on the admissions process.

Privilege: Enjoying the Benefits of a Small School Without Being in One

Pamela's peer group, who are among the highest-performing white female students, chose not to enroll in a school-within-a-school ("small school") program, because they preferred to leave their schedules flexible for specialized and advanced classes and because they did not wish to share all of their classes with the same cohort of students. However, by the time Pamela was a junior, she discovered that she was taking many classes with the same group of students. This happened largely because some of her AP classes and specialized electives like Latin and choreography were offered just once a day, so taking these classes set the rest of her schedule. Thus, Pamela tended to share her classes and highly qualified teachers with other high-achieving students. Shadowing Pamela for a day each semester was like being in a small school for highly motivated, college-bound, mostly white students. The only time I saw large numbers of students of color or felt as if we were in a large, diverse high school was when we walked through the hallways during passing period or went out to the courtyard at lunchtime.

Pamela's friends were predominantly students from her classes—they were entirely white and college bound. Her group of friends ate lunch together every day on the steps of the school's Community Theater in the main courtyard. Her closest friends socialized outside class as well, and all went to the senior prom together in what she called a "limo-bus," big enough for twenty-two students. In her senior-year exit interview as part of the Diversity Project Class of 2000 study, Pamela commented that she had "branched out," saying that "all the cliques seemed to sort of meld together, and, like, everyone's sort of, like, hanging out with everyone else and not worrying about who's supposed to be in what group." But in Pamela's case, "branching out" to include "everyone" simply meant socializing with other groups of white students who ate lunch on the theater steps.

That Pamela's friends overlapped so much with her classmates is significant, because her network of friends constituted a source of social capital. Berkeley High School's unofficial tracking system, which began in ninth grade, had created a cohort of students who spent the whole school day together and casually exchanged information—over lunch and during dance rehearsals—about the college application and admissions process or about who got into AP English and who did not. Even social chit-chat had exchange value for college. During one shadow day, I noted that most of Pamela's social conversations revolved around whose names were listed on the AP class rosters for next semester, who got what SAT scores, and who was applying to which colleges. She and her friends knew each other's GPAs and grades in specific classes, and Pamela could readily tell me how her record compared to those of her closest friends, with whom she was competing for admission to college.

Privilege: Access to Private College Preparatory Resources

Outside the context of Berkeley High, Pamela had access to a vast array of private college preparatory resources. She enrolled in private SAT preparatory classes in which she took numerous practice tests under timed conditions and learned test-taking strategies to maximize her score. She took the SAT once, but took the SAT IIs (subject area tests required by many colleges) multiple times. She reported, "I took math and writing. I took Math IIC [the more difficult test] twice, and I did really bad both times. So I took Math IC the third time. And I took writing three times. I took Biology and Chemistry too. I didn't take Latin."

Pamela knew from talking to friends and from her private college adviser that she could take the SAT II tests as many times as she wanted and put the scores on hold until she decided which three highest subject area scores to submit to the college admissions offices. Her parents hired a tutor to prepare for the SAT IIs. She also took a national Latin exam three times, stating that she did "pretty good. I got gold the first time and silver the second time."

When asked what her private college adviser did for her, Pamela said that the adviser first met with her during her sophomore year to get a sense of her personality and goals, then thought about which colleges might be most suitable for her. Her adviser kept her knowledge base up-to-date by visiting dozens of colleges a year and was in communication with many of the top colleges that are popular with local students. In Pamela's junior and senior years, her college adviser guided her through the SAT and admissions process, helped her with her college essays, and determined which would be her "stretch" school (where she was least likely to be accepted) and her "fallback" school (where she would definitely be accepted and could attend if she were rejected by all other schools). In one interview response about her college adviser, Pamela explained:

Pamela: The first time I met with her was sometime in tenth grade. And then at the end of junior year, I was meeting with her a bunch because we were talking about what colleges I was thinking about, and my SATs, and stuff like that. And then recently, I've also been meeting with her. She was basically helping me write my essay for the UCs, because she goes to seminars . . . with UC admissions officers who stand up and basically tell them what they want to hear.

Interviewer: What do they want to hear?

Pamela: It depends on which topic you have. But for Topic A, which is what I did, it's basically, "Tell us about your accomplishments." Like list all of your accomplishments that you'll bring to the university. Like they basically—since you don't have an interview and because you don't have additional questions like, "What extracurricular activities have meant the most to you?"— which is what most private schools have—they want to know everything, basically. Really general—general in some ways, but then you talk about every single event, like, "I did this and this and this." . . . They want to know everything, but they also want to get a sense of who you are from your writing. So you don't just want to say, "I did this and this and this." You want to say why you did it and what it's meant to you, and that kind of stuff.

Interviewer: One or two pages? And then what are the other questions?

Pamela: Write about a creative achievement that you've done. And then write about a significant event that has influenced your life. So, yes, she [college adviser] helped me with that also.

It is evident from this and other exchanges that Pamela's college adviser provides a great deal of detailed, nuanced information that helps student clients to package themselves for the admissions officers. The essays described above were for the UC system, and through working with her college adviser, Pamela was even able to distinguish between the essay questions on the UC application and the questions "most private schools" ask.

Pamela's College Outcome: Admission to Her Stretch School

In the end—through a combination of advice from her private college adviser, her SAT preparatory class, her ability to take the SAT II subject area tests several times and submit only her highest scores, and her overall high school record, complete with nine semesters of AP classes—Pamela was admitted to her stretch school, UCLA (University of California, Los Angeles). She commented that this made taking the AP science classes and advanced Latin—classes she disliked—well worth the sacrifice. She envisioned finishing college in four years, going on to graduate school, and becoming a successful child psychologist with her own practice.

Kevin: A Disadvantaged "Regular Track" Student Strives for College

Kevin, unlike Pamela, did not see attending Berkeley High School as a choice. A product of Berkeley public schools and living below the poverty line, there was never any question that Kevin would go to Berkeley High. Always a good student earning high grades, Kevin entered Berkeley High School at grade level in math (Algebra I). He proceeded to take the classes he needed to graduate from high school, earning 273 course credits—well over the 220-credit graduation requirement. He also met the minimum "A through F" requirements for admissions eligibility to the University of California, as follows:

- Two years of history/social science (*Kevin took three years*)
- Four years of English (*Kevin took four years*)
- Three years of math, with four years recommended (*Kevin took four years*)

- Two years of laboratory science, with three years recommended (*Kevin took three years*)
- Two years of foreign language, with three years recommended (*Kevin took three years*)
- One year of college preparatory electives (*Kevin took three and a half years*)

Kevin essentially followed the standard course sequence in all of his academic areas and chose Spanish as his foreign language elective. The rest of his electives reflected personal interests. For example, as an expression of his interest in his Asian identity, Kevin took classes in Asian and Asian American literature. A talented visual artist, Kevin took a number of art-related classes, including advanced drawing, photography, and modern art history, as well as an acting workshop class.

During his interviews, Kevin often spoke about his determination to go to a four-year university, possibly a UC campus. His motivation was not for himself but for his mother. In one junior-year interview, Kevin explained,

> My goal is to bring my mom out the ghetto. That's my goal. Yeah. That's, that's why I'm going to college. That's why I'm doing all that stuff. Not for the American dream—just to get my mom out the ghetto. Just to, just to bring her out. And, you know, just to let *her* experience the American dream. Just to—help her. I want to help her.

Kevin went on to say that he had to consciously set college as his goal, because he felt he was unlike the middle-class Asian Americans who came from backgrounds where college was a given. Comparing Southeast Asian students like himself with the middle-class Asian Americans, he said,

> Because, like, they were, like, Chinese and, like, the Japanese, and the supposed upper-class, better Asians, you know. They—they're getting the really good grades and the high SAT scores and stuff. . . .

I just seemed to notice that folks like us, we get into gangs, and, some of us care [about school] while some of us, uh, like a lot of us are right now, you know, "I don't really care, I go to community college, blah blah blah." You know, "I just get a job," you know, it's like that. . . . Just, you know, get D's in all my classes and just get out of here, you know. . . . A lot of them are Southeast Asian. . . . But then a lot of these people, too, though, live around my area, and they live around, you know, like semi-ghettoish, you know. And that's like, that's how they were raised. They're like, you know, "I don't really care." I mean, because the system's already going to bring them down anyway.

Out of devotion to his mother, Kevin refused to let the system "bring him down," and he worked hard to prepare for college. In his entire family, only his uncle, who had come to the United States from France, had ever gone to college. Although his mother supported his efforts to go to college, it was unfamiliar territory for her and for Kevin.

Disadvantage: No Access to Crucial College-Going Information

Unlike Pamela who had a private counselor, Kevin had no access to certain crucial college-going information, including the importance of taking at least one AP class, information about how to pursue honors mathematics, or how to apply for the best college scholarships. These are all aspects of cultural capital that were readily available to Pamela through her friends, family, and private college adviser. But for Kevin, who had little social and cultural capital and depended on the school to guide him through the college preparation process, the deficiencies in the system for poor and working-class students of color became all too apparent.

Why and How to Take AP Classes. Unlike Pamela, Kevin did not load his schedule with classes that he may have disliked but would have enhanced his high school transcript for college. This is in part because, despite his hard work and his record of nearly straight A's, Kevin's counselor never told him about the advantages of taking AP classes for which he was clearly qualified. As a result, Kevin—whose friends were mostly in regular classes, whose mother never went to college, and who lacked the social and cultural capital of students like Pamela—took no AP classes in high school. Since AP classes offer a bonus for college admissions and an extra GPA point in UC admissions, this had an adverse effect on Kevin's college resumé. Kevin commented,

> I never heard about AP classes. I heard about honors classes, but I haven't heard about AP, and how, like, Cal [UC Berkeley] and UCLA, and like all the other UCs, they're, like, they look great, it looks good on your transcript, you know. And I didn't hear about it until sophomore or junior year, and that's basically like, I was in the mode where like I'm just going to do regular classes and just try to get through that. I wasn't going to try to work harder. And that threw me off. . . . Since I never heard about it, like, eighth grade or freshman year, . . . nobody instructed me on that. That's why I'm kind of pissed about that. And then, like, I didn't get to start thinking, like, work *real* hard. . . . It just threw me off, and I was, like, I can't do it, 'cause I'm already struggling with these regular classes, how am I going to do AP?

When asked why this made him "pissed" and angry, Kevin simply replied, "Because some people get an advantage—and some people don't."

Kevin heard about AP classes in a casual conversational exchange with junior-year classmates: "People were like, 'Hey, are you going out for AP Chem and AP Bio?' I'm like, 'AP, it's like what?' . . . And they started telling me about it, I'm like, 'Awww,' you know. . . . Shoot, it's too late for that now, you know. I can't do it now." In reality, it was not too late for Kevin to think about taking at least one or two AP classes. However, without a counselor or informed adult to guide and encourage him, Kevin was left with the impression that other students were already too far ahead of him, and it was "too late." As Kevin put it, "I didn't know how to get into them—like what the hell is an AP class, you know? And it was like that lack of, like, I guess, communication or lack of information that was coming to me."

Kevin suffered the consequences of uneven distribution of information, a form of social capital, and he lacked access to networks of informed adults. These constitute a distinct disadvantage in the competitive college application process that even a high-achieving student like Kevin cannot overcome. Besides taking a toll on his college resumé, this lack of information in the face of students who took such information for granted made Kevin feel somewhat demoralized. In hindsight, he said, "You could say that even if somebody had told me about AP classes [much earlier], it's like I was, like, I probably felt outside of that whole little ring of AP class students. They're, like, so above academically, you know? And it's like how can I compete with that? That was my mentality, you know?"

How to Get into Honors Math.   AP classes were not the only area in which Kevin was disadvantaged by his lack of access to information about how the school worked. Although Kevin was placed at grade level in ninth-grade math, he qualified to go into the honors section of second-year algebra during his junior year. He explained,

> Actually, I should have gotten the algebra honors, like, uh, the one before trig[onometry], right? Or the one before Math Analysis, and they didn't put me in. I mean, I got like really high grades and stuff. I got A's and stuff. They never put me in, and I was, like—. . . . And then I just heard to get into honors you have to get, like, you have to ask your teacher for a recommendation and you have to take a test, and I didn't hear about these things. . . . And then my friend got into honors, too, and I don't think he even took a test and he got in, put in somehow. I'm like, "What?" I was, like, so confused. I was, "Yeah, what's the deal with this," you know?

Kevin's assessment of his college readiness was based not only on his lack of AP classes but on his position within the regular college preparatory track—"steerage" class, to use Alfie Kohn's (1998) ocean liner analogy—in a school where privileged students are concentrated on a first-class track to college. Once again, he expresses his feelings of inferiority and betrayal, but this time more in terms of his chances of being accepted at "a better college":

> Yeah, just sometimes I, I feel inferior to them. Like, I remember like in freshman year, me and my friends . . . we were, like, in the same ethnic studies class, and . . . we both got A's and stuff, you know. And I was, like, yeah, you know, like, kind of on the same level and stuff. But then, like, I . . . found out about all the classes he was taking. He's right now, like, he's taking calculus, and he's about to go to Cal to do math, and he's taking all AP courses next year. And I'm, like, huh? And I'm taking all these regular classes, and so, in a way I feel inferior to him. Or, I feel like, it's like I don't have a chance compared to him into getting into a better college, you know. . . . It's just like, you know, a setback. Yeah, kind of scared . . . going into college and stuff. 'Cause like the majority of college students like, well, to the colleges I want to go to, it's like, you know, they're, they're—more prepared.

Kevin's case is a good example of the limitations on how far a strong student with good grades can go if he starts high school at grade level. Kevin would have qualified for AP English or AP science, assuming he passed the entrance exams, and if he had taken just one more semester of Spanish (a class in which he received all A's), he would have automatically reached AP Spanish. However, unless he started ninth grade above grade level in math, he would not have been able to reach AP Calculus, AP Statistics, or AP Physics by senior year.

Disadvantage: Possessing the Wrong Kind of Cultural Capital

Kevin was on his own when it came to finding out about financial aid for college. He said, "I was searching for every scholarship I could find, even the national ones which no one ever really gets, like the Publishers Clearinghouse Sweepstakes." That Kevin included Publishers Clearinghouse as a college scholarship opportunity speaks to the absence of financial-aid counseling available to him. Then Kevin heard about a particular scholarship that would provide full support to one deserving student from "practically every local high school." But when he asked the newly appointed Berkeley High college adviser about the program,

> She said this scholarship was geared more toward people who *really needed it*, for example, this one girl . . . [who] takes care of all her sisters and brothers at home, all the while being a good student. That made me just not want to apply because I knew that as much as I thought I have been through and achieved, it wasn't as much as the girl she told me about. It didn't hit me until later, but I questioned: Well, how come she assumed that I didn't have similar, if not worse, circumstances? It's real silly to compare and argue whose suffering is much worse, but it was the fact that she assumed my situation is what bugged me the most. I don't know if it was racial. Maybe she assumed that I was well off because I went to her office every day, deeming persistent people or people that were really adamant about going to college as people who were well off. But me, I'm just tired of assumptions. Hopefully, the assumptions that [the college adviser] made came from my actions, not my appearance or race. Most likely, it was all those factors—my persistence to go to the office, my inquiries, my race, my appearance, my way of speaking—combined.

Kevin's remark about his "appearance or race" refers to the possibility that he might have been judged on the basis of the model minority myth, which sets Asian Americans apart from other racial minorities with claims that they are the successful, hard-working minority that has "made it" in America. It is a dangerous but deeply embedded myth that could make Kevin seem unworthy of economic assistance based solely on his physical appearance and racial attributes (Lee, 1996).

Whether the model minority myth came into play or not, Kevin's story of the discrimination he faced when he went to the only college adviser available to him for advice on a crucial UC scholarship speaks volumes about the ways in which students may be judged on the basis of their cultural capital, or lack thereof (Wacquant, 1998). Unless the counselor is motivated to ensure that students like Kevin receive the extra help they need, they are forced to rely on their own abilities and limited insider knowledge to navigate the system.

The college adviser's response took Kevin aback and caused him not to apply for this scholarship, for which he was clearly qual-ified and deserving. For students who rely entirely on the school sys-tem to provide vital college information and support, such assumptions and acts of discrimination can be costly.

Kevin's College Outcome: UC Bound in Spite of, Not Because of, His Position

Asked where he was applying to college, Kevin replied, "Of course all the UCs, and then I don't know about Ivy Leagues, because . . . they're all AP, you know, they're just all competitive." But because UC admissions gives extra weight to grades in AP classes, Kevin was disadvantaged in gaining admission to the top tier of the state's public institutions of higher education as well. This fact was not lost on Kevin, who said, "Since I want to go to all these UCs and stuff, it's like, everybody has done at least a AP course."

In the end, however, Kevin was admitted to UC Berkeley, the most selective and prestigious of all UC campuses. Fortunately for Kevin, the admissions officers apparently took into account the economic disadvantages his family faced, the strength of his grades and his application essays, and his record of using his artistic talents in areas of Asian community service. UC Berkeley admitted him for "second-round" spring 2001 enrollment, with his fall semester classes taken in a special UC extension program for those on spring admissions. However, in this era of Proposition 209 and the UC Regents' parallel ban on affirmative action, Kevin was in no way assured of admission to UC Berkeley, and in many ways he simply beat the odds.

Conclusion

Pamela's experience shows how privilege—in the form of economic, social, and cultural capital—provides unfair advantage to a student who otherwise might not have made it to UCLA. Kevin's experience illustrates the difficulties encountered by a strong and persistent student who lacks all three forms of capital, and made it to UC Berkeley with a little bit of luck.

Pamela's story also speaks to the damage done to what Ms. Lee, at the beginning of this chapter, called the "high-end kids," by spending four years of high school in this culture that places a premium on getting ahead at the expense of others. For one thing, Pamela sacrificed her present—her own curiosities and passions about learning—to a future promise; she sacrificed personal and immediate interests for external and delayed reward. She learned to take classes she disliked or found boring, based on the promise of an exciting college experience where she believed such trade-offs would be a thing of the past. And finally, she internalized the elitist rationale for reserving the most challenging classes for students like herself and declared Berkeley High School's efforts at detracking a failure.

Kevin's story too speaks to damage done—not only to his college prospects but also to his sense of self. Instead of opening a new door for him, Kevin's discovery of the value of AP classes served to make him feel less equal, less competitive than his peers who shared his detracked ninth-grade classes but then moved seamlessly to the honors track. His encounter with the college adviser caused him to drop his quest for the full UC Berkeley scholarship, even though he knew the college adviser's assumptions that he was undeserving were wrong. Kevin's astute recognition of the unfairness of this systematic denial of access to college-bound information, classes, and resources caused him to become angry and critical, but also to doubt his own ability to succeed in college.

However, it is not enough to reveal the inequities in a school system built on privilege, stratification, and differentiation of student learning and outcomes. Those who benefit most from such a system, when challenged, find ways to defend and preserve it (Oakes, Wells, Jones, and Datnow, 1997). Thus in December 1999, a Berkeley High teacher responded to an e-tree dialogue among parents who complained that too much attention was spent on low-performing students and that teachers failed to adequately challenge the high-performing students, such as their own children. This chapter ends with the following excerpt from an open letter from this teacher, simply signed "Teacher X":

We talk a lot about diversity at Berkeley High School, about struggling to make the school work for every student. The shame of our school is that it is still two distinct schools: one that works quite well for the more privileged and mostly white students and one that represents failure and frustration. I suppose it is part of the hypocrisy of liberal Berkeley that we all love bragging about our integrated high school but put so much focus on erecting the barriers.

Think about what you are modeling for your student. If you are a white parent who spends all your energy positioning him or her, pushing for the highest AP class, complaining about the lack of rigor—and you never ask your student how the African American students in his or her class are doing, how he or she is getting along with Chicano/Latino students—perhaps you are modeling everything we are trying to work against. We need to build real community at the high school because that is the kind of world we want our children to live in. If we want them to simply excel, to leave classmates behind and live in gated communities, then we should only push for their success. But teenagers can dream, and they dream of a better world. I like to think most people who go into teaching do it because they want to help young people create that world. We could use a little help here.

3

THE DISCIPLINE GAP AND THE NORMALIZATION OF FAILURE

Anne Gregory, Kysa Nygreen, Dana Moran

Ray: Ms. Dinkins, man, she just didn't like me.

Interviewer: Why not?

Ray: I mean, I don't want to say nothing about no racial, but when I do say it, it's the truth though, 'cause she ain't ever kicked out no white people. I remember one situation, and I know my partner Jimmy remember it too, wherever he at, but um, [pause] we went up in there, the bell had just rung, right? And we was just outside the door, and the bell had just rung, right? Right. And we, we open the door, come in, and she's like, "You guys you gotta be here when the bell rings, you gotta go to OCS [on-campus suspension]. Go." You know, "Leave." You know, just like that! Right? So we're walking out, and these two white girls, you know, they're supposed to be doing cool up in that class, I guess. I don't know, getting A's or whatever they be doing. You know, when they come in the door, the teacher's all, "Hurry up, hurry up, you're about to miss the assignment," you know? I mean, but, man. But, you know, Mr. Jackson [in the on-campus suspension office], he knows what's up, you know?

Interviewer: So what did Mr. Jackson do about it?

Ray: I mean, he didn't even trip, 'cause he know I be up in there every single day—knows what's up, man, so he don't even trip.

Ray, an African American graduate of the class of 2000, appears unmoved as he tells this story. His tone is matter-of-fact, as though the run-in with Ms. Dinkins and the quiet resignation of Mr. Jackson were commonplace. In fact, Ray's story may be typical. A closer look at the Berkeley High School discipline system reveals countless stories in which students—the majority of whom are African American—are removed from spaces of learning and placed into spaces of punishment. Their stories reveal an approach to discipline that focuses on separating "bad" kids from "good" kids, while ignoring the racial implications of the practice. Meanwhile, the need to find ways to reengage students with learning, especially those who are most frequently punished, is rarely considered.

In this respect, BHS is like thousands of other schools throughout the United States that use school discipline policies as a strategy for removing disruptive students (Ferguson, 2000). Such policies are aimed primarily at identifying and removing "problem" students, rather than considering why students enact such behavior or what might be done to reconnect them to the educational aims of school (Ayers, Dohrn, and Ayers, 2001). Like many other schools, BHS has been stuck in a vicious cycle of reproduction. It disproportionately punishes its neediest students by denying them the opportunity to learn, and it does so even though there is no evidence that it succeeds at either changing student behavior or improving the climate for learning. This is not to say that students like Ray do not engage in problematic behavior that must be addressed. Rather, the school's inability to address the needs of students like Ray likely contributes to the myriad discipline problems plaguing BHS.

In this chapter, we argue that the problems related to school discipline—which include relatively minor offenses such as tardiness and classroom disruption, as well as more serious offenses such as fighting, aggression toward school staff, and drug dealing—demand a systematic, schoolwide, coherent, and organized response coordinated and supported by the central administration. We critically examine why a school that has been plagued by these kinds of disturbances has been unable to develop such a response, and we ask how the failure to address discipline issues, which are, as we will show, fundamentally racial issues, relates to the achievement gap at the school.

We argue that because these issues affect a predictable subset of the student population—lower-income, low-achieving, black students—communitywide concern and action have been slow in coming. We also consider how and why the behavior of students like Ray comes to be seen as normal and natural in a school that has grown accustomed to the idea that black students fail and act out in disproportionate numbers. We ask why a middle-class white student behaving like Ray—and such students do exist at BHS—might be less likely to receive the same kind of treatment. By understanding how widespread poor achievement, oppositional behavior, and pervasive class cutting among lower-income black students is seen as normal and natural, we hope to point to promising ways to disrupt these entrenched patterns.

As we approach this topic, we also take a critical look at the expectations held by others—teachers, administrators, parents, security guards—who are implicated in the failure of black students. We ask why, in a community that is widely known as politically progressive, BHS produces racialized patterns of discipline and achievement that are identical to what we see in schools throughout the country (Miller, 1995; Gordon, Piana, and Keleher, 2000). This chapter's focus on African American students reflects the Berkeley High School discipline patterns, which shows that they have the greatest overrepresentation in discipline referrals—when teachers refer students for disciplinary measures including on-campus suspension. Although Latinos are also overrepresented in discipline referrals in some school districts, this is not the case at Berkeley High School.

In addressing this question, we focus on the role of ideology in producing, sustaining, and legitimizing these outcomes. In other words, we look at assumptions and beliefs that are ingrained in our cultural landscape—so ingrained that we often fail to recognize them. Because of these collective and unspoken assumptions, we are not surprised when we walk into the on-campus suspension room and see mostly black and brown faces there. Nor are we surprised to see spaces of punishment that are clearly designated and isolated from spaces of education. After all, the school's approach to punishment and its racialized academic outcomes conform to broader societal patterns that have been in place for so long in so many parts of the United States that failure becomes normalized.

This chapter draws on the research of the Diversity Project's Discipline Committee—a team of teachers, graduate students, school safety officers, and community members. The committee was created in 1999 to investigate the factors that influence racial disparities in discipline in hopes that through such an inquiry, we might be able to recommend strategies for addressing the problem. An analysis of numerical data on disciplinary referrals for suspension and expulsion was used to uncover trends in the number of formal discipline consequences over the years. We examined the reasons offered by school staff for such disparate patterns, and we analyzed the representation of males, females, grade levels, and racial and ethnic groups in the official discipline records. We also conducted semistructured interviews with twenty teachers who ranged in teaching experience and academic department. We sought to better understand their perceptions of the racialized discipline system, their discipline strategies, and what type of support they receive to run more effective classrooms. We also worked with what we were told would be the last generation of students who were involuntarily transferred out of Berkeley High School and mandated to attend East Campus Continuation High School, an alternative school, hoping to gain insight into how and why these students had fallen through the cracks of BHS. We relied on public records, aggregated school records, a student survey, and formal interviews with ten involuntary transfer students, including Ray. This chapter also draws on our own anecdotal experience; we have worked extensively in a variety of roles with students at Berkeley High School or East Campus.

Failing Students or a Failing System? Ray's Journey Through the Discipline System

We begin our exploration of discipline at Berkeley High School with Ray's journey through the discipline system. After numerous rules infractions and conflicts with teachers and other students, Ray makes it to the end of the discipline line—he is "involuntarily transferred" from Berkeley High School to East Campus. For three decades, East Campus served as a de facto last step in the BHS discipline system. BHS students who fell more than a semester behind in credits could be involuntarily transferred to East Campus. Located a half-mile south of Berkeley High and serving a fluctuating enrollment of 100 to 150 students, East Campus offered a shortened school day and basic remedial classes for students whose behavior or attendance caused them to be removed from BHS. Students widely regarded East Campus as a "dumping ground" for "bad kids," and in a district that takes pride in its commitment to integration, it was nearly 80 percent black.

In 2000, the school district attempted to revamp the image of the school. The old, deteriorating bungalows that housed the school were abandoned. Students and teachers were moved to a freshly painted, neatly landscaped, and attractive facility located directly across the street, and the school's name was changed from East Campus to Berkeley Alternative High School (BAHS). According to the district's plan, it was to become a small alternative school offering a more intimate learning environment to a voluntary student population. In the fall of 2000, BAHS recruited its first voluntary freshman class, emphasizing its new school-to-career curriculum and small school setting, and the district began to phase out the process of involuntary transfer. However, at the time of our research, East Campus received students with histories of low achievement, disciplinary referrals, persistent class cutting, and truancy. Ray explains,

I got transferred because attendance. I racked up a lot of absences. Really, I racked up hella absences in one class, you know, like fifty or sixty. And then I was cutting other classes you know, during the time. So it added up to over a hundred. And then I was getting referrals. And, I was doing hella stuff. I mean, I wasn't getting into no fights or nothing, you know, 'cause I'm a laid-back person, you feel, I'm cool with everybody. But you know, it was just, it was my attendance and my attitude toward the teachers, you know, the teachers didn't like my attitude because I'm not gonna let a teacher talk to me any way he wants to. . . . So that was just, that was the reason I got kicked out.

One might wonder how Ray could accumulate "fifty or sixty" absences in one class and why no action was taken earlier to address his truancy. As is true for many other students at BHS, Ray tells us that his cutting began the first semester of his freshman year. He had signed up for basketball to fulfill his physical education requirement but was placed in a dance class instead. In what might seem like an understandable decision for a ninth-grade boy in that situation, Ray simply avoided the dance class. He explains:

I talked to my counselor and she was like, "Well, um, you got to go talk to the teacher" or whatnot. So I went to go talk to the teacher and she was like "um yeah, man, you should have just been transferred," or whatnot. So then I talked to the counselor and she never transferred me, you know, she didn't transfer me until hella late, you feel? . . . She didn't actually change me from the class till it was about over. So, all them absences were still there on my transcript, 'cause I was still enrolled in the class. I don't know why they didn't take me off the roll sheet, you know. I mean I didn't go to that class from the jump. It's not like I showed up on the first day. I showed up like two months later, so she should have been took me off the roll sheet.

Although Ray attended his other classes, he could not remember any attempts by the school to intervene and find out why he was cutting the dance class. Like other BHS students, his parents received an automated telephone message to let them know he had missed a class. But for a savvy youngster like Ray, this was hardly an effective means of addressing his absence from class. He explains:

> Oh, they had a recording. They got a little voice-recording thing. It says, "Your child has been absent either one or more classes. To excuse these absences call this number." They call your house around six, seven o'clock, in alphabetical order. So you know, I just be home and, like, answer the phone or whatever. 'Cause I know when they're gonna call, you know, about six or seven o'clock. All you got to do is answer the phone. First you say, "Hello," and it says, "Hello, this is Berkeley High," and then you just say a couple words, and then you hang up. And after you hang up, then it made its call. If you hang up before it actually says something, it will call you back. Or if you didn't answer the phone at all, it will call you back. So you have to actually say something, answer the phone and say something.

By detailing exactly how to get around this system of parental notification, Ray explains the ease with which students who need this home-school communication the most can easily learn to circumvent it. Besides the automated message, Ray recalls:

> I don't remember any of my teachers ever calling the house to see what's going on. I don't remember that ever happening. Not even Ms. Dinkins, that teacher that used to give me a referral every day. She never asked to talk to my grandma. Only time I ever had a conference was when I was leaving. So that was the only time my grandma actually came up there to the school and actually talked to them, and she was surprised to see all the stuff that I was doing or not doing, and to see all the times that I was cutting.

When asked whether any of his friends ever had parent conferences, Ray replied,

> Really, though, it was nobody. I can't think of anyone who got a parent conference at BHS. At East Campus, yeah, but not up at the High. Them parent conferences were for, like, students that actually were there, but maybe who missed a couple days, you know, had a couple little mistakes. But me [shaking his head], I was just like, f_!. And so it was just like "f_! you too."

Ray notes that his grandmother was "surprised" to learn of his poor record, but by that time, Ray was already being transferred to the continuation school.

While we recognize that Ray's story is his own account and interpretation of what happened, our research findings and those of the Diversity Project overall suggest that the journey Ray describes is commonplace at BHS. Thus, we believe there is much to learn from Ray's story. First, Ray points to a lack of follow-up on students when they are sent out of class or consistently cut class. Although Ray claims Ms. Dinkins kicked him out "every single day," he does not recall any action taken to intervene in the situation, to confront the issue with Ray and his teachers, or to hold a parent conference. Nor was there any intervention when he cut his dance class "fifty or sixty times." Ray reports he never got a personal call home from a teacher, OCS officer, counselor, or administrator. The first time Ray confronted the consequences of his actions was the day he received his report card at the end of the semester, when he received an F in both the dance class and Ms. Dinkins's class. After only one semester of high school, Ray had already become one more in a continuous stream of low-income, African American students who was behind academically, and on his way to the segregated school for misbehaving students, East Campus.

In a final comment, Ray explains why he thinks East Campus had a disproportionate number of African American students. He alludes to the spiraling cycle of low expectations, defiant behavior, and self-fulfilling prophecies, which culminates in pushing African American students out of the school:

> The majority of us [black people], you feel, we don't believe in laws, rules, and all that, actually some school trying tell us, you know, what to do. And we're like, "Whatever," you feel? I mean, we're like, "Whatever, man, I'm gonna do what I wanna do," so we start cutting. And we don't get that counselor or that teacher telling us, like, "Man, you about to fail. I mean, you ain't about to pass the ninth grade." You know, we don't get that. So, it's kind of like, you do it, you feel, and then we actually don't know the consequences of it.

In detailing Ray's story, we must caution against misreading it as an indictment of individual teachers or counselors for failing to make personal calls home. We recognize that many teachers, safety officers, counselors, and other staff members regularly go above and beyond to reach out to particular students and their parents. But given the pervasiveness of disengagement and low achievement, these isolated efforts of well-meaning individuals simply cannot reach all of the students in need. Furthermore, BHS teachers lack the time and resources (such as access to telephones at school) to undertake such an enormous task on their own. Even Ray points out that "teachers don't got the time to know every single student. It's just too many kids in a class. And the counselors, even worse. Counselors got like five hundred students each."

We recognize that Ray is not a powerless victim in this cycle of events. Ray knew he was cutting and getting kicked out of classes, and he must have known there would eventually be consequences for his behavior. At the same time, as a first-semester freshman, Ray was at an age when many teens make poor choices. With no effort to reach a parent or to intervene in his pattern of cutting, the school essentially allowed Ray to continue making poor choices that would have severe consequences. Ray bears at least a portion of personal responsibility for his choices, but it is also clear that Ray's status as a low-income, African American male robbed him of the second chances that are routinely available to middle-class white students who make similarly poor choices.

We chose Ray as a starting point for this analysis of discipline at BHS because he fits the profile of the typical student who is most likely to get into trouble and to fail academically: an African American male ninth grader who has trouble adjusting to the freedom of Berkeley High School. Data collected by the Diversity Project revealed that these students are at greater risk of failure. Even before the project carried out its research, it was widely known that these students require more guidance, direction, and structure than the school offers. Yet over the years, little has been done to make changes in the operation of the school to address the needs of such students. Although inaction may not be an indication of racism, the inability of administrators to enact systems of prevention and intervention for such students is, at minimum, a sign of benign neglect.

Weaving Through the Discipline System: An Overview of Discipline at BHS

A stroll through Berkeley High School on almost any school day provides a quick portrait of the racial contours of the discipline system and its many holes (although since 2001 or so, changes have taken place to reduce the number of students hanging out during the school day). Safety officers, stretched thin over the seventeen acres of campus, patrol the halls and communicate to one another by radio. Often their voices are relaxed and nonchalant, but occasionally their tone is serious and a sense of urgency comes through when they have need to rush to the scene of a conflict or disturbance. To deter class cutters or intercept strangers, teachers are posted in pairs at the main hallway thoroughfares and intersections during class time. Also armed with radios but often isolated in a distant wing of the school, many of them dread playing the part of police officer as they patrol and occasionally confront students wandering the halls.

Policing the halls at BHS is a game of cat and mouse, one in which the cats are outnumbered and most have largely given up the chase. Most students figure out rather quickly that as long as they keep moving or speak as though they have a legitimate reason to be out of class, they can wander the halls indefinitely. The buildings, which span city blocks, provide plenty of places for young people to hide, and numerous destinations and routes for a forty-five-minute stroll. Groups who prefer not to wander know the spots where they can simply hang out and "chill" without being apprehended—the stairwells, in or near the old gym, on the bleachers in the new gym, between the buildings, at tables in the outdoor lunch area, or in the Martin Luther King Jr. Park behind city hall. There have been times in the past when things became so chaotic at the school that many students stopped trying to hide, and some brazenly sat directly under the windows of the vice principals' and safety manager's offices. Sometimes so many students were in the halls that it was hard to tell if classes were in session.

What is striking is not just that there are so many students hanging around the campus while classes are supposed to be in session or that they manage to do so in groups often as large as ten or more. What catches the attention of visitors is that most of the students seen outside during class time are African American. Other students, including high-achieving white students, also cut class, but they are more likely to leave campus and sit in MLK Park adjacent to the campus or go to a nearby coffee shop where they can hang out for hours without being bothered. Many white students know that if they walk the halls with a sense of mission, they will not fit the profile of a class cutter and will be less likely to be stopped.

In contrast, black students, who by sheer frequency of infraction embody the profile of the class cutter, are more likely to do so with a sense of nonchalance and even defiance. They travel in groups, and their conversations can often be overheard in classrooms. They are the mice in the game with campus security guards, only many of them show no fear of being caught. They have no fear because the students who cut are typically doing poorly in their classes already, and the sanctions that would be imposed if they were apprehended (in-school suspension) are largely inconsequential to them.

The truancy and attendance problem is not limited to the campus but spills out into the larger community. The sprawling campus has many points of entry, and although it is not accessible to traffic, a major street—Bancroft Avenue—cuts across its center. Throughout the years, there have been attempts to close the campus by building a fence, but the community has generally opposed these measures as too repressive and heavy-handed. In addition, due to the design of the campus, it would be logistically impossible to maintain a closed campus without posting guards at dozens of locations. The campus is completely porous, and it is hemorrhaging students.

Nearby businesses in the downtown area along Shattuck Avenue regard the students as a mixed blessing. Many rely on them for business, particularly at lunchtime, but they also resent them when they arrive in large, loud groups and intimidate the regular adult customers with their presence. Some students hang out in groups on the street, laughing and harassing passers-by, while others are nearly indistinguishable from the more sophisticated college students, pausing to enjoy a cup of coffee while studying or talking with friends. Even farther away—on the famous Telegraph Avenue at the doorstep of the university—BHS students can be found shopping, eating, and walking up and down the street.

Seeing so many students out of school while school is in session might lead those less familiar with Berkeley to assume that attending class is optional. What the outsiders do not realize is that the students were simply taking advantage of a system that had no immediate response at that time for students who missed class on a regular basis.

This does not mean that the discipline system fails to punish students. Some students, like Ray, are eventually caught by the discipline system and banished to East Campus. The students who are targeted for punishment are disproportionately African American and low achievers. Hence, like the gap in achievement, a gap in discipline divides the school along racial and socioeconomic lines.

Supported by a collection of rules and regulations that are inconsistently enforced, the discipline system's primary function, in practice, seems to be to weed out and exclude "bad kids" from the classrooms. Like the courses that segregate them by ability and academic performance, BHS disciplinary practices segregate and isolate a disproportionate number of black students into spaces of punishment. Whether in school or outside it, these spaces are reserved for students whom the school cannot handle or control. Once on the path of separation, disciplined students are pushed farther and farther away from the school, and in the process they become further removed from the opportunities that a high school education is supposed to provide.

First Steps: On- and Off-Campus Suspensions

Many African American students walking through the halls during class time are actually heading toward OCS, the first line of defense in the discipline system. Like many other schools throughout the country, BHS established OCS in 1980s to reduce the number of students it was suspending and sending home. The idea was to create a detention center where students could be punished for misbehavior but still be allowed to engage in learning.

Upon arrival at the OCS room, an observer might see some students giving a cheerful greeting to the program manager. An African American man with an imposing presence, the OCS manager was an ordained minister who saw his role as more of a counselor than a jailor. As the students file in, some are so accustomed to spending their days here that they shrug their shoulders in resignation as they throw their book bags to the floor and take their seats to sit out their punishment. The newcomers may occasionally start up conversations with the OCS manager, using him as a sounding board to express outrage at the teacher who banished them and explaining how unfair it was. The majority of students listen politely as the manager of the program explains the importance of respectful behavior, even when students feel they have been wronged.

OCS takes place in a classroom that has been designated as a punishment space. Often referred to as a "holding tank," students are sent to OCS for a class period or for the entire school day when a teacher or staff member can no longer handle them in the classroom. Few students use their time in OCS to catch up on schoolwork. Instead, it is usually a space for simply watching the clock until the period of punishment has expired. An idea that once seemed promising—keeping students at school rather than sending them home—has morphed into something else: a holding tank for passing the time.

A typical visit to the OCS room reveals the well-known but scarcely acknowledged fact that African Americans occupy the vast majority of seats. In the fall semester of 1998, for example, 70 percent of the two thousand OCS referrals went to African American students, who made up only 38 percent of the total student body. In the fall of 1999, this figure increased to 76 percent. Latino students are the second highest in terms of representation in OCS, followed by white and Asian students, who are vastly underrepresented.

In addition to being sent to OCS, many students are sent off-campus to serve a traditional out-of-school suspension. In 1998–99, there were 297 of these off-campus suspensions. African American students were again disproportionately represented for both the 1997–98 and 1998–99 school years, making up 67 percent and 68 percent of all suspensions, respectively.

Many teachers believed there were "only a handful of trouble-makers," although our research found that the problem was actually widespread. For example, when we began our study, an administrator estimated that only about 5 percent of the students caused all the trouble. But we found that 87 percent ($N = 403$) of students suspended in 1997–98 were suspended only once that year. We cannot attribute the bulk of the suspensions to the same students, who were getting into trouble over and over again. In cases where students were suspended multiple times, however, African Americans were again overrepresented. In 1997–98, 45 out of 54 students who were suspended more than once were African American (83 percent), and in 1998–99, 18 out of 22 repeaters were African American (82 percent).

Students can be referred over and over into the system without anyone taking action to figure out why this is occurring or what might be done to prevent it. In fact, when we were doing our research, we discovered that no one was designated to be responsible for monitoring discipline data. Even as the school began collecting better data, there was no systematic flagging of students with repeated disciplinary problems. From 1998 to 1999, we found some students with as many as thirty referrals to OCS. While informal intervention may have occurred, there was nothing in place to systematically identify these individuals. In some cases, students were repeatedly referred to OCS by the same teacher, yet there is no record that the conflict between the teacher and student was ever investigated by an administrator. Furthermore, while sitting out their punishment in OCS, students received no tutoring or academic skill building. As far as we could discern, basic communication related to discipline did not occur; teachers, counselors, and safety officers were not notified in a systematic manner when their students were suspended or referred to OCS.

Our investigation of referral records revealed that the most common reason for students to be sent to OCS was disruption and defiance. This same pattern held for a majority of the off-campus suspensions issued in 1998. The preponderance of such incidents suggests that conflict between students and teachers or other authority figures often serves as the entry point for students into the discipline system. The sheer number of these incidents over a three-year period (1996–1999) indicates that such conflict is fairly widespread, and not necessarily due to a handful of aggressive students or ineffective teachers. The data also suggest that focusing on a few deviant individuals will not address the scope of the problem.

The disruption/defiance category is a broad and subjective one, encompassing many different kinds of imaginable offenses. A Berkeley High discipline document from 1999 attempts to clarify the types of behaviors that could lead to disciplinary action for defiance/disruption: "Refusing to comply with requests of school personnel is considered defiance. This may include refusing to identify oneself, refusing to stop when requested or to move when requested, arguing, shouting, etc."

Despite this attempt to clarify the vague offense, subjectivity is inevitable when individual staff members determine whether they perceive an action or behavior as defiant and challenging to authority. The ambiguity of the offense and the fact that adults are allowed to make the accusation without any requirement that they substantiate the claim leaves room for misperception, overreaction, and racial bias. In fact, we found considerable variation in how teachers interpret this category.

The written referral forms that teachers must fill out to send a student away clearly reveal the wide-ranging interpretation of what behaviors are considered defiant. Some referrals describe hostility directed at the teachers, such as verbal threats or name-calling. Others speak to a more subtle perception of an affront to teacher authority, like not having a pencil for class, making hoops with wads of paper in the garbage can, or talking to a friend during class. While one can imagine how any of these seemingly minor infractions might be disruptive to a classroom, the sheer volume of cases reported suggests that something bigger must be going on.

Because of the tendency to attribute the problem to the individual student, the possibility that teachers might contribute to the conflict is rarely considered. Even when a teacher refers a large number of students to OCS on a regular basis, it is rare for teacher support or evaluation to occur. One teacher, Ms. A, reflected on her own role in negative interactions with students:

> Ms. A: I was having a problem with a particular student and I tried everything I could. I referred her to OCS; I tried to get her tutors. None of that helped. I tried to get a lot of different things to get going. . . . Finally, at the end, at the beginning of the second semester, I found another teacher who agreed to take her. I figured maybe it was just my class. Maybe it was just my style.

Interviewer: Do you think it had reached the point where it became something between the two of you?

Ms. A: Yeah.

Some teachers become more effective in their interactions with students as they gain more experience on the job. One teacher talked about developing a different strategy of intervention with students. She says, "Last year was nuts. But, um, I would say that aside from the backup class, I was sending students out, you know, at least once or twice a week last year. . . . And this year, maybe I've sent three students out for the entire year." Her new strategy is to intervene before it "escalates to the level of OCS." She explains, "The way I do things is first I talk to the student. And then I talk to the parent. And then I talk to the student and the parent together. And then I'll refer to OCS. But, so, that's my new thing." It is worth noting that this teacher developed a strategy that proved to be effective, but she did so on her own. Sadly, such successful strategies are often developed in isolation from other teachers, so the benefits do not reach the entire school.

The Last Step: East Campus

Students who have reached the end of the discipline line often wind up being involuntarily transferred to East Campus. Ray describes his classmates at East Campus in the following way:

> The students at East Campus? You can call them failures, so-called dropouts or whatnot. You can call them people, people that really didn't care for Berkeley High, didn't like the school system, didn't like the rules. Or you could just say people that just basically didn't like Berkeley High. Or basically, got kicked out of Berkeley High for not going to school, fighting, grades, or other things. Just people that didn't get accepted into the Berkeley High system, so Berkeley High kicked them out.

He goes on to explain:

> It was all black people in that school. It was only, look, when I was going there, it was all black people and Mexicans. Well, it was majority black people, you feel, I'd say at least 70 percent black people. Maybe 20 percent Mexicans, you feel? Five percent, maybe not even that, nah, it was only like two white people, you know, white boys. One of them, Joey, you feel, he was cool. And then there was Lexy, that was the only Chinese person. And then there was Massoud, and he was, I don't even know what category to put him in. But it was mostly black people, mostly black people, and then Mexicans too.

East Campus is a phantom school in Berkeley. Most residents do not even know that the school exists unless they work there or have a child in school there. In a community that takes great pride in being one of the first districts in the nation to integrate its schools voluntarily, it is ironic that such a highly segregated school would go unnoticed. That Ray can count and name the nonblack or Latino students at East Campus demonstrates that, like OCS, the racial composition of the students sent there is obvious. Why the district and community accept a school that functions largely as a dumping ground for young people deemed unmanageable at the larger BHS is an issue that requires further analysis.

In the 1970s, the school was called McKinley, and it served a predominantly white student population. According to one veteran teacher who worked there, "It was for hippie kids who couldn't handle the structure and rules of BHS. It was a cool place to work because the kids were bright but unconventional." By the 1999–2000 school year, African Americans made up 74 percent of the official student population compared to 38 percent at BHS. It appears that during the 1980s, the school ceased to function as an alternative educational setting and instead was primarily used as a site for students regarded as incorrigible. When we conducted our research, East Campus was also segregated in terms of socio-economic status, with an overrepresentation of low-income students as compared to BHS and the Berkeley Unified School District as a whole.

Despite the hard work of many of the teachers and staff who work there, the use of involuntary transfers as a means of enrolling students created the perception that East Campus was a "dumping ground for throwaway kids." This image was not lost on the students, whose attitude toward the school tended to be markedly negative. During our observations at the school, students routinely arrived at class late and unprepared. They appeared to come and go as they pleased, and they rarely showed enthusiasm for classroom activities. In interviews with students, it was clear that grades did not seem to matter to most of them. Instead, they were preoccupied with getting credits toward graduation.

Most of the students did not perceive the school as a place for intellectual and personal growth, but rather as a place to put in time and get out as soon as possible. As students weave through OCS, suspension, and East Campus, many of these disciplined students moved further away from seeing school as a place where they would be challenged and have the opportunity to fulfill personal goals. Interestingly, all of the students sent to East Campus are old enough to quit school if they want to; in order to be sent there, a student must be at least sixteen—the legal age for withdrawal. Yet despite their records of trouble and failure, they continue to come. Although all of the indications are that the educational system has given up on them, it appears that the students have not yet given up on themselves. Though most do so half-heartedly, they continue their education, realizing that obtaining a high school diploma will be important to them later in life.

Punishment schools like the old East Campus are common throughout the country. They typically serve students who are deemed a threat to the education or safety of others, and it is not a coincidence that these are generally also the neediest students, the ones who come from the most difficult personal and social circumstances (Noguera, 2003). As the school district attempts to reform the school from one focused on punishment to one that offers genuine educational opportunities, the key issue will be to ensure that it does not once again become a dumping ground. Only time will tell if this pitfall can be avoided.

Beyond developing alternative settings for troubled students, it is important for schools to devise strategies that make it possible to prevent students from entering the discipline system and becoming trapped in a negative spiral of punishment and failure. Students typically end up at schools like East Campus after several years of discipline problems in traditional schools—problems that initially are often minor but develop into major issues because the underlying causes are not addressed. For educators and others who watch as so many low-income youth of color become ensnared by these negative trajectories, we must ask why more is not done to intervene early, before the cycle of failure appears irreversible. We now turn to this question.

Failure Becomes Normal

During our numerous trips to the district administrative offices to document the discipline gap, we had many occasions to chat informally with clerks and staff. In one compelling instance, a staff member told us a story about a man who used to go to school board meetings and express his outrage at the number of black students being suspended. He would use the district's own data and demand to know why mostly black students were being suspended and expelled. He apparently did this somewhat regularly, and without ever getting a satisfactory response. This, we were told, happened over thirty years ago.

Racialized patterns of school discipline are not a recent phenomenon at BHS. While we carried out our research examining two years of discipline data, many at the school kept reminding us that these trends have been in place for decades. With such a history, it may be surprising that a large-scale initiative has not been sustained over the years to address and attempt to subvert these patterns. The consistency of racialized discipline patterns, coupled with the lack of systematic and sustained efforts to devise effective practices to intervene early when trouble first appears, suggests that these outcomes are accepted to some degree as normal and therefore tolerable.

The reform and intervention efforts that have been tried over the years have been erratic and generally occurred as a result of volunteer efforts devised by frustrated teachers, parents, and community members. Numerous committees have discussed the discipline problems at the school. While we were carrying out research at BHS in 1999, a committee was established to devise a policy for students who are tardy to class. The policy appeared to show promise and had the buy-in of teachers. However, it was implemented for one semester and then abruptly abandoned when a new principal was hired. This situation was not uncommon; with high staff turnover and changing administrative priorities, initiatives frequently get stalled, dropped, or forgotten altogether.

Ironically, this occurs even when new programs and interventions seem to be working. Other support programs sought to become more connected with the discipline system. For several years, a conflict mediation program for both student-student conflict and teacher-student conflict struggled to establish itself and become widely used as a resource for teachers, students, and administrators. Like the policy on tardiness, this initiative initially showed promise, but it was plagued by underuse and a lack of active involvement from the administration. A lack of stability has befallen anger management groups, which have tended to come and go over the years.

At BHS there has been no shortage of willingness to experiment in the search for solutions to school discipline problems. Rather, what has been lacking is the organizational leadership to ensure that new initiatives are evaluated, good programs are maintained, and the resolve to alter established patterns is not dissipated.

Innovative programs have been implemented with the best of intentions, but typically they have only been able to hover at the edges of the problem, while the larger discipline system has remained intact. In the spring of 2000, the Discipline Committee of the Diversity Project shared findings from its research with BHS faculty and the community. We showed graphs and tables documenting the widespread nature of discipline problems and the disparities of the discipline gap, and we challenged the effectiveness of the policies being used to address discipline problems at the school. We shared comments from students and teachers illustrating the pervasiveness of the problem, and we presented data showing how the lack of structure and support for needy students contributed to the underlying causes of the large number of discipline problems at the school. As we made these presentations, we discovered a disturbing trend: for the most part, the findings we presented failed to evoke surprise, much less a sense of urgency that something had to be done by either the community or the school.

After these presentations, we asked ourselves how it could be that in a progressive community like Berkeley, facts like those we presented would not be a cause for more concern. The only explanation we could come up with was that the figures we shared reflected what the faculty and community had come to consider as normal and natural. Whether we were talking about the achievement gap or the discipline gap, the disparities among groups have become so commonplace that they are taken for granted. Nationwide, in study after study, the research about discipline and race produces findings that merely "prove the obvious": African American and Latino students are more likely to get into trouble. This fact is so well known and so deeply ingrained in the national consciousness that it often stirs little interest or concern (Gordon, Piana, and Keleher, 2000).

What is obvious to so many people is the expectation that a specific, predictable subset of students will consistently become academic failures, troublemakers, and discipline problems. We refer to this expectation as the *normalization of failure*, which operates at the level of taken-for-granted assumptions and beliefs. Complacency and passive acceptance are by-products of normalization, and the degree to which the normalization of failure can be challenged and uprooted will play a large role in determining whether schools will continue to mete out a disproportionate amount of punishment to poor black and brown students.

Our research at East Campus showed how the normalization of failure can affect student identity. During one of our visits, a substitute teacher at Berkeley Alternative High School—the former East Campus—recalled a student who exclaimed, "This is East Campus. We don't *do* work here!" The student was new and had never attended East Campus, and yet the negative assumptions and expectations behind the normalization of failure had become her own. Her objection to being made to work while in a school that she knew serves as a dumping ground for bad students illustrates the depth of the problem. Students who have been labeled failures invariably internalize the label, and over time it can profoundly shape how students see themselves.

For this reason, any effort to alter discipline patterns and counter the normalization of failure must also include an effort to empower students to think critically about their taken-for-granted assumptions of success and failure. Helping students to develop a critical consciousness about the cycle of punishment and its social implications must be a central feature of a school's discipline policy.

One of the goals of the Diversity Project was to expose and challenge the normalization of failure and the dominant assumptions that reinforce it. One way we tried to accomplish this was to look at the achievement gap and the discipline gap through a different lens—one that refused to accept these gaps as normal or natural. In other words, we strove to make the familiar appear strange, to "problematize" or "denaturalize" the inequalities that are generally taken for granted. By problematizing the familiar, we hoped to demonstrate that patterns of inequity persist to a large extent because of our consent and acquiescence as a community. We further hoped that illuminating this consent would begin to galvanize the collective will to address the issues more forcefully. We hoped our research might make it possible to alter the tendency to locate behavioral problems within individuals, by making it possible for people to see how the structure of schooling helped to produce the behaviors. Once people could see this, we hoped they might seek to make changes in the organizational practices used to manage the institution.

We close this chapter with a discussion of two prominent ideological assumptions that we believe underpin the normalization of failure for black students at BHS. First is the assumption that discipline policies should attempt to identify and isolate the "bad kids" from the "good kids" so the latter group can get an education; the second is the assumption that the cause of discipline problems is located within individuals—students who misbehave, teachers who fail to maintain order in their classrooms, administrators who fail to address discipline problems effectively—rather than the structures. These assumptions inform the logic that guides how discipline is handled at the school, and they influence the interventions that are employed to address the issue. We argue that these assumptions are problematic, but because they are treated as conventional wisdom, they have the effect of overshadowing all other approaches that might be taken to address the discipline and achievement gaps. We now discuss each of these assumptions in depth as they arise through the school's approach to discipline.

Separating the "Bad Kids" from the "Good Kids"

At Berkeley High School, as is true at many other schools across the country, disciplinary procedures tend not to reengage students in the learning process or address the root causes of misbehavior. On the contrary, disciplinary procedures seem primarily occupied with identifying, separating, and punishing the offenders. This emphasis suggests the aim of discipline is not to help all students learn well but rather to remove the "bad kids" from the learning environment and contain them elsewhere.

Often the people responsible for implementing these policies are well intentioned: they want schools to be safe, classrooms to be orderly, and students to learn self-discipline and self-control. However, given the consequences of these policies on students who are targeted for discipline and the failure of these practices to achieve their stated goals, intentions are less relevant than impact. Approaches that rely on segregating and excluding students typically target a particular subset of the population—low-income black students—and relieve teachers and staff from the responsibility of reengaging these students in learning (Noguera, 1995). Such practices invariably reinforce stereotypes about "good kids" and "bad kids" and end up reproducing the same inequalities they were put in place to counteract.

The net result of these policies and practices is that the disciplined students are moved farther and farther away from spaces of learning and into spaces of punishment. School discipline policy focuses on the identification and segregation of "problem" students rather than the engagement of all students to learning. In this model, which resembles society's approach to criminal behavior, innovations in policy are directed at better or earlier identification of "problem" students. This policy is based on an implicit assumption that students can be divided into "good kids" and "bad kids" and that the discipline problem can be solved by removing a few "bad apples" from the spaces of learning.

At least theoretically, East Campus as a small school could have served as a setting for positive intervention for students with greater academic and social needs. The small school environment makes it possible for personal relationships between teachers and students to develop, and individual help for students who had fallen behind academically can be more easily provided. Nearly every student with whom we spoke had positive feelings about the closely knit school environment, the personal relationships with teachers and the counselor, and the extra help they received at the school.

Unfortunately, the practice of involuntary transfer to East Campus, which was still being used at the time that we carried out this research, undermined the potential for the school to function as an effective alternative learning environment. Moreover, several obstacles ensured that East Campus could not serve as a sufficient intervention. High student turnover, truancy, and low academic skills were among the most significant of these obstacles. Our study found that East Campus students were low achieving long before they arrived there. Low academic skills were compounded by high levels of truancy and student turnover, making it impossible for teachers to establish consistent classroom routines or implement progressive curricula building on previous lessons and long-term class projects (Nygreen, 2005).

All of these conditions combined to ensure that despite the efforts of many dedicated staff members, East Campus could not serve as an effective academic intervention for the neediest of students. While the benefits of a smaller school helped some students who might not otherwise have done so to catch up and graduate, for many others being sent to East Campus was "too little too late." In fact, for too many students, it is an example of how a well-intentioned effort to help students can end up reproducing the same inequalities it was created to overcome. In segregating "problem" students into a different space, East Campus marginalized and stigmatized them by taking away the opportunity for college-preparatory course work and creating, in the eyes of the community, "a school for dropouts."

Individuals Are the Problem

When we presented the findings from our research on discipline to the school staff, particularly the data showing the large number of referrals to OCS, several teachers said they wanted to know "who is doing this." Rather than sparking a discussion about how to rethink the entire disciplinary system at the school, some staff members wanted to direct attention to a subset of teachers who issued the greatest number of referrals, in an attempt to penalize these individuals. Similarly, when we presented data on suspensions, several teachers argued that the high rate of referrals could be explained by a small number of difficult students who were constantly getting into trouble.

The notion that a small number of individuals are responsible for the problems confronting the school is similar to the widespread belief in our society that the cause of problems like crime can be attributed to a relatively small number of deviant individuals (Currie, 1985) or "bad apples." As a society, we address crime through punishment targeted at individual criminals, the assumption being that if deviants are incarcerated, law-abiding citizens will be able to live in a safe and orderly society. This approach ignores that the line separating criminals from law-abiding citizens is not well defined; occasionally people who have never committed crimes do so. That the penal systems in the United States are notorious for their high rates of recidivism—more often than not, they fail to rehabilitate and instead produce more dangerous and hardened criminals—has rarely prompted a willingness to reform the criminal justice system (Skolnick and Dilulio, 2000). Likewise, the possibility that we might reduce crime through prevention is rarely considered, and we are not willing to consider that reducing poverty by increasing employment and raising wages might actually deter the incidence of crime (Currie, 1985).

At schools across the United States, discipline policies closely resemble the strategies used to address criminality in society. Misbehaving students are targeted for punishment that typically consists of varying forms of exclusion—detention, suspension, and expulsion. Discussions of "problem" behaviors rarely take into account the multilayered context that includes teacher-student interactions, school climate, school structures, and community and societal experiences. Even in a liberal community like Berkeley, the individual-oriented approach tends to dominate the way in which discipline problems are handled. Such assumptions lead us to ignore the influence of environmental and structural factors—in this case, disorganization at the school and a permissive school culture. As long as this assumption persists, approaches to discipline will continue to focus on individualized interventions, while overarching institutional patterns of the school and broader structural inequalities go unchanged and unnoticed.

In our interviews with school staff, several told us that they recognized that ineffective rules, a permissive school culture, and the sheer size of the school itself contributed to the discipline problems they most frequently encounter. Nonetheless, in discussions about discipline, they were less likely to consider ways of addressing larger systemic issues, especially as they relate to the discipline gap (Gregory and Mosely, 2004). As a consequence, the school remains trapped in an approach to discipline that many adults recognize as ineffective in improving student behavior or making the school safer or more orderly. Like most other schools across the country, they stick with this approach not because it works but because it is what they have always done.

The Social Impact of Ideological Assumptions

BHS—like most other high schools across the country—addresses school discipline in much the same way that our society addresses crime. In both cases, the approach is guided by the same ideological assumptions: (1) the problem of misbehavior/crime can be addressed by identifying and removing the offenders, and (2) the cause of misbehavior/crime exists within the individual offenders. Clearly, these two assumptions complement each other well. If "criminality" is a quality located inside individual people, then the logical way to reduce crime is to remove those people and segregate them in distinct punishment spaces. In other words, if we can just eliminate the "bad apples" from the bunch, the problem can be solved. In this paradigm, fighting crime becomes an exercise of identifying those "bad apples," or what criminologists have called the search for the "criminal type" (Platt, 1974). When this paradigm is applied to school discipline, educators and scholars are led down the road of searching for new and improved ways to identify the "bad kids" faster, more accurately, and earlier in their school careers.

The problem with this approach, we believe, is that it fails to address the ways in which social structures contribute to, and in fact produce, certain kinds of behavior labeled as criminal or defiant. Notably absent from the national conversation on crime, for example, is a serious examination of economic inequality, the lack of living-wage jobs in the legal economy, and the failure of public education to provide a pathway to social mobility. In the case of school discipline, we believe the underlying social causes of classroom misbehavior include these broad social inequalities as well as school-level policies and school culture, described in this chapter. An authentic commitment to prevention must include a rigorous exploration of these underlying causes and a serious schoolwide effort to address those that are within the scope of the school's power. In order to examine these social and school-level causes of classroom defiance, however, we must first be willing to give up our assumptions about school discipline, which hold that discipline problems are caused by individual "bad kids" who must be removed.

Eradicating the Discipline Gap and the Normalization of Failure

After each year of data collection, the Diversity Project presented its findings on race and achievement to the Berkeley School Board and school staff. We had disaggregated data regarding GPA, course enrollment, enrollment in advanced science courses, and school discipline. Most staff members listened politely, and many were interested in discussing how the findings could be used to address some of the long-standing problems at the school. However, some staff were unmoved by the data. They had an explanation already in their heads for the racial disparities, one that placed the blame squarely on the children and their families, and they responded with indignation to the suggestion that the school might do something to intervene and alter the outcomes. One staff member incredulously declared that everyone had known of these problems for more than twenty-five years. The response of James Williams, our codirector at the time, was simple: "Then why hasn't anything been done about it?"

Like the disparities in academic performance, the disproportionate punishment meted out to minority students at BHS has been normalized, and staff at the school have grown accustomed over time to the idea that certain students (especially African

Americans) will get into trouble and fail academically. Normalization and the tendency to treat behavior problems on an individual, case-by-case basis prevent the school from addressing the institutional factors such as the permissive school culture and the absence of effective systems for dealing with behavior problems in a preventive fashion that might make it possible to produce long-term changes in school outcomes. Among school staff, normalization contributes to complacency and acceptance of the status quo. Normalization affects the students as well. It creates an environment in which oppositional behavior among students of color is taken for granted as natural and inevitable by students and teachers alike.

However, historical patterns of unequal outcomes and disparate treatment of students at Berkeley High School need not be seen as either inevitable or natural. The normalization of failure is both a cause and a result of sustained inequality at BHS, and it must be challenged at the level of collective action. Assumptions about failure as normal must be addressed in a direct and concerted manner. Such assumptions are often deeply embedded in our cultural landscape, and new policies aimed at prevention and early intervention, while needed, will not by themselves change the patterns of punishment and misbehavior. The normalization of failure must be addressed through sustained public dialogue among stakeholders—parents, teachers, administrators, and students—who have not had much experience addressing sensitive issues in racially mixed groups. Without open and honest discussion about these issues, it is unlikely that any proposed solution, regardless of how meritorious it might be, will work, because it does not have the support and buy-in from the relevant stakeholders. The Diversity Project initiated a process for constructive dialogue on these important issues. The challenge now confronting BHS and schools like it around the country is to sustain the dialogue and prevent the status quo from remaining normalized and unquestioned.

Part Two

AGENCY IN THE FIGHT FOR EQUITY

4

CHANGING TEACHER PRACTICE AND STUDENT OUTCOMES

Pharmicia M. Mosely

I entered graduate school as a burned-out and frustrated young, urban high school teacher. I had worked for three years in a San Francisco high school that served mostly black, Latino, and Asian students. The staff was overwhelmingly white, and many teachers expressed frustration with their inability to meet the needs of students of color who struggled in their classes. I went to graduate school hoping that it would help me learn how to help teachers like those I had worked with and, as a result, help the students to be more successful in school.

As I began graduate school, I joined the Diversity Project, a collaborative research and reform initiative based at Berkeley High School. I wanted to learn how to use research as a tool to assist schools in addressing the problems they faced, and I welcomed the opportunity to become immersed once again in the everyday routines of a high school, this time as a researcher. I chose to help with the research and work of the project's Professional Development Committee, because this was the group that was working most directly with teachers and dealing with issues related to instruction and teacher-student relationships. I was excited to have an opportunity to work with teachers and a school that mirrored my previous experience.

From the beginning, the Diversity Project placed teacher professional development at the center of its strategy for using research to transform Berkeley High School. We knew that changes to structures, policies, or programs would do little to change patterns of student achievement unless we could find ways to change and improve the teaching. Central to this change was an effort to devise strategies for changing the beliefs and assumptions teachers held about students of color and academic achievement.

Several challenges related to teaching were obvious from the start of our work. The school had embarked on a limited effort to reduce tracking, and we also knew that many teachers lacked experience teaching heterogeneous classes. We also knew, from existing data, that a number of students entered BHS in the ninth grade reading well below grade level, but the school had few teachers with the skills to address literacy at the secondary level. Finally, the one-on-one interactions between teachers and students—especially when there were differences in race, class, language, and culture—were often strained, and these strained relationships also seemed to have direct bearing on the outcomes of students of color.

I began working with the project in 1998. From the beginning, I worked closely with teachers, particularly those who served on the Core Team of the project, in devising strategies to engage teachers in research related to classroom practice. In the pages that follow, I provide an overview and analysis of the research and professional development work carried out by the Diversity Project from September 1996 through June 2002. This is followed by personal narratives from teachers who worked with the Diversity Project, including reflections related to their work with the project and their efforts to engage in reform at BHS.

Year 1: 1996-97

In January 1997, the Diversity Project introduced itself at a staff development day by organizing a panel of racially diverse Berkeley High students. The purpose of the panel was to allow a group of students to present their ideas and experiences concerning why so many students experienced such high rates of failure at the school. Although the stories that the students told were familiar—students who gave up because they were bored, distracted, or simply unprepared to handle the rigors of a class—the discussion itself was remarkable. More than one hundred teachers listened attentively as students spoke honestly and openly about the reasons for their failure. Teachers posed questions and challenged students to acknowledge their responsibility for failing a class, but they also listened without becoming defensive as students described being turned off by teachers who lectured and left little room for questions or rarely stopped to ask if students understood the material being covered. The dialogue that ensued between teachers and students was the first small step in a process of reflection that teachers would engage in about how to help all students to be more successful.

In one exchange during this dialogue, a teacher asked, "What do teachers do that motivates you?" One Latino male student insightfully replied:

> You need to focus on what's right. Not every student is doing everything wrong. There's something that they're doing right. You can focus on that, and that will motivate them. Don't treat me like a child; don't patronize me. Tell me what I'm doing wrong, but tell me how to fix it. If I get 70 percent on a test, tell me yeah, I did well on this part, but you need to bring this [part] up. 'Cause I know a lot of teachers who mark in red big letters across my page what I'm doing wrong, what I need to fix. And that's it. And it seems like they didn't read the good parts. I did something *right*.

So unusual was this opportunity for students and teachers to talk about these problems face-to-face, and so poignant and critical were the student voices that, four years later, teachers were still referring to this as one of the best staff development days ever held at Berkeley High.

During the same morning session, the Diversity Project organized two panels of teachers who held unrehearsed discussions in front of the entire faculty. The discussions focused on the challenges they faced in teaching classes of students with mixed abilities. They also included an exchange of successful strategies that teachers used with heterogeneous classes at Berkeley High. Although these discussions were less candid than the student panel, they nevertheless represented a significant departure from the way things were typically done at the school. For the first time in many years, teachers were talking about what they do in the classroom, and in so doing, they were reducing the isolation of teachers and making instruction more transparent.

Later that semester, the Diversity Project's Professional Development Committee began an action research project to identify the forms of diversity-related training and professional development that the staff at Berkeley High felt was needed. The committee developed two surveys—one for teachers and one for classified staff—noncertificated service staff such as clerical, custodial, and campus security personnel. The teacher survey explored the experiences teachers found most helpful for professional development and fostering reflective practice. It was also designed to identify sources of strength within the existing faculty and staff in order to determine who could be called on to help address various issues in teacher-student relations that many teachers found problematic. Such issues included classroom management, cooperative learning, and teaching heterogeneous classes.

Some themes emerged from our analysis of data from eighty-nine teacher surveys. Two findings were particularly compelling. First, in response to the question, "Do you have any difficulty teaching students whose race and class background is different from your own?" over 80 percent of the teachers said no. Berkeley High School teachers who completed the survey (89 out of the 180 teachers in the school) tended to view student academic performance as more dependent on social factors outside their control, such as family support, prior schooling, or socioeconomic class background, than on race or gender. This seemed to suggest that teachers minimized the role that racial and gender stereotypes might play in their own pedagogical practices. However, although teachers indicated that they believed race and class were not obstacles to teaching all students, in response to another question, it became clear that there was more to this issue. We asked, "Which students do you typically have the most difficulty working with in your classes?" Seventy-four percent of the teachers responded that low-income minority students, especially African Americans, posed the greatest challenge for them.

In analyzing their responses, we were not only struck by the apparent contradiction in these findings but also surprised that teachers reported success in teaching all students, given the high rates of D's and F's among Latino and African American students. At a schoolwide professional development meeting held in May 1997, at the end of our first year of work at the school, we presented findings from the survey with BHS teachers. As teachers examined the data that were displayed on large charts, they too were struck by the obvious contradictions, but most were at a loss over what should be done to address it.

In an attempt to help teachers confront these issues, the Professional Development Committee decided to work with teachers in developing customized professional development (CPD) plans, in which each teacher specified exactly what kind of support and training he or she needed. The CPD plans were to be piloted in Year 2.

Year 2: 1997-98

Seven teachers agreed to work with the Diversity Project on the CPD pilot in an effort to improve teaching at the school. The committee included newer and veteran teachers, men and women, white teachers and teachers of color, from a range of subject areas—math, science, history, Spanish, English as a Second Language, Chicano/ Latino studies, and ethnic studies. The CPD plans were based on a peer coaching model of pairing teachers who would work together over the course of several months. The Diversity Project would provide the teachers with the opportunity to observe each other's classrooms (this required paying for substitute teachers) and with time to meet. In addition, the project provided one graduate student researcher for each teacher pair. The classroom observations were to be followed by a time for providing constructive feedback in a private setting, so that teachers would have ample opportunity to learn from each other.

Interestingly, although the teachers who volunteered to work on the CPD project saw themselves as fair and basically committed to supporting students of color, the observations revealed significant differences in the ways in which they interacted with students. Despite the pilot teachers' perceptions that they served all students equally, some peer coaches observed instances of inadvertent bias in classroom interaction, communication, and curriculum presentation that seemed to marginalize students of color. The most common example was a willingness to allow students of color who were disengaged from classroom activities to sit quietly in the back of the classroom as long as they were not disruptive. Out of a desire to avoid putting students on the spot and embarrassing them, some teachers were in effect allowing students to choose not to learn. Fortunately, there were also examples of teaching practices that appeared to be effective with all students, and these could be shared with other teachers.

This process was an eye-opening one for all involved. By observing each other's classrooms, engaging in dialogue about what they observed, and honestly analyzing their own practices within a collegial environment, teachers were learning to deal with issues of race, culture, and equality in a positive way. One teacher commented:

> My partner in the peer coaching/CPD was a veteran science teacher and also department chair. As a social studies teacher, this pairing at first seemed strange to me, and I wondered if we would be mismatched. This turned out to not be the case. While our styles of teaching differ and our subject matter differs even more, I found both the observations and pre- and post-meetings to be very useful. . . . My participation in the peer coaching/CPD model has allowed me to learn from observing another teacher and has forced me to do some critical reflection about the impact of my own identity (including ethnicity, gender, income, learning style, etc.) on the dynamics

of my classroom and the patterns of success and failure of my students. It has given me access to current research on diversity and equity issues in the classroom and provided a context for my own analysis of my teaching practice.

Comments like this one were common among the teachers who participated in the pilot. It seemed clear that peer mentoring around customized professional development was an effective way to provide teachers with the support they needed. For years, teachers had tackled these issues in isolation and struggled to find ways to address the obstacles on their own. Now they had the opportunity to discuss their work in a safe and constructive setting, and by all indications, it seemed to be helpful. The question was how to make it possible for such an approach to involve a larger number of teachers at the school.

Year 3: 1998-99

Given that the costs and time involved with the pilot made it difficult to replicate on a larger scale, we sought to find other ways to engage a broader number of teachers, still using lessons learned from the pilot as we attempted to advance the work. In the project's third year, the Professional Development Committee turned its attention from peer coaching to developing ways to involve the entire faculty of 180 teachers in addressing issues of teaching heterogeneous classes and teaching across cultures. Many teachers indicated in their surveys that they wanted more training in these areas, so the interest was clear. Moreover, the Diversity Project believed that we had to help teachers identify effective teaching practices and curricula that could be used in heterogeneous classrooms. We also wanted to help teachers overcome the obstacles that made it difficult for some of them to be effective with students of color. To accomplish these goals, we launched a broader strategy for professional development, involving a larger number of teachers at the school.

The staff development program took place in two phases. In the first phase, twelve lead teachers were selected to participate in a two-week seminar in the summer of 1998. They were asked to plan a year-long series of workshops and focused in-service activities for teachers schoolwide. In the second phase, which took place during the school year, the twelve lead teachers, joined by other faculty interested in playing a leadership role in staff development, conducted several workshops on themes identified over the summer. These workshops covered a range of issues, including classroom management through intellectual engagement, devising assignments that work in an equitable classroom, teaching basic skills across the curriculum, sheltered English to support language-minority students, building safety nets for sensitive classroom conversations, setting high standards for all students, assessment and fair grading practices, using dramatic simulations to liven up the classroom, and teaching students to work cooperatively.

The workshops were held throughout the school year, and teachers were allowed to choose to attend the sessions of greatest interest or relevance to them. The Professional Development Team that coordinated and planned the workshops recognized that some areas of teacher practice are harder to deal with than others. We knew, for example, that race plays a critical role in learning and classroom interactions, yet this subject is often difficult to discuss openly. To get around this difficulty, the workshops focused on how issues of race typically arise in classrooms.

Issues related to classroom management, and challenges to the Eurocentric curriculum of many courses, were addressed explicitly. Teachers discussed how these issues come up in their classrooms. They asked themselves how they might embrace the diversity in their classrooms and use it as a learning opportunity for all. Finally, they discussed how to begin to address these issues within the high school community. The workshops were developed to begin an ongoing dialogue among teachers about the ways in which issues related to diversity had an impact on their teaching. The workshops also provided an opportunity to stimulate schoolwide sharing of best practices. At a school like BHS where such conversations had not occurred for many years, these meetings among teachers proved to be a catalyst for more far-reaching changes at the school.

There was, of course, a major flaw with this professional development strategy: involvement was voluntary and left to the choice and preference of individual teachers. Several teachers suggested that the ones who needed this help the most would be least likely to attend. We understood this problem. Teachers who denied the significance of race issues in their teaching or explained the issue of low achievement as a "cultural" problem caused by unmotivated students and negligent parents would be less likely to attend. Similarly, teachers who lacked a desire to improve their classroom effectiveness simply because they were less invested in their own careers, and therefore less interested in enhancing their efficacy in the classroom, were also less likely to participate. For these reasons, we plotted a different strategy in the fourth year.

Year 4: 1999-2000

Although the fifty-eight teachers who participated in the workshops uniformly expressed support for this approach to professional development, we found that the workshop approach was not sustainable. The commitment to improve individual teacher practice was not shared by the entire staff, and many teachers were unwilling to stay after school to participate in an activity for which they would not receive compensation.

For this reason, the Diversity Project decided to launch a different professional development model: Action Research for Teachers (ART). For this new initiative, a group of twenty interested teachers were enlisted to critically examine their own practice. The idea was to start the work with this group of twenty, then add new groups of similar size as the work took hold and could be sustained.

Again, we wanted to create a setting where teachers could learn from each other as they reflected on their own practice. To accomplish this goal, we designed the meetings so that teachers could discuss strategies that had proven effective in soliciting student engagement within their own classrooms. We hoped that teachers would model best practices that addressed a variety of learning styles and student needs. Once exposed to new instructional strategies, teachers would be asked to try these practices in their own classrooms. We would then examine the impact of these practices on student engagement, under the assumption that engagement is the first step to learning.

A major shortcoming of this process was that it relied on teachers' providing input on what they felt they needed in order to improve their teaching. We realized that if the teachers were unaware of weaknesses in their teaching, they might not seek help to correct them. Moreover, the effort to improve teaching was only loosely connected to analysis of student achievement. That is, we did not analyze data from standardized tests to ascertain specific skill areas where students appeared deficient, nor did we examine student work as we proposed ideas for addressing perceived teaching problems. The strategy we adopted was similar to many other professional development initiatives: it was based on only a vague sense of what it would take to improve the quality of teaching (Elmore, 2002). By failing to make explicit the link between teaching and learning, it became substantially less likely that we would be able to use this intervention to further efforts to close the achievement gap.

We also knew that the model would not help us reach the teachers who were most resistant to change, since participation was voluntary. For those who participated, the ART strategy seemed to work. Lead teachers modeled strategies for the participants, who in turn attempted to implement new strategies in their own classrooms and reported back to the whole group about how it went. Group discussions were lively, candid, and open. Teachers freely offered examples of success and failure, and when they described challenges they faced in reaching all of their students, they received help from their colleagues in thinking through how to reach them.

Years 5 and 6: 2000-02

In the fall of 2000, the ART planning team learned of a "cycle of inquiry" model employed by the Bay Area School Reform

Collaborative. This process requires teachers to identify a specific problem in their classroom and develop an action plan to address that problem. Unlike the first year of ART, during which teachers tried out generic best practices, the cycle of inquiry allowed teachers to focus changes aimed at addressing the racial achievement gap within the context of their classrooms. The shift to a more generative model allowed the planning team to outline a basic process of inquiry, but gave teachers the ability to choose the focus of the research as it pertained to their particular circumstances.

Graduate student researchers from UC Berkeley continued to work with BHS teachers on small-scale projects, but most of the ongoing work to improve teaching through teacher research was carried out by the teachers themselves. Several teachers were quite familiar with and adept at qualitative research methods, so there was no doubt that some of the teacher-led efforts to support professional development could proceed.

However, the real challenge confronting teachers is to ensure that old routines and patterns of behavior do not take hold again. Blaming students for poor academic performance, without ever asking how their learning is related to the quality of instruction provided, is a common practice, and unless it can be challenged, efforts to raise student achievement are unlikely to succeed. Even when it is clear that certain teaching strategies (such as excessive reliance on lecture and passive learning) are ineffective with students, teachers may rely on these methods simply because they are comfortable with them and have relied on them in the past. Breaking the routine through critical reflection and a careful review of student assessments is essential if teacher effectiveness is to improve.

Teachers as Agents of Change

Through my four years of work with the Diversity Project (1998–2002), I came into contact with many teachers and had an opportunity to talk to them about the triumphs and challenges they faced. I realized that for many teachers, any affiliation with the Diversity Project served as a form of professional development, not just work on the Professional Development Committee or ART. Many teachers worked with research committees related to the Diversity Project, such as the studies of the class of 2000 and of school disciplinary practices, or the analysis of existing interventions, such as the detracked freshman core and some of the small learning communities.

As part of the professional development process, teachers were expected to share their experiences and lessons learned. One aspect of this reporting that I observed was that not all teachers' voices were valued at all times. For example, voices of teachers of color were valued in discussions of race and achievement in terms of problem solving (Mosely, 2003). All teachers' voices were valued in large Bay Area-wide school reform meetings. But teachers reported feeling that their views were not valued in the same way at Berkeley High. They could go out and tell other schools about their work, but staff at their site were less interested. Part of the contribution that the Diversity Project made to the school was to help center teachers' voices in discussions of school reform. We helped teachers share what was happening in their classrooms in a way that was safe and honest.

The Professional Is Personal

I entered graduate school hoping to find a "professional development solution" for problems that white teachers face in helping students of color; in fact, I learned much more. Through working with the teachers at Berkeley High, I realized that reflecting on and analyzing one's classroom practice and beliefs is a personal endeavor. Our Professional Development Committee tried to have open and truthful dialogues about race that address teachers' personal beliefs and professional practices. These discussions varied in intensity and effectiveness.

One of our key findings was that these discussions are essential to the process of school reform. Teachers need to have a clear understanding of where they stand in relationship to their students and colleagues. Given that Berkeley High is so racially diverse and given the persistence of disparities in achievement that break down along racial lines, teachers must link their personal beliefs about race and achievement to their own classroom practice. In the end we found that ART helped provide the structure for teachers to do that. Nevertheless, the question remains: How can such work be sustained?

Six years later, we return to the core belief of the Diversity Project: that teacher reflection and research is an essential part of eliminating the achievement gap. This belief is rooted in our understanding that school change is not just about altering the processes and systems that guide schooling. It is also about battling macro forces like institutional racism, and doing that by addressing the microlevel classroom interactions between teachers and students.

In order to truly understand what is happening in classrooms, we turn directly to Berkeley High teachers, in the hope that their reflections and insights will help others concerned with finding ways to promote teacher initiative in the effort to improve teaching and to achieve greater equity for students.

Teacher Voices

Finding and Keeping the Conscience of Berkeley High

Dana Michiko Moran

In 1993, after teaching for seven years at a public high school in central Los Angeles, I was on my way to teach at Berkeley High School, my alma mater from many years before. My job was to teach ethnic studies and serve as the part-time (0.2 full time equivalent, FTE) Racial Harmony Coordinator—a title invented by the principal, but one that I could never actually bring myself to use. It was through my "coordinating of racial harmony" (still an unfinished job) that I met the people who would become the leaders of the BHS Diversity Project. From the perspective of a teacher at Berkeley High, it has been my experience that the project has both modeled some unique and powerful methods of research and provided much-needed support for teachers in search of more equitable outcomes at our school.

In 1994, PBS aired a documentary, *School Colors*, that depicted the racial divisions and ethnic tensions that characterize Berkeley High School. Intending to coincide with the fortieth anniversary of *Brown* v. *Board of Education*, the documentary asked, "How far have we come in desegregating schools?" The answer was, it seemed, "not very far." Students and staff felt maligned by the film and by the representation of the school. Although no one could claim that anything in the video was outright false, they insisted that much of what works well at BHS was intentionally left out. Feelings of betrayal toward the film crew were high since the community had allowed them access to virtually every aspect of campus life, including classrooms, student meetings, parent meetings, and personal interviews.

The Diversity Project began its work two years after *School Colors* was released. Because of the controversy surrounding the film, the atmosphere at the school was still strained when it came to open discussions of issues related to race and diversity. Nonetheless, the project set out to investigate and understand patterns of social separation and academic achievement (or failure) that broke down along racial lines. To say that we were greeted with suspicion would be an understatement. Today, however, our data are well respected in the school community and frequently sought by those attempting to examine the problems of equity at Berkeley High. This transition has happened for a number of reasons.

First, the Diversity Project has always made it a priority to fund teacher release time. Time is a teacher's most valuable resource, and in order for our partnership to be truly collaborative, teachers had to be involved in a way that was not merely extra work. Raising the funds to pay for time so that teachers could participate in leading the project was costly. At the height of our data collection, we funded 1.2 FTE at a cost of close to $50,000 per year. The project's willingness to commit the resources needed to make this possible is a testament to the seriousness of its commitment to collaborative research.

As a teacher-researcher, I found this time to be invaluable. It allowed me time during the school day to meet with my research committee, interview staff and students, track down administrators, analyze data with graduate students, and compile reports and presentations. We spent a great deal of time outside school as well, but the buyout time during the school day was essential for us to make and maintain contact with students and school personnel. I would not have been able to interview and shadow students, administrators, or other teachers if I had been confined to my classroom all day.

This respect for teachers' time, and the inclusion of teachers as full partners in designing, collecting, and analyzing the data, is an important hallmark of the Diversity Project. We envisioned ourselves as part of the school community, a true partnership between school and university, so the active participation of different stakeholders was essential. Our Extended Team included teachers from virtually every department in the school and with varying levels of experience (one teacher was in her first year; others had more than thirty years of experience). The Extended Team, which served as an advisory body, also included elected members of the Berkeley School Board, students, parents, classified staff (for example, secretaries and safety officers), counselors, administrators, and community members. This inclusiveness of key stakeholders was another important factor in our success and gave legitimacy to our findings.

From the beginning, the Diversity Project always involved parents, students, and teachers in every aspect of the work. Having participant researchers keeps us honest, and it also gives us both insider and outsider perspectives. The presence of these stakeholders pushed us to probe deeply in our analysis of the data. It also turned out that this approach made our findings more authentic and more complex when we presented our findings to BHS staff and the community and held discussions of what it all means. We never "studied" anything without listening to those being studied. While it would be incorrect to say that everyone has always been happy with the conclusions of our research, it would be fair to say that we sought multiple perspectives and that those efforts were respected and appreciated. When we began, a teacher told me that she suspected the Diversity Project was setting up Berkeley High to be fodder for another public lashing, probably in the form of a book. Four years later, in a meeting of administrators and department chairs, another teacher described the project as "the conscience of the school."

The truth is that BHS always had a conscience; what it lacked was a vehicle for expressing concerns about equity and fairness at the school. In this respect, one of the most important accomplishments of the Diversity Project was that it brought together like-minded people who sought to reverse the patterns of failure at Berkeley High. Prior to the project's creation, it was easy for teachers who were concerned by the failure of so many students of color to feel alienated and even somewhat crazy, especially when so many people touted Berkeley High's successes. It was common for the school's advocates to quote figures about college attendance and how many of our graduates went on to Harvard and other prestigious universities.

As a BHS student, I experienced those successes. I was evidence of them. I went to class, did well, and graduated from UC Berkeley. The system worked for me. But when I returned as a teacher, I saw struggle and failure, and lots of it. I saw the success too, but it was as if the failure was invisible, or worse, inevitable. It was the family secret that everyone knew but nobody talked about—not necessarily because they were afraid of it, but because they had become used to it. When it seemed that so many others at Berkeley High were at peace with the academic divide, or felt powerless to do anything about it, the project drew people from various corners of the school and community who shared the distress, saw the failure, and sought to change it. This group has grown steadily larger over the years, and new consistent voices for change have emerged.

I have been scolded, chastised, and verbally attacked for "emphasizing the negative" and "overstating the problem," in relation to my work with the project and the issues of equity at Berkeley High. We are constantly reminded that, after all, minority students at Berkeley High perform better than their counterparts at other schools. Our current difficulties with the Western Association of Schools and Colleges (the entity that accredits high schools and colleges and that granted BHS a minimal one-year accreditation) are frequently blamed on a self-study report that "focused on the negative aspects" of the school, on the failure of the school to educate and serve large segments of its population. A school board member once accused us of calling white people racist and blaming them because we pointed out that these failures were mostly for black and Latino students.

My colleagues in the Diversity Project shared the sense of urgency and outrage in response to such nonsense and allowed me to feel less crazy and more optimistic. The parents, students, graduate students, staff members, and other teachers of the Diversity Project have continually impressed and inspired me and made me believe that change is possible, even at Berkeley High, where the patterns of success and failure have been entrenched and unspoken since I was a student there over twenty-five years ago.

There are some things we did not do well, and many things we did not do at all, but the project created a focal point for reform-minded people and gave them a place to come together. Participating in such a broad-based effort to challenge the status quo has created a community of teachers, parents, and staff who will not let these issues go away and will continue to lend their insights, energies, and talents to creating a new reality for our school, my school, Berkeley High.

There Are No Pedagogical Solutions to Political (or Racial) Problems

La Shawn Routé Chatmon

Leaving Berkeley High School was the hardest thing I have ever done in my professional life. During the years I worked there, I had taken on many different roles at the school: I was a teacher in the African American and Ethnic Studies Department; I was the student activities director; I was principal of summer school; and in the last two years, I was the codirector of the Diversity Project. I was also a cheerleading coach, the African American studies adviser, a

Black Academic Motivator, and the coordinator of Richard D. Navies Week, an intensive week-long series of educational events sponsored by the African American Studies Department. Throughout all of this, I never stopped teaching. I loved our students. I sat on too many committees and leadership teams to count; led my colleagues in workshops and research; participated in and conducted focus groups; stood up and sat down in unbearable; unproductive staff development meetings; and presented work from the Diversity Project at regional and national meetings.

In everything I did, I tried to be the diplomatic professional, to remain steady and trustworthy. I tried to maintain a sense of integrity and lost my temper only when I reached a point of frustration and had no other good alternative. I respected my colleagues. I believed deeply in the possibility of a better Berkeley High. But after only five years (which felt like ten), I packed my books, papers, displays, student work, and photos and walked briskly down the halls for the last time. When I left, I was hurt, disillusioned, tired, and angry.

In my last year, I had begun to make public comments in conversations about the importance of teachers not being complicit in reproducing the same outcomes year after year. I asserted that the most insidious form of racism we perpetuated in our school was that we opened our doors every year and did the same exact things, often pretending to expect different results. As a school community, we were, in my mind, as visionless as a person driving in fog at zero visibility. There was not one common principle for which our staff agreed to abide by, not one stance we could take about the nature of teaching and learning, not one agreement about the root of the achievement gap or what we could do about it. And with every idiotic and cowardly decision we made as a school and school board, my hope in the possibility of change and increased student achievement diminished. How we functioned from day to day and why so many good people allowed the situation to go on without taking the actions we knew could make the school a better place for all students had become a growing source of wonderment and disappointment for me.

The first time I was made aware of the achievement gap at Berkeley High was in a staff meeting—the ones with 100 to 125 folks packed in a library at the end of a long day, papers being graded, backs to each other, newspapers being read. The assistant principal had stuffed our boxes with the semester "D&F" reports, which noted the number of students with one or more D or F grades on their report card. The numbers were unfathomable: upwards of 60 percent of the D and F rates were for African American and Latino students.

The staff expressed outrage and righteous indignation. After the meeting, people talked for days about the data and what they suggested, and then suddenly, as if a storm had passed, the conversations came to an end, not because we had figured out what to do but simply because we had moved on to something else. In hindsight, I have many theories about why we were all able to get back to work, but at the time I thought, "These people are crazy!" I joined the Diversity Project the following year, my second year at the high school, because I wanted to push the conversation forward.

As a Diversity Project team member, I was actively involved in two committees: the Professional Development Committee, later to become Action Research for Teachers (ART), and the Parent Outreach Committee. My lessons from both experiences run deep, and I will be ever grateful for the opportunity to work with such extraordinary men and women committed to interrupting patterns of underachievement. In the first two years, the Diversity Project operated with the following theory of action: if we found out from teachers what their pedagogical strengths and challenges were (we used surveys to get this information) and developed a curriculum to meet teacher-identified needs, then staff development would be more authentic and relevant to classroom practice. We believed that such an approach would compel teachers to take what they learned (with support from the project and other teachers) and implement new strategies in their classrooms, which would result in increased achievement. I was involved in planning staff development with twelve of my colleagues.

My awakening came not in implementing professional development, but rather through the process by which the Professional Development Committee developed its work. Led by one of the project's graduate students and a veteran and noted teacher leader in the school, this diverse group worked for several weeks in the summer to develop a curriculum for the school year. We managed to bring together a collection of individuals who under normal conditions may not have volunteered to be in the same room together for three weeks. What was revealed in the process of many discussions about the joys and pains of teaching—teaching from our various positions, as women, as men, and African Americans, Latinos, Asians, whites, gays and lesbians—is that there was much more at play than the delivery of content in our classrooms.

Teachers shared their stories, their assumptions, their fears, their anger, and their expectations for their students. It was an amazing and difficult journey, but through our frank and honest discussions, we emerged as allies in the work and more committed to making a difference in our classrooms and throughout the rest of the school. I will never forget one of our group members, in the midst of an intense conversation about race and achievement, saying out loud, "I am so glad that I am not African American."

It was my work on both of these committees that inspired the title of this essay—a phrase that I heard in a professional development consortium where the keynote speaker was Asa Hilliard. In *The Maroon Within Us*, Hilliard asserts that "there are no pedagogical barriers to teaching and learning when willing people are prepared and made available to children."

With all the data that the Diversity Project was able to gather in the school, the issue of Berkeley's design never came into sharp relief during my tenure. Should we have expected that many teachers and staff members too align themselves to a common vision of student achievement? Was it realistic to believe that even in a school where so many things were not going well that young people could actually learn to use their minds well? At the time, I believed these things were possible. It took me a while to become disillusioned.

I had been encouraged to dream and to think the best about what could be accomplished through education. As a former teaching fellow in Brown University master's program, I came to Berkeley High School believing that it could be a better place for all students. I started teaching in the summer of 1995 and at the time did not see why so many of my colleagues acted as though it was so hard to serve the needs of all students. I did not understand why it was so difficult to make simple decisions about changes that we all knew needed to occur, and I could not figure out why no one wanted to lead, why people sounded so angry all the time, or why adults did not just "do the right thing."

Despite the questions that began to nag at me, I loved teaching. Our students were incredible. Working with them every day for five years, including summers, was by far the best and most rewarding part of my work.

If you believe, after all this talk of how challenging it was—the reproduction of failure, the critical incidents, the racist and sexist comments endured—that I did not love that place and fought every day as if it would be my last day, you would be sorely missing the point. Change is messy, hard as hell, and takes time. It is not only practice that one is ever trying to interrupt in schools—it is culture (adult and student); it is expectations and beliefs (adult and student); it is the very design of a school that fights back in all its reproductive nature. It is negotiating family and community expectations and values (that are often competing). It is not simple work, or high schools all across the country would have done it already.

I See Myself as an Ally

Miriam Klein Stahl

Being a part of the Diversity Project kept me in the teaching profession. I started working as an art teacher at Berkeley High School in 1995 at the age of twenty-four. When I was hired, the Art Department had not taken on a new teacher in thirty years. I was new to BHS and new to teaching. The high school had no support system in place for incoming teachers. I felt isolated and overwhelmed in a classroom that the maintenance department also used as storage space.

During my first year, other teachers talked to me only to ask for my hall pass when they mistook me for a student in the hallways. Around this time, the Diversity Project made a presentation at a staff meeting that interested and distressed me. I was impressed by this grand effort to document the achievement gap and the social separation at the high school. Conversely, I was completely disillusioned to be part of an institution that perpetuated the inequalities of our larger society. Overall, in this presentation I saw a community working together for equity, and I wanted to be part of this collaboration.

In my second year of teaching, I joined the Diversity Project as a member of the Class of 2000 Committee chaired by Jean Yonemura Wing. Jean encouraged me to assist in gathering research on the class of 2000. At times I was uncertain, feeling safe only in the territory of the arts, but I was willing to try if the research outcomes would improve the culture and academic outcomes at the school. As my involvement in the project expanded, my room became a hub of activity that centered around our work. Teachers and researchers came and went throughout the day to pick up tape recorders and data collection materials. All the while, we conversed about our experiences and observations.

Jean gave me the task of helping her organize teachers and community members to interview and shadow students. Shadowing students became the most meaningful professional development I have had as a teacher. Through this process of observation and reflection, I became part of a community of Berkeley High staff, researchers, students, and parents working toward closing the achievement gap. Most important, I had the rare opportunity to see the school from a student perspective. Focusing my observations on the student and not the teacher was a challenge. I was curious to see how other teachers worked, but if I had entered the classroom as a colleague to observe teaching practices, I would have completely missed the opportunity of viewing the school from the student point of view.

Over the four years I worked on the project, I shadowed three students (two for the Class of 2000 Committee and one for Action Research for Teachers). Although each of the three students had a very different high school experience in terms of access to challenging classes and their feeling of social acceptance, one common thread was the incredible amount of time they needed to spend focusing on listening skills. Even the best and most engaging teachers spent most of the forty-five-minute classes talking. Every day students attend six classes, with the majority of the content delivered in a lecture style and with a complete disconnect from the previous class. I was able to see the instant at which the student could no longer rely on his or her listening skills and would need to get a drink of water or sharpen a pencil or secretly listen to headphones. Their apparent disinterest in some cases was correlated with the lesson being presented, but at other times, it seemed that the student just needed to move around or talk to someone. Both of these behaviors are unacceptable in the academic environment. By the end of the shadow days, I too found it hard to concentrate or pick up on what was happening with the students because I was so burned out from navigating around such a huge school with so many different academic expectations and social interactions in the hallways and at lunch.

Through shadowing and interviewing, I learned both general and specific aspects of the student's experiences at BHS. One common link to success or failure that I saw with all three students was their relative connection or disconnection to support within the school, whether that support came from an individual or special program. The first student I shadowed was Raul, a middle-achieving Latino junior in the class of 2000. Every day he would take the bathroom pass in his science class so that he could go by the library and say hello to a woman on the library staff. I noticed that many Latino students felt a connection to this woman, who was one of just four Latinas on the BHS staff. He told me that she was one of two adults at the high school who cared for him. The other person he felt a connection to was the director of the Computer Academy, a small school program within Berkeley High. Raul went to her when he needed a pencil or was having problems in a class.

The second student I shadowed was Lily, a high-achieving white female, also a junior in the class of 2000. She was enrolled in Advanced Placement courses and had access to tutoring that helped her to succeed. When she was going through the emotions of coming out as a lesbian, Lily's grades began to drop. She found support in a staff member in the Berkeley High Health Center who was the director of the Peer Health Educators program, a group of students who educate other students about AIDS and other sexually transmitted diseases. Lily became a peer health educator. From this empowering connection, she began to get back on the track of high achievement.

The last student I shadowed felt absolutely no connection to school. Jake was a low-achieving white student who was failing all of his classes. Shadowing Jake gave me the opportunity to see what students do when they cut class. After the first class of the day, I caught the public transit bus with Jake and one of his friends and rode to the Smoke House burger stand for french fries. When we got back to school for fourth period, I went to the bathroom, and when I came back, he had slipped out of class and was gone for the rest of the day (missing three more classes). Later I found out he went to smoke pot in the park with two friends. One activity where Jake found success was creating some pretty amazing graffiti around Berkeley. Jake never succeeded or made a connection to BHS, but he was fortunate to have parents who recognized his artistic ability and had the resources to send him to a small private arts school in Napa, where he excelled in academics through the umbrella of visual art.

I have always believed that the visual and performing arts are vital to youth education. As an artist and a teacher, I have spent most of my life fighting for the validity of the arts in education; but only after shadowing students did I realize how essential the social and physical aspects of the arts classes are in contrast to the static immobility that I found in most academic classes. Some of the only classroom spaces in the school in which students can move around and talk to each other are in the dance studio and darkroom. There also seems to be a community spirit in art classes, where in academics there is often an underlying sense of competitiveness.

The work of the project helped me to modify my teaching through reflection on the research we made, shadowing of students, and the wisdom of my colleagues. The codirector of the Diversity Project, Lashawn Routé-Chatmon, once said in a meeting with administrators, "*Equity* does not mean 'the same.'" Modifications I have made in my classroom stem from that statement. Now, when I check for understanding on a new lesson, I do not move on until I know that every student comprehends the new concept or technique. Sometimes that means working with a student one-on-one for forty minutes or pairing up students to check each other for understanding. I have found positive outcomes in communicating the strengths of my students with teachers in classes where the same students are finding nothing but failure. Being part of the project heightened my knowledge of school and community resources. If I have a student who is struggling to succeed, I can check if the student is accessing such resources as free tutoring, free or reduced-fee lunch vouchers, college and academic counselors, the health center, or small school options.

Being part of the project opened up my consciousness to the possibility that I could be an agent of change at BHS and help create a larger network with a community of people committed to equity in our school. I went into teaching with the idea that I could be an ally for gay and lesbian students. I quickly found success in being that ally, but also found it to be a narrow scope of the student population. Instead of feeling that I could offer support to a specific group of students, I learned how to intentionally create a more equitable classroom by recognizing the diversity of needs of all of my students. In a broader scope beyond my classroom, this meant looking at education as a whole and figuring out how to seek and allocate funding for the arts and other programs that provide services to students who come to us without resources.

Overall, my involvement in the Diversity Project not only helped me to become a better teacher in my classroom; it also widened my perspective on education as a whole and the broader issues that affect our young people and communities. Finally, I discovered the extraordinary potential of working collaboratively with a spectrum of students, parents, educators, and community members to make positive change in our schools.

Learning to Question My Own Teaching

Tamara Friedman

I graduated from Berkeley High School in 1988 and returned less than ten years later as a new teacher. I have been teaching Spanish and English as a Second Language at the high school since 1994. I first became involved in the Diversity Project as an Extended Team member in my third year of teaching in 1997. I was attracted to the project's initial goal of creating an "irreversible momentum for change" and addressing the existing "achievement gap" at the high school. I was involved with the project for four years, during which time I served on the Extended Team and worked as a graduate student researcher and as a teacher on the project's Core Team. Over the years, my work with the project has informed my teaching and my involvement at the school in many ways.

When I began working with the project, I was new to the concept of action research and the methods of qualitative research. My first role was as a member of the Taking Stock Committee. Our job was to carry out a qualitative research project investigating extracurricular activities at the high school. We were interested in seeing how these activities might contribute to increased separation of students of different racial, social, and economic backgrounds. In addition, we hoped to gain insight into how these nonclassroom activities may in fact exacerbate the disparity in achievement along racial and ethnic lines at BHS.

This first research experience was a fascinating learning process for all of us on the committee. None of us had a background in qualitative research, and we found ourselves in the position of trying to create a study that would allow us to bring feedback to the staff and school community in a meaningful and useful way. Ultimately we were able to create a study that included interviews with both students and staff advisers, in conjunction with quantitative documentation of how different students were involved in extracurricular activities. The information we gathered allowed us to come back to the staff and school and begin a discussion about how these programs function to reinforce narrowly defined identities for students of different backgrounds at BHS.

For example, we found that white students were more likely to participate in the more academic extracurricular activities, while students of color were more likely to participate in social clubs, sports, and cultural activities. In terms of sports, there was a clear separation of students of different racial and ethnic backgrounds. Some sports, like golf, lacrosse, and swimming, were considered "white sports," while others, such as football and basketball, were predominantly "African American sports." The most interesting piece to me as a teacher was that almost none of the staff advisers perceived this separation as problematic in any way. In addition, most advisers did not feel responsible for creating more inclusive recruitment and retention practices.

As an introduction to the Diversity Project, my work on Taking Stock supported a personal hypothesis that BHS works subtly in many ways to separate students and reinforce limiting identities for most students. In general, white students are seen as, *and* see themselves as, academic and college bound, whereas many students of color are seen as, *and* often see themselves as, athletes and socializers. While clearly these are overgeneralizations, it seems important to try to understand the identities that students create for themselves and how the school setting works to constantly reinforce these restrictive definitions of identity.

As I continued to work on the project, I also decided to return to school in a Ph.D. program in UC Berkeley's Graduate School of Education. I went back to school in part due to my involvement with the project, which had created a personal interest in methods of qualitative research, action research, and schoolwide change. As an English as a Second Language teacher, I also was particularly interested in learning more about the English Language Learner (ELL) population.

My continued work with the project allowed me to stay connected to the high school in a meaningful way. I was simultaneously involved in my own research for graduate school and work with the project. On my own, in the ELL Department, I was looking at how the school both creates and limits opportunities for ELL students to use English in meaningful contexts for successful language acquisition. For the project, I worked throughout the year on a research study documenting the implementation of the detracked freshman English/history core.

In the case of my own research, I continued to see the ways in which BHS has an impact on student identity and ultimately student achievement by maintaining strong lines of separation between different groups of students. In my work with the project, I began to see that even attempts to bring students together in heterogeneous groupings are often ill conceived and can actually push the lines of separation in both academic achievement and social interactions. Our work with the freshman core revealed that the teachers understood the purpose of heterogeneity as primarily social, and not an academic intervention. Few teachers saw the purpose of heterogeneous classes as one of addressing the achievement gap and viewed these classes as an opportunity for students of different backgrounds to interact socially. Students were perceptive of this purpose and reported many core classes as nonacademic and less than challenging.

My final official work with the project took place when I returned to teaching at the high school the following year. I worked with a group of project members to create a plan for professional development for teachers. The goal was to create a plan that would incorporate our research from previous years into a comprehensive model of professional development geared toward addressing the achievement gap at BHS. Included in our work was a summer institute, which engaged several BHS teachers in dialogue about how to address the achievement gap directly through our classroom practices. The following fall, we opened school with an all-day in-service for the entire staff, addressing teaching practices that promoted the success of all students.

After four years of working with the project, I resigned from the Core Team. My decision to leave was in part due to my disillusionment with the process of schoolwide change. I felt that while perhaps we, the project, had succeeded in creating a heightened awareness among staff of some of the issues contributing to the achievement gap at BHS, we had also fallen short of instituting meaningful schoolwide programs and had not ultimately created an "irreversible momentum for change." However, as I look back on my time with the Diversity Project, I recognize that my own involvement in research and study over the years has informed my practice as a classroom teacher in many important and powerful ways.

Last year I had the opportunity to teach an off-semester Spanish 1 course—a course that would normally be taught in the fall—during spring semester. Off-semester classes generally serve students who have failed to pass a Spanish course one or more times. I was stunned on the first day to see that all of my students were students of color and all of them were taking the course for a second or third time. While the work of the project is always infused into my theoretical base for teaching, it was not until I was faced with this shocking reminder of BHS's achievement gap that I could truly appreciate all of our work and its relevance to my teaching practices.

During this semester-long course, I found myself constantly struggling against students' negative perceptions of themselves in the school setting, fighting against other teachers' perceptions of them as students, and battling my own built-in perceptions of students of color in a remedial course. Throughout the semester, I had many opportunities for frank conversations with the students about why they felt they were in this course and how they felt about being there. Almost unanimously, they saw the class as one for "dummies and failures," and therefore considered themselves to be part of a "lower-achieving" group. From the work they did, I was able to discern that almost all of these students were in fact fully capable of doing the course work, but frequently chose not to do it.

When I questioned students about why they thought they were not completing work or succeeding in my class or other classes (if that was the case), I got poignant reminders of all of our research over the years. Students constantly referred to the fact that being a student was not cool at BHS; it was a "white thing." Students also shared stories of teachers who made automatic assumptions about them as students from the outset of the school year. In addition, all of the students in this class complained of having class schedules that were not stimulating or rigorous and classes where there were low (if any) expectations of them.

I tried to incorporate the student feedback into my instruction and teaching practices by maintaining high expectations, attempting to create meaningful and rigorous course work, and holding students accountable. For some students, this strategy worked. However, for many others, the modifications I made in my approach to teaching were not enough. The rate of failure in my class was not significantly better than that of most other off-semester courses, and several students did not "make it" in the end.

Certainly I would like to believe that my informed teaching practices in this situation helped some students to be successful. However, I came away from this recent experience feeling as though one teacher (or teachers in general) cannot have an impact on a historical and institutional reinforcement of the achievement gap. Perhaps the most disturbing piece of this experience was the realization that low student achievement among students of color at BHS is often not based on lack of preparedness, as it seems to be in other school settings. Many students of color come to BHS prepared, reading at grade level, with support of educated parents and families, and they still do not achieve. Like the rest of the school, my students learn to see themselves as nonachievers, and this learning is directly tied to the way in which race operates at our school.

In the light of experiences like the one I had with my off-semester Spanish class, it is difficult to maintain a positive outlook and hope for meaningful change. However, at the very least, I feel that I have an impact on student achievement by continuing always to question and adapt my own teaching practices, in addition to questioning and attempting to change the practices of our larger institution. I do fear that as a teacher in an institution that so blatantly works to reinforce such disparity in achievement among students of different racial, ethnic, and socioeconomic backgrounds, I am complicit in maintaining the status quo.

The Perfect Marriage: Intuition Meets Action Research

Leslie Anne Plettner

In *Teaching: Making Sense of an Uncertain Craft* (1992), Joseph P. McDonald eloquently points to the one certainty of teaching: that it is uncertain. As a classroom teacher, I am uncertain about most things: Which students will or will not understand the reading assignment, and why? How can I make the reading assignments and homework interesting and accessible to as many students as possible? Why does Jamal not turn in his homework? Why does Nicole, who is usually fully engaged, seem disengaged today? Is she ill? Did she have family problems last night? How will her mood and my response to her bear on what she takes from class today? Why do some members of the class seem alive from the discussion, while others seem threatened by its intimacy and intensity?

Having received my teacher training at Mills College, which prioritizes training teachers for inquiry, I felt confident not only in understanding the importance of being a reflective practitioner of teaching, but also in understanding how to effectively use inquiry in my teaching. My training at Mills focused on developing a general inquiry approach to teaching. Although we discussed action research as a model of inquiry, we never explored in detail the process of doing action research. Nevertheless, when I was asked by the Diversity Project to be a lead teacher in training teachers how to use inquiry-based action research to help close the achievement gap, I enthusiastically accepted the challenge, and I anticipated my understanding of inquiry would change little. I was wrong.

The First Date

My experiences as a classroom teacher over the last five years have made me feel certain about two things. First, given the uncertainty of teaching, inquiry is the centerpiece of understanding. Therefore, learning is at the center of teaching. Second, although I feel my stance as a reflective practitioner has taught me a great deal about teaching, I have come to realize that the longer I teach, the less I know. The less I know, the more questions I have. I think an inquiry-based approach to teaching is immeasurably valuable, but the acknowledgment of knowing so little can leave me feeling both vulnerable and intimidated. I have been searching for a tool that will simultaneously recognize inquiry as the centerpiece of teaching and provide me with agency and direction in my place of vulnerability and intimidation.

While it seems that the power of intuition has not been sufficiently recognized by many Western societies, it has served me well as a teacher. By allowing observations to rest in my heart and my mind, I have been able to transform those observations into useful knowledge that guides my teaching. Although such knowledge cannot be measured by numbers or other forms of quantitative data, I feel that intuition-based knowledge is critical to good teaching. Nevertheless, as a classroom teacher, I have learned that intuition is sometimes misleading and therefore is not enough. It needs a partner.

The Engagement: Doing Action Research

This year I taught U.S. history, women's studies, and ethnic studies. I situated my own research in my U.S. history class. In an effort to close the achievement gap, my three other team members and I identified a high-leverage skill that we felt students needed in order to have success in our classrooms: homework completion.

We picked homework completion for two primary reasons. First, doing homework helps students develop discipline and time management skills, useful skills for everyone in the workforce. Second, by reading and writing about history or doing other homework assignments based on classroom activities, a student is more likely to have a deeper understanding of the material and participate more in class. Because we assumed these reasons to be true, homework weighs heavily in our grading; in my class, it is worth 40 percent of a student's grade. My team and I wanted to help students complete more homework. By doing so, students are more likely to understand the material and hopefully receive, at minimum, a passing grade.

Our team worked together to grasp why students did not turn in homework. Based on teacher experience, we developed and administered a student survey. Students categorically identified time management as the reason for not turning in homework. With confidence, we constructed an action plan with measurable goals. According to the surveys, we assumed that students merely needed to learn how to structure homework into their lives. We assumed that students would complete their homework if they (1) did homework during a regular time period, (2) did homework in a regular space, and (3) rewarded themselves for doing their homework. We interviewed students to check in with them and make appropriate arrangements to apply the time management strategies.

The student interviews were unquestionably compelling. They opened my eyes, forced me to challenge my assumptions, and pushed me closer to understanding homework completion and equity. In part, my intuition is based on my own experiences as a student. I think this is natural and, unless constantly monitored, unavoidable. By doing action research, I learned that my natural instincts can sometimes be deceptive. I was a successful high school student who received all A's except for one B. I never liked geometry. I understood most things fairly easily, and when I did not, I requested help or stubbornly persisted until I understood. Because students identified time management as the barrier to homework completion, I assumed they should do what I did: I did homework during a regular time at a regular place and I gave myself rewards or study breaks. My students revealed a different, more complicated story. Although I was disappointed that I had oversimplified the problem, using data to learn indubitably exhilarated me.

Two out of three of my Chicana female students did make time to do their homework every night, but for a variety of reasons, they struggled to complete it. Because Celia needed on average more time to process information, she simply needed more time to do her home-work. She immediately mentioned the schedule of a neighboring high school, El Cerrito, which covers a year in a semester through block scheduling and students take just three classes per semester, as an alternative that would help her complete her homework. Seven classes at BHS, coupled with the time needed for her to process infor-mation, made it difficult for her to complete her homework. In addi-tion, Celia regularly became frustrated with assignments, and with no assistance available at home, she would simply give up and move on to the next assignment, never completing the one she had started. It quickly became clear to me that Celia needed more than just time management skills to complete her homework. She needed more time or fewer classes, tutoring, and a tenacious attitude.

Rosa also made time to do her homework but struggled to com-plete it. Rosa identifies as being very curious and a perfectionist. When she begins to study, she becomes full of questions. She wants to know everything. Although she often spends considerable time on an assignment, her curiosity often takes her off track, and she is unable to complete the assignment. Also, Rosa feels she needs to do an assignment perfectly. Often when she begins an assignment, she gets stuck and feels that her response is inadequate, so she never fin-ishes. Similar to Celia, she needs to learn to be persistent and move past her frustration. To her advantage, Rosa's mother provides sig-nificant tutoring and enables Rosa to complete some of her assign-ments. But Rosa feels dependent on her mother. Her inability to complete her homework has caused Rosa great worry, and she fears that this is causing depression, which makes it even more difficult for her to complete her homework.

Rosa and Celia helped me realize that time management issues may in fact serve as a mask for an inability to complete homework. While students may identify time management as the reason for not completing homework, a closer look reveals deeper issues that can include depression, personal dispositions, and learning styles that make it difficult for students to process information in ways asked by their schools and teachers.

Another finding includes an issue difficult to solve through a time management plan: traveling long distances to and from school. Two of my students (an African American male and a Chicana female) traveled great distances to and from school. One student lives in Richmond, a few miles outside Berkeley, and the other in the neighboring city of Oakland. On average, each spends between two and three and one-half hours traveling each day. Both students emphasized how tired they were when returning home. They often fell asleep when doing homework. Sleep deprivation contributed to their inability to complete homework. In addition, Taishan (African American male) worked out for football after school, so he often did not get home until 7:30 P.M. Both his exhaustion and lack of time made it extremely difficult for him to complete homework.

Learning to do action research and becoming a more reflective teacher were two skills that I learned through my participation in the Diversity Project. I also learned the importance of working with like-minded individuals and the value of forming alliances with different constituencies—students, parents, and community. We still have a lot of work to do at BHS, but I feel that if more teachers can be encouraged to reflect on what they do and if we can find ways to reduce teacher isolation, we will be in a better position to help the school achieve its potential.

How to Win Friends and Influence Conservatives (and Become a Better Teacher)

Susannah Bell

I love to win arguments, but unfortunately, I am usually not very successful in arguments. My words get tangled up in my passions so that I forget the importance of a calm, reasoned position, and my opponent wins by default. Not long ago, however, I won an argument (the subject about which I was deeply passionate) with my conservative brother-in-law. The subject of the debate was affirmative action, and my brother-in-law was making the typical right-wing assertions. Among them, he stated that there is no longer a need for affirmative action because all students already have equal opportunities. Right away I knew I had him, because I was able to provide evidence to the contrary—evidence I had gathered from my experience shadowing a student at Berkeley High School as part of the Diversity Project's class of 2000 study.

The student I shadowed, Ayana, was a female African American senior who performed at an above-average academic level and took part in many extracurricular activities, including athletics. I interviewed Ayana on several occasions, and twice during the school year I followed her through her day, observing her in both academic and social settings. This enlightening experience not only gave me the evidence (and confidence) to calmly argue my position with my brother-in-law, but it and other Diversity Project activities helped me to see why there was still an achievement gap at our school and in my classroom. Through these experiences, I was able to enhance my own teaching considerably.

The most valuable part of the experience was the objectivity with which I was able to observe classroom instruction and interaction between teacher and student. By evaluating what in my opinion was right and what was wrong in the classrooms of Berkeley High School, I was better able to gauge what was right and what was wrong in my own classroom.

During the shadowing experience, Ayana's teachers were aware of my purpose in their classrooms, but they did not know which of their students I was observing. The most fascinating thing I noticed about Ayana was that she displayed two very distinct personalities, depending on the class. If she liked the class, she was bubbly, energetic, and focused. If she did not like the class, she appeared lethargic, disinterested, and distracted. And after the first few classes, I did not have to observe Ayana's expression and body language to tell whether she liked a class. In most cases, I silently agreed with her, and it had nothing to do with whether the subject matter was interesting to me. What mattered was the climate and tone set by the instructor.

I am a thirty-four-year-old instructor with thirteen years of teaching experience and have always considered myself a professional.

Nonetheless, during the shadowing experience, I was tempted to behave inappropriately in some of the classrooms I visited. Not surprisingly, these were the classes in which Ayana fell asleep or chatted with friends while the teacher was attempting to conduct the lesson. These classes seemed to have at least one of the following characteristics: the mode of instruction was dull, repetitive, unchallenging, and predictable; the instructor displayed a patronizing tone in his or her delivery and interaction with the students; and a lack of classroom equity was clearly evident.

In an English class, for example, the teacher started to discuss a story she had assigned the previous day. When it became apparent that very few students had read the story, she instructed them to read it aloud, each student reading a paragraph in turn until the story was finished. At the end, the teacher began posing the story questions that followed the text. Although many of the students, including Ayana, raised their hands, the teacher virtually ignored them, instead repeatedly calling on the same three or four (Caucasian) students. It was hardly surprising to notice Ayana yawning and propping her head up by the second half of the period. When I asked Ayana if this was a typical activity, she replied that it was.

In Ayana's math class, I observed a similar lack of classroom equity, as well as other factors that made the climate of the class intolerable in my opinion. In this class, the teacher, a white male, was inappropriately chummy, even flirtatious, with his white female students. He virtually ignored the other students, except during a discussion in which he seemed to encourage Ayana's participation, but then goaded and patronized her when she was unsure of herself. As a result, Ayana became visibly withdrawn.

Later, when the students were supposed to be working on their assignment, most of the students, including Ayana, were noisy and unproductive. At the end of the period, however, Ayana was attempting to understand the lesson so that she could complete the homework, while the rest of the class was lined up at the door waiting for the bell to ring. Ayana tried repeatedly to get the attention of the teacher, who was chatting with a group of white girls waiting at the door. She called him by name at least four times, and when he finally came over to help her, the bell rang. When I asked Ayana if she thought this was a challenging class, she replied that it was not.

The challenging classes, clearly Ayana's favorites, shared three qualities to account for their success, which primarily involved the climate and tone set by the instructor. In these classes, the teacher displayed rapport with students, but balanced with firm expectation; the teacher found ways to make the subject matter engaging; and the teacher challenged *all* students.

One class in particular exemplified these qualities and was perhaps the best teaching I have seen in my career. This was a double-period physics class taught by a white female in her late thirties. At the beginning of the period, the students worked on a review sheet for a test being given the following day. The atmosphere was relaxed and productive as the teacher floated around the classroom, helping students by using real-world applications to clarify the material. The rare instance of off-task behavior was immediately remedied when the teacher stood near the students and gave them a glance of quiet authority and an encouraging smile. To help some students figure out a problem, she set up an experiment on the spot. During the second period of this double-period class, she led a discussion about a recent field trip to Great America amusement park in which the students completed a unit on the physics of the roller coaster. The atmosphere crackled with energy and enthusiasm as every student in the ethnically diverse class contributed something to the discussion. This stimulating environment made me wish I could return to high school, so it was no surprise that this was Ayana's favorite class, even though it was also her most challenging one.

Through the experience of shadowing Ayana, as well as through participation in Action Research for Teachers (ART), I was able to enhance my own teaching and address the achievement gap in my classroom. The shadowing experience provided me with the opportunity to bring some degree of objectivity to my teaching that I had not previously possessed.

One ART workshop facilitator encouraged me to use an observation instrument to record data on my own teaching practices concerning a particularly challenging class, and after using the instrument for a few weeks, I noticed a marked improvement in the students' behavior. The Diversity Project shadowing experience as well as the ART workshops also allowed me to raise the bar for all my students while making learning more meaningful for them. As a result, I implemented new teaching practices to promote more student investment and greater equity in the classroom. For example, I used ideas from the ART workshop on student publishing to implement a thematic Web site project for my American literature class of juniors in the Computer Academy, a small school program within BHS. The achievement level of the students in this class rose dramatically as a result of this project; many of the students would not have passed the course without it, and I attribute their success to the sense of investment and pride in their work that is now a part of the public domain.

In the argument I had with my brother-in-law, I shared the story of my shadowing experience to demonstrate the continued inequities in education. He said that he had never heard hard evidence to demonstrate inequities that still exist in education, and that his opinion was based on "what he saw on the news." I do not know if I changed his opinion about affirmative action, but I do think I opened the door. The most important thing I won through my participation in the Diversity Project was not an argument, however. It was a new perspective on teaching and learning that I believe will make a difference for my students and will also help in a small way to narrow the achievement gap at Berkeley High School.

Spending a Day as a Student

Magi Discoe

Spending a day as a student at Berkeley High reminded me once more that our current high school model is the worst possible way to teach children. When the Diversity Project offered teachers the opportunity to shadow students for a day at Berkeley High, I jumped at the chance.

My own experience in high school had been one of alienation and difficulty. Now I was a seasoned teacher, an insider in a system I once hated. I had been a socially isolated and academically unsuccessful special education student, and high school had been torture for me. The young woman I was to shadow, by contrast, was a successful student. She was taking Latin, AP classes, and in general other classes chosen by students who have been able to advance in the system. As I awaited the day I would shadow my student, I wondered if I would see her school experience as wildly different from my own. Would it be more enjoyable? More friendly, even "clubby"? I hoped I was about to take a look into the secret world I had missed as a student. I hoped I would finally have the Real High School Experience.

I did not. By the time I dragged myself through three forty-five-minute classes, I was jumping out of my skin. By midday, I had little memory of the discussions held way back in first-period class. By the end of fourth period, I was wondering if I could somehow get sick and cut the other two classes. I just couldn't sit still. And that one skill, *sitting still*, is the sine qua non of success in high school. Students who cannot do that cannot succeed in our educational system.

Here I must digress a moment lest I overstate my case. It is true that self-control and self-discipline are critical skills needed to accomplish anything in life. And the ability to sit still is one form of self-discipline: it helps us focus our attention in certain situations. But when we make this ability into the primary and indispensable demonstration of self-discipline, we encourage students to become shallow and apathetic.

The problem was not the teachers. They were good by conventional standards. They knew their material, they were concerned for the students, and they worked hard to make the lessons cogent and interesting. The students helped. They learned to prompt the teacher for information. They asked questions designed to show knowledge and give the impression of curiosity—nothing really risky and nothing that could be seen as ignorant. They were rewarded with the focus and approval of the teacher. And each forty-five-minute period had its own subject matter, its own passion. But just when things began to get interesting, it was on to the next class, with more sitting and listening, and more passive learning. I knew that if it was a struggle for me to stay alert, the student I was shadowing had to be struggling too.

I compare these AP classes with my own ninth-grade integrated science class. Most ninth graders simply cannot sit still for seven hours, cannot be passive, and do not know what kind of questions to ask. But if they are to be successful in this system, they must learn to do these things. This is the form of self-discipline expected in this environment. Those who do not learn it will drop out or gravitate to the lower-level rowdy classes. They will fight the system by not learning. They will work together to create an environment where success means to succeed in not learning what the system wants them to learn. Those who learn self-discipline in some other context—sports or some private passion—may stand a chance of becoming successful. Those who are not so lucky will fall further and further behind.

I discovered education in college when I was thirty-eight years old. My education before then had consisted of several abortive attempts at community college and three years at UCLA—all leading to the feeling, "I just can't do this anymore." So I gave up on education. Instead, I traveled and supported myself at a series of unskilled-labor types of work.

Then, in my early thirties, I found something I wanted to do: I wanted to be a paramedic. I went back to school for paramedic training. I enjoyed that. The lessons I learned were practical and immediately rewarding. During the ten years I worked as a paramedic, I got in the habit of learning. I had to.

It was not until I went back to college again in my late thirties that I became really enamored of education. At that late date, I realized I had been tricked: I might have loved learning all along had it been an exploration. I discovered that I needed more time to think about things if I was to learn well, and that I would learn best by following an interest. And that is ultimately why I became a teacher: I wanted students to realize, as I had finally realized, the excitement of learning.

I am now a seasoned teacher. I teach afternoon classes. By the time they get to my class, the students have been slugging away all morning. I have just taken them from lunch. (I teach science, the Kingdom of Curricular Content.) After shadowing my student, I realized that I would not be able to do what my students must do. I could not go from class to class for seven hours, each hour a new thought. I could not sit still that long. The system we provide for our children is fractured. The miracle is that so many children go to high school and are successful there.

I believe we should be asking ourselves the big questions. Should we even have high school, or should we put all our resources into earlier grades and have no student leave middle school without basic academic skills? What is the purpose of high school? As a staff, we are divided as to our purpose. Are we providing academic knowledge? Better citizens? Do we want to encourage adaptation to a system that values passivity and success, or should we encourage defiance and social action? Does "social action" have meaning without an academic core? What alternatives could we provide to students besides the academic model of high school? We have too many tasks, too many agendas.

My shadowing day in school brought up many more questions than answers. It made me uncomfortably aware of the contradictions within my own beliefs about education and about my own teaching. Visiting other classrooms, as both a teacher and a student, has been more thought provoking than any in-service lesson possibly could be. I appreciate the opportunity.

Realized Potentials

James Dopman

I joined Action Research for Teachers (ART) because I wanted a mirror for my own teaching. With little professional contact besides the monthly mandated faculty meeting, a teacher has little oppor-tunity to reflect on his or her practice in the presence of other teachers whom they admire and respect. I am fully aware and fear-ful of the possibility of developing poor teaching techniques for the mere fact of having no one else to learn from and to push my think-ing. ART does this in the company of reform-minded teachers who are interested in much more than maintaining the status quo. Indeed, it is the energy and collegiality toward a vision of a better school that encourages inquiry and reflection to become a natural part of my teaching.

ART has profoundly influenced my practice. As a second-year teacher, I am beginning to see that one of the major systemic obsta-cles toward educational equity for students is the lack of reflection on the part of teachers. Many educators subscribe to the centuries-old model of "delivering knowledge" to the empty heads of stu-dents. Furthermore, this model decrees that if those students do not succeed, it is not because of the teacher but because of the student.

In my teaching credential program, I was introduced to the con-cept of teacher-centered versus student-centered causes for failure. ART elaborated on this idea and made it and other concepts more practical. Considering I have been a part of ART most of my full-time teaching experience (a year and a half), ART has been an invaluable part of my maturation into the teaching profession. It has been a bridge that connects theory to practice.

A large part of how ART has affected my practice can be summed up in one word: reflection. Reflecting on how a lesson went or how my students are interpreting an essay assignment gives me insight into why a student may succeed, or not succeed, in my classroom. Instead of feeling insecure about critiquing my own teaching, as some teachers do, I feel empowered to know that there is something within my abilities with which I might be able to effect change. Without ART, I feel fairly certain that instead of developing inquiry as a habit of mind, I would have developed the subtle habits that have existed for decades and inevitably perpetu-ate a racialized achievement gap.

My high-leverage assessment this year is tests. With standardized testing, exit exams, and classroom quizzes, I felt that this is an area that I wanted to focus on in terms of understanding the achievement gap. Most of these assessments have a high-stakes component: entrance to college, exit from high school, and overall grade point average. Considering the systemwide importance of testing, it is imperative that teachers understand why a student passes or fails to pass the tests, regardless of teachers' personal feelings on the validity of tests.

The main variable that led me to choose tests was that they made up a significant portion of my students' grades, as they do in many other teachers' classrooms. While a student can pass the class without performing exceptionally well on tests, it is rare that a student completes all homework, participates, takes thorough notes, and then bombs a test. Tests are usually a barometer for larger issues.

The two causes of the achievement gap in tests that I chose to focus on were poor test design (a teacher-centered cause) and lack of study skills (a student-centered cause). With poor test design, the main chunk of the mini-action was to go through the three tests that my students took and assess which questions they missed most of the time. My other two prongs to corroborate that poor test design was the cause of the achievement gap was to have a teacher and a nonteacher edit the test for clarity of instruction and evaluate the questions. I concluded that poor test design did contribute somewhat to wrong answers here and there, but it did not explain why a disproportionate number of students of color failed while my white students generally succeeded.

The other cause, lack of study skills, provided more insight into the racialized achievement gap in my classroom. Although the decision to study is inherently a student's choice, knowing *how* to study is something that is teachable and therefore possibly a teacher-centered cause. The first piece of information that I collected was a survey in which I asked students: "Do you study for tests? If yes, how long? If no, why not?"

The second question asked them what techniques they used to study. The higher-achieving students had more comments like, "Yes, depends on the test." Answers like these seem to indicate that these students had a clearer understanding of themselves as students. In other words, they appeared to be more easily able to evaluate what they needed to do in order to get the best grade they could get. In contrast, my low-achieving students' responses communicated a disconnect with what they needed to do in order to do well on tests. Instead of determining how much time they needed to study based on a self-assessment of their own proficiency in a subject, many made blanket comments, such as "studying for half an hour every day." Another frequent comment from my low-achieving students was admitting that boredom stops studying or prevents it from even beginning.

My other two triangulating pieces of information were correlating the survey information with their test scores and making spot calls home to parents to find out if their student studied for the final exam. Correlation of the survey data with test performance provided conclusive results. Those who gave ambivalent answers on studying had much lower test results than students who were much more confident in their ability to figure out how much they needed to study. The calls home were not as telling because the parents' answers were not consistent; some parents had no idea there was a test, while others knew that there was a test but were not aware if their child was studying. Thus, as is usual for inquiry into our own teaching practice, I am already asking more questions than I have answers.

I feel that I have some evidence that study habits have a causal relationship with test performance. What is less clear is which aspect of studying is the cause. Is it the ability to study? The ability to figure out how long to study? Or the ability to overcome boredom (an intrinsic feeling) to force oneself to study in order to get good grades (an extrinsic carrot)?

However, one of my major problems with the cycle of inquiry is my tendency to jump out of the mini-cycle and then the larger cycle itself. In the course of evaluating study skills as they apply to test taking, my intuition leads me to believe that the cause of the racialized achievement gap is something bigger. Maybe this is so obvious that it is hard for me to ignore. When I reflect on the main difference between students who academically succeed and those who do not, the answer is always "buy-in." High-achieving students buy into the fact that they have to jump through institutional hoops in order for society to deem them a success. One of these hoops is studying for tests, even if it is boring or takes two-and-a-half hours.

As a result, I have another cause that I am currently evaluating: the cumulative lack of attention within a unit leading up to a test is more a cause of poor test scores than anything else. Comments on high-achieving students' surveys such as, "I don't study because I already know the material," are from students who are more frequently engaged in the class. This leads me to conclude that if a student is not engaged for ten minutes each class period within a unit, that equals a whole lot of time during which they were not getting the material they need in order to do well on tests.

Of course, I may find that it is easiest to control for study skills. One of the facts about which I frequently remind teacher participants is that there are multiple reasons that a student does poorly on any given high-leverage assessment. Controlling for one variable is easier said than done. As a teacher with inquiry quickly becoming an essential habit of mind, I want all my students' potentials to be realized, not squashed because their public educational experience has not taken on the burden of helping them to see how wonderful learning can be.

Teachers are undoubtedly one of the most important elements in any school change efforts, and they may be the most difficult to reach. Each teacher is the king or queen in his or her classroom, and despite the efforts of administrators to influence classroom practice through evaluation and professional development, shaping what happens in the classroom is very difficult.

Teachers also play a role in perpetuating the achievement gap. They do this through lowered standards and expectations; by giving some students more attention and encouragement than others; and through the passion, organization, and skill they bring to their teaching. Teachers can be unconscious in their complicity with respect to the reproduction of inequality, or they can simply accept the failure of large numbers of students as normal and blame the students for their failure. However, there is also a possibility that teachers can serve as agents of change by reaching out across the differences that separate them from their students with respect to race, class, culture, and age and opening doors for students who have come to see themselves as failures and underachievers.

The Diversity Project tried to help teachers make the latter choice. We did so by bringing teachers together, showing respect for the work they do, and giving them the opportunity to reflect on their work so that they might find ways to critique it and improve on it. We may have been naive in what we thought could be accomplished from such an approach, for certainly the achievement gap at BHS is alive and well and much more needs to be done. But it is also true that a critical mass of teachers at BHS are now committed to working toward greater equity at the school, are less afraid to engage students and parents on sensitive issues related to achievement, and are more willing to challenge colleagues they know are not playing a positive role at the school.

Clearly more is needed, but the Diversity Project was never envisioned as a process leading to a specific change in a set period of time. Rather, it provided teachers with a way to bring to light the gross inequities that are operative at the school, in the hope that by drawing attention to these and the ways in which the adults who work there are implicated in their maintenance, we might be better able to do something about it. Whether this can occur or whether the project's strategy and goals were merely a pipe dream remains to be seen. But this is the unfinished business of the school, and it will be up to new teachers, students, and parents to make sure that the school does not return to its previous complacency.

5

CREATING DEMAND FOR EQUITY

Transforming the Role of Parents in Schools

LaShawn Routé Chatmon, Katrina Scott-George,
Anne K. Okahara, Emma Haydée Fuentes,
Jean Yonemura Wing, Pedro A. Noguera

Parents are frequently cited as the ultimate cause of disparities in student achievement. As a child's first teacher, parents generally have a strong influence on learning during early childhood. These influences, clearly manifest in the development of early literacy skills (Adger, Snow and Christian, 2002), shape the intellectual foundation for future cognitive development. Parental influences on learning and academic achievement do not end after infancy but continue throughout adolescence. Several researchers have shown that the educational and socioeconomic background of parents plays a decisive role in the formation of student attitudes and habits toward school (Lareau, 2000; Epstein and Hollifield, 1996). Richard Rothstein (2004) has argued recently that middle-class, college-educated parents provide their children with such a wide range of advantages that it is nearly impossible for schools to counter the effects to create a level educational playing field.

From the start, the Diversity Project recognized that parents play an important role in shaping the educational experiences of their children. However, unlike researchers who perceive working-class parents and parents of color as a hindrance to the achievement of students, we believed that under the right conditions, these parents could play a powerful role in advancing their children's educational interests. In addition, because we understood that the achievement gap at Berkeley High School was not merely an educational issue but also a political one, we understood that no change at the school would be possible without the active involvement of parents.

This chapter analyzes the role of parents in the Diversity Project. It is an analysis written in part by parents who were active at the school and played a significant role in setting the direction of the project and its work (Scott-George). The other authors worked as teachers (Routé-Chatmon) and researchers (Fuentes, Okahara, and Wing) who focused their energies on issues of concern to parents at Berkeley High School (BHS). Together, we examine how parents of color at BHS went from being marginal and excluded from the educational process to becoming active participants in decision making at the school. The experience of parents in the Diversity Project is in essence a story about the politics of equity and the politics of empowerment.

From the Margin to the Center: Engaging Parents as Partners

When the project commenced its work in 1996, prevailing attitudes among the BHS staff toward the racial achievement gap ranged from authentic concern to resignation and complacency. Those who held the latter view could offer a wide array of reasons to explain why students of color were not doing particularly well at BHS. High on the list was the belief that their parents were not attentive or concerned enough about their children's academic performance. Several pointed to the absence of parents of color at back-to-school night and other school events as prime evidence that black and Latino parents were uninterested in the education of their children.

Given the prevalence of such attitudes toward the parents of students of color, the Diversity Project recognized that if the school was going to change, the relationship between the school and the parents of students who were least served would also have to change. We believed that parents, in addition to becoming more involved in the education of their children, had to become engaged in the decision making of the school in order to assert the educational rights of their children. For this reason, the Diversity Project included parents in its leadership from the very beginning. The research strategy we developed was aimed at achieving two goals: (1) understanding parental attitudes and experiences at BHS so that we might gain insights into how the school might need to be changed to accommodate their needs and concerns, and (2) using the research process to facilitate an increase in parental involvement at the school.

Our approach to working with parents was influenced by the ideas of educational philosopher John Dewey (1995), who argued with respect to the role of parents: "What the best and wisest parent wants for his own child, that must be what the community wants for all of its children. Any other ideal for our schools is narrow and unlovely; acted upon, it destroys our democracy" (p. 7).

We understood that in order to create a school that treated the education of every student as important, BHS would have to engage parents in new and different ways. We knew that powerful forces worked to maintain unequal learning opportunities at the school (Wells and Oakes, 1996; Oakes, Wells, Jones, and Datnow, 1997), and we knew that the fight to challenge these deeply entrenched practices ultimately would have to be led by parents.

Finding new ways to involve parents of color at BHS meant working against a long history of alienation and exclusion from the school and district. Past efforts to promote integration and address the educational needs of students of color in Berkeley had been led by well-intentioned educators and activists who saw the fight against de facto segregation and racial inequality as "the right thing to do." Unlike cities like Boston and Philadelphia, parents of color were not at the forefront of efforts to end segregated schooling in Berkeley. Those who were saw integration as an important social value, but knew little about the educational changes that would need to occur if racial integration of schools was to result in a genuine improvement in educational opportunities for students of color. Those who led desegregation in Berkeley did not recognize or understand the need to empower parents of color so that they could play an active role in the education of their children. Consequently, parents of color were left out of the educational process, even as Berkeley undertook voluntary desegregation efforts in 1968 (Kirp, 1982).

In the years that followed busing and desegregation of Berkeley schools, African American parents—motivated by hope that integration would provide their children with the education they needed—handed over their children to institutions and people who did not know them, did not acknowledge their culture and values, did not know their community or parents, and in too many cases did not love them. By the 1990s, unfulfilled promises and years of negative experiences with Berkeley's public schools had generated considerable distrust and hostility among many parents of color. The Diversity Project sought to rectify this history of marginalization by working with parents so that they could become active advocates and agents for change at the school.

We embarked on this task, recognizing that efforts to engage parents at the school would encounter significant obstacles. Working-class parents typically lack the time and flexibility to be at school when important meetings take place. Even if meetings are held in the evenings, parents who have worked hard all day and have small children at home are often reluctant to come to the school in the evening. In addition, lack of transportation, lack of translation services, lack of child care, and a basic lack of information regarding how decisions are made and how the school functions create additional obstacles that are not easily overcome. We understood that these obstacles were real, but we also knew that we would have to find ways to overcome them.

Our work was based on the following questions: How do parents engage in schools in ways that authentically call into question systems and practices that contribute to the failure of students and achieve the same results year after year? What do parents need to know to serve as effective advocates for their children's success? What do parents of color expect of their children and of the school, and how do these parents define success for their children? Finally, how do parents address and confront issues of power, racism, sexism, and classism in ways that lead to lasting changes at the school?

As these questions suggest, the kind of parent involvement we envisioned goes well beyond bake sales, PTA meetings, and parent representation on shared governance committees. We wanted parents to be genuine partners in the educational process. We wanted their concerns to be taken seriously, and we wanted to make it possible for them to work with other parents to create popular demand for the type of transformational education they wanted to see for their children. What follows is an account of the Diversity Project's evolving strategy to create such demand among parents—demand for something that conventional wisdom said they did not want.

From Parent Outreach to Organized Communities: The Diversity Project's Evolving Strategy

Parent involvement has been hailed as vital to promoting academic success, especially so for poor and minority students (Lareau, 1989; Epstein and Hollifield, 1996). However, the experiences and treatment of different groups of parents at Berkeley High School historically have varied widely based on the race and class of parents, with poor and working-class parents of color facing numerous obstacles that have made it difficult for them to play an effective role. In the same way that the school marginalizes many African American, Latino, immigrant, and low-income students, the parents of these students are often distanced from school activities. The distancing is due in part to linguistic and cultural differences that separate parents from BHS staff, but also due to a basic lack of power on the part of parents of color within the school community. Recognizing the need for parents of color to be more effectively engaged at the school, the Diversity Project chose to confront these issues directly.

When individual parents from disadvantaged groups attempt to advocate for their children and intervene on their behalf, they are often rebuffed, silenced, and further marginalized (Valdés, 1996; Shirley, 1997). This exclusion can take a variety of forms—some overt and deliberate, and some inadvertent. In contrast, the parents whose children have traditionally experienced the greatest degree of academic success have exercised the greatest degree of influence at the school. They are more likely to be represented on school decision-making bodies, and they are also more likely to have a keen understanding of how to get what they want from the school and how to get the attention of the school and district administrative leaders. Such parents are typically white and well educated. They come from the more affluent neighborhoods in Berkeley, and when they engage the school, they do so with a sense of entitlement and a clear understanding of their rights (Valdés, 1996; Shirley, 1997).

Disparities in power and privilege contribute to disparate treatment of parents, which in turn contributes to patterns of disparate achievement among students. Parents who do not understand how the system works, have trouble speaking English, or are not familiar with the technical lingo that professional educators use, can be easily confused, dismissed, and disregarded. Underlying this treatment is a set of stereotypes and assumptions about the values and beliefs of parents of color whose children may be struggling academically or behaviorally.

In schoolwide focus groups conducted by the Diversity Project in the 1996–97 school year, teachers shared their views about obstacles that prevented all students from meeting teacher expectations. Responses were quite broad, spanning a range of topics including school structure, policies, and culture. Numerous responses related to perceived deficiencies among the parents of struggling students. For example:

- A perception that parents of color are not adequately involved in the school
- A belief that many parents of color are not good role models
- An assumption that parents of color do not provide guidance to their children
- A belief that parents of color do not encourage, support, and set high expectations for their children

Ironically, despite acknowledging a lack of contact or familiarity with parents of color, a significant number of BHS teachers stated that the academic difficulty of students could be traced in part back to poor parenting, parental devaluing of education, and deficiencies found in the home. These beliefs were based largely on assumptions, stereotypes, and generalizations, not experience. Most teachers had relatively little contact with parents of students of color, and the contact they did have tended to be limited. Thus, many teachers formed opinions based on assumptions such as the belief that parents of successful students participate in school (which is not true for many successful white and Asian students), or the belief that all parents and students have equal access to information regarding school policies and rules and that most struggling students come from troubled homes.

Of course, the tendency to blame parents and shift responsibility to the parents for the academic failure of students is widespread. Pedro Noguera (1999) observes, "As is true with the public discourse over many social problems that affect the poor, the cause of academic failure is most often located first in the individual student, then with the family, and finally with the schools" (p. 19). However, despite considerable evidence to the contrary, the prevailing belief among many BHS teachers toward students of color who were struggling academically is that their parents "just don't care." Over the course of four years of research carried out at the school, the Diversity Project uncovered evidence from a variety of sources that revealed just the opposite.

For example, the annual class of 2000 survey conducted during the 1998–99 academic year posed the following question: "My parents/guardians think getting good grades is: a) the most important thing; b) extremely important; c) very important; d) somewhat important; or e) not important." Interestingly, the highest proportion of students reporting that their parents think getting good grades is "the most important thing" were African American (45 percent), and by far the lowest proportion were white (12 percent). Even when combined with the response of "extremely important," white students still lagged behind all other racial/ethnic subgroups, especially African Americans and Chicanos/Latinos. Although there may be several ways to interpret these data, the responses to this survey question certainly suggest that most students of color believe their parents place considerable importance on their per- formance in school (Table 5.1).

Recognizing the discrepancy between teacher assumptions about parents and student beliefs about parental expectations, the Diversity Project undertook a research strategy aimed at eliciting information from the parents themselves. We deliberately designed a research strategy that would simultaneously create conditions and opportunities for parents of color to become organized so that they could demand changes at the school. We knew that the push for greater equity was most likely to come from those parents whose children were least well served at Berkeley High School—parents who were marginalized within the high school community, whose voices were seldom if ever heard, and who were widely viewed as "those parents who just don't care." We believed that without the wisdom and organized political strength of parents of African American, Latino, language-minority, and lower-achieving stu- dents, transformative change toward achieving diversity with equity would be impossible.

Following are a series of theories of change that guided the work of the Diversity Project at different points in time, as we sought to organize marginalized parents as a crucial force for equity reform.

THEORY ONE: *If you reach out to parents and ask them what their expe- rience has been and what they would like to see changed, they will tell you. And if you make that information public, the school will respond.*

The Diversity Project established the Parent Outreach Com- mittee in the summer of 1997 to carry out its research agenda among parents of color and parents of lower-achieving students. Like the project's research committees, Parent Outreach included Latina/o, African American, Asian American, and white parents,

Table 5.1 Berkeley High School Class of 2000 Survey Responses on Parents' Opinion on the Importance of Good Grades, 1998–99 School Year

My Parents/Guardians Think Getting Good Grades is:	African American (n = 167)	Chicano/ Latino (n = 30)	Asian American (n = 55)	Multiracial (n = 78)	Other (n = 29)	White (n = 191)
The most important thing	45%	40%	27%	32%	41%	12%
Extremely important	36%	43%	34%	24%	27%	34%
Total	81%	83%	61%	56%	68%	46%

as well as teachers, administrators, classified staff, and researchers from the university. Some members of the committee occupied dual roles—they were both BHS staff and parents—and this provided the committee with a unique vantage point from which to study the issues.

The main work of the Parent Outreach Committee consisted of organizing a series of focus groups that would specifically target the parents of students who were doing poorly academically. The goal was to use the focus groups to solicit the concerns parents had about the school and then to synthesize what we learned. We wanted to be sure that these parent concerns could be considered by the principal's Strategic Planning Work Group (a staff-based group empowered in spring 1998 to draft a five-year plan for Berkeley High). In this way, we hoped to use the research as a tool to increase the likelihood that the voices and concerns of parents of color would begin to influence the direction of the school.

We saw the focus groups as part of the project's action research strategy. We envisioned the research process as a vehicle for mobilizing parents of color. The theory of change underlying the strategy was that as parents expressed their concerns and ideas for school change, they would also see the need to become organized so that they could influence the direction of the school as a political force that could no longer be ignored. Our role as researchers was to lay the groundwork for what would ultimately become an ongoing, parent-led, diverse, and broad-based movement of parent activism at the high school.

Michelle Fine (1993) echoes our thinking: "Unless parents are organized as a political body, parental involvement projects will devolve into a swamp of crisis intervention, leaving neither a legacy of empowerment nor a hint of systemic change" (p. 707). Furthermore, we believed that without the knowledge and wisdom of parents of African American, Latino, language-minority, and lower-achieving students on how to meet the educational needs of their children, any plans for transformative change would be fundamentally flawed. Noguera explains an additional reason for organizing parents:

> We recognized that those who benefited under the present circumstances might perceive themselves as having a vested interest in preserving the status quo and therefore might be less likely to support change that produces greater equity. Moreover, as we carried out our work we positioned ourselves as facilitators of discussion rather than as advocates for a particular agenda because we sought to prevent ourselves from becoming trapped in a polarized conflict over change at the school. Hence, organizing African American and Latino parents would provide us with a means to insure that the change effort was not dependent upon our advocacy and also counterbalance the influence that would be exerted by the opponents of change [1999, p. 35].

In the early stages of organizing the focus groups, the Parent Outreach Committee identified four target groups for outreach: (1) parents of African American students, (2) parents of Latino students, (3) parents of Asian students, and (4) parents of lower-achieving students in general. Interestingly, as the committee discussed outreach strategies and decided to focus separately on each of the targeted communities of parents, we realized that not all African American students (or, for that matter, Latino or Asian students) had parents from the same racial/ethnic background. Students from racially mixed families and students who had been adopted, for example, often had parents from different backgrounds. While we saw value in creating focus groups that brought together parents from similar backgrounds (our assumption was that this would lead to more honest and candid conversations), we also knew that we could not exclude parents whose children were affected, regardless of their background. We also knew that it was important to have the focus groups facilitated by "insiders"— parents whose standing in the community provided them with a degree of trust and legitimacy among other parents. Such individuals, we reasoned, would increase the likelihood of generating strong parental participation.

This strategy proved successful in reaching parents of Latino and African American students. To increase the numbers of those who could participate, we organized focus group meetings in homes, churches, and community centers, so that the meetings were accessible. At each set of meetings, we typically provided food, child care, and translation services so that there would be few barriers to participation. Despite these efforts, we were least successful in engaging immigrant parents of lower-achieving Asian students. Lack of language proficiency in any Asian language, the absence of ties to the leaders within these groups, and the nonexistence of a common community, language, or identity among the various Asian nationalities challenged our outreach efforts with this constituency.

Language was an important consideration in our outreach to Latino parents. School records indicated that 80 percent of students designated as Latino were from homes where Spanish was the primary language. The committee thus recognized the need to conduct outreach to the Latino parents in Spanish and to conduct the focus groups in Spanish as well. It stood to reason that the "insiders" we would recruit to the Latino Outreach subcommittee would be Spanish speakers, and so it made sense for this subcommittee, wherever possible, to conduct all of its business in Spanish. The children of the subcommittee members represented a broad range of academic experiences, including those who would later matriculate to the University of California, as well as those who struggled to earn passing grades and stay in school.

The remainder of the Parent Outreach Committee assumed responsibility for reaching out to parents of African American students and for organizing the African American focus groups, as well as multiracial focus groups of parents of lower-achieving students.

The structure and work of the Parent Outreach Committee and its subcommittees encouraged collaboration, participation at varying levels, and the development of parent leadership. In the focus groups, we posed the following questions:

- What has been your experience as a parent at Berkeley High School?
- What do you need from the school to better support your child's academic and personal growth at Berkeley High School?
- What are your suggestions for positive change at Berkeley High School?

These questions were used to spark discussions that often covered a broad range of topics. The feedback from parents was thoughtful, passionate, and insightful. Parents addressed a wide range of concerns, including problems related to school organization and structure, unfair school policies, ineffective operating systems and procedures, the lack of effective student academic support, a negative school climate and culture, poor teaching and the lack of cultural diversity in the school curriculum, inadequate counseling and academic placement, and lack of attention to school safety. Repeatedly parents talked about difficulties their students experienced in making the transition from the smaller middle schools to the large, impersonal high school. Most frequently they described the school's unresponsiveness to their own questions and concerns and its lack of an effective early warning system to inform them about their children's attendance or grades. They also spoke of difficulties in contacting teachers and other staff, along with a host of unresolved issues that had a negative impact on student academic performance.

What became clear is that while parents had a lot to say about problems at the school, the school's institutional procedures for how parents should engage with teachers and other personnel were at odds with what parents of color needed or had in mind. This contributed to these parents' often experiencing strained and even hostile relations with the school. A mother of one African American male student who later became a leader in the Diversity Project's Parent Outreach efforts coined a term, "The Pissed-Off Theory," to describe her experiences and observations related to home–school relations for parents of color in the school district. She explained, "By the time parents of color get to school, they're pissed off. They typically find out way too late that something is wrong, so by the time they get to the school, they're angry, and teachers are going to know it."

By the end of the school year, the Parent Outreach Committee had successfully conducted eighteen focus groups: six among parents of Latino students conducted in Spanish, nine among parents of African American students, one among Asian parents of various national origins conducted in English with translation, and two among parents of lower-achieving students of all races. In all, more than 180 parents participated. As one mother of an African American student expressed, "Well, we certainly blew the myth out of the water that parents of color just don't care!"

Ultimately the focus groups created a public space where parents felt heard and understood within a small and supportive atmosphere. They were able to share their concerns and cast their troubles not simply as an indication of their own shortcomings as parents, but to see the ways in which the structures and culture of schooling at Berkeley High School contributed. The focus groups also made it possible for parents to see that the difficulties they encountered as individuals were part of a larger pattern of institutional indifference to the needs of their children.

As expected, the focus groups served an important research function. All of the parent input was transcribed, categorized, and summarized in report form. The report was forwarded to the principal's Strategic Planning Work Group. The data made it clear that not only did these parents care about the education their children received, but many were also unhappy about blatant forms of inequity at the school.

The research strategy also proved to be an effective organizing strategy. At a community forum in May 1998, called to solicit responses to the draft strategic plan, nearly half the parents in attendance were African American and Latino, and the vast majority had participated in the Diversity Project's parent focus groups. At a school where parents of color are generally absent from school events, this outpouring drew considerable attention. Because they had participated in the focus groups, many of the parents raised concerns about the strategic planning process, which excluded parents, and posed questions about how they would be included in decision making. Afterward, several teachers commented that this was the first meeting they had ever attended in which the parent composition matched that of the student body.

THEORY TWO: *Parents can advocate for themselves and on behalf of their children, and their role in the school should be institutionalized for long-term impact.*

In the focus groups, parents consistently raised the need to continue meeting and organizing. While the focus groups affirmed that parents were not alone in their concerns, the experience also drew attention to the need to institutionalize the involvement of marginalized parents of color. Following up on this sentiment during the 1998–99 school year, the Parent Outreach Committee secured start-up funding to establish the Parent Resource Center at Berkeley High. The center opened its doors in the fall of 1999 and was staffed by two part-time parent liaisons.

The Parent Resource Center was seen as a way of responding to the various needs expressed by parents through the development of a structure that could improve parents' interaction with the school. Irma Parker, the lead parent liaison since spring 2000, explains the logic behind this strategy:

> One of our charges from the Diversity Project was to help get disenfranchised parents to feel more welcome in the school, and to help

them navigate the high school and advocate for their children. But the Diversity Project also recommended that we should start talking to these parents and form a parent group, basically for parents of African American and Latino students, because they were the kids that were mostly affected.

We realized the critical importance of providing assistance to parents who were dealing with immediate school-related problems and crises. At the same time, we realized that dealing with individual crises would never be sufficient to solve the systemic inequities at the high school and create broad-based parent demand for change. Furthermore, a parent center, no matter how well staffed, could never serve all of the hundreds of parents in need. For this reason, the Parent Resource Center was, by design, part of an inside-outside advocacy model.

As an institutionalized "inside" advocacy model, the center has served as a point of contact for many individual parents and families who previously did not know how to interact with the school. It helps parents arrange meetings with teachers and administrators, answers questions about school and district policies, and provides assistance to parents who are experiencing difficulty with their children. In addition, the center has hosted numerous, well-attended Saturday workshops, drawing sixty to eighty parents at a time to discuss topics such as teen anger management, college funding, student rights, teen depression, parent-teen communications, kids and the law, attention-deficit/hyperactivity disorder, learning disabilities, small schools, and when and how race makes a difference in students' experiences at school. In 2003, the Parent Resource Center initiated the Positive Minds group mentoring program for at-risk young men, which Parker says "has turned around their lives and made it much easier, not only for these kids, but for teachers in the classrooms who were having problems with these kids." The center also has collaborated with city government and other public agencies in devising strategies for soliciting parental input on a variety of youth-related issues. At the suggestion of teachers, the Parent

Resource Center has planned and conducted a professional development workshop for school staff on how to communicate effectively with parents.

Parker concludes,

> I think that the Parent Resource Center has been a saving grace for disenfranchised parents. So many parents come in now, and they're just happy to know that whatever their concerns are, somebody's going to value them and work with them in a timely manner, or just listen. You know, a lot of people just call—sometimes their kids run away, their kids are on drugs. And we're dealing with all kinds of things. I think that basically the high school, and for sure the district, does not know the scope of the work we do in here. It's much, much more than just answering the phone and referring parents to different rooms or taking a note to your kid. That's the least thing we do here. We do some heavy-duty work here. So I think it's just an amazing place.

Even after the Diversity Project ceased its work in 2002, the Parent Resource Center has continued, though its existence remains precarious because financial support for the center is based on soft money from grants and donations. It has demonstrated the value of institutionalizing a place where disenfranchised parents can get answers to their questions and develop strategies to advocate for their children. However, the systemic problems remain, along with the need to continue organizing to create the demand for change.

THEORY THREE: *Working with the school has not produced sufficient demand. We must present the school and district with an organized community armed with a vision of what we want schools to look like, with outcomes we care about.*

Picking up where the Diversity Project left off, two parent groups—Parents of Children of African Descent (PCAD) and Berkeley Organizing Congregations for Action (BOCA)—began organizing within the African American and Latino communities, respectively. These groups have relied heavily on the research carried out by the Diversity Project as they have taken on the difficult process of transforming the role of parents in schools.

In the fall of 2000, with support from the Parent Resource Center, a new organization of parents came together and signaled a new chapter of grassroots mobilization of parents of color fighting for equity. Many of these parents, who named themselves Parents of Children of African Descent, had worked together at various Berkeley elementary and middle schools and ended up at Berkeley High. Many were parents of ninth graders in the class of 2004 who encountered academic difficulty shortly after arriving at the school. Irma Parker recalls, "For some reason, when we got to Berkeley High, we thought that things might be a bit different here and we wouldn't have as many problems. But we encountered *more* problems—not only with our kids, but we found that there were other kids that were having even worse problems."

The PCAD Steering Committee contacted the Diversity Project and swiftly but carefully studied all of our data and reports on the inequities and disparities uncovered in the class of 2000 study. At the same time, they began collecting data on the high failure rate for class of 2004 ninth graders, who were disproportionately students of color. Through their research, they discovered that as many as 150 freshmen were receiving F's in two or more of their core academic classes during their first semester of high school and 250 were receiving at least one F. Without emergency intervention, PCAD saw that it was unlikely that these students would graduate from high school, much less go on to college.

Armed with Diversity Project research and recommendations and with their own data in hand, PCAD moved into action. PCAD went to the school board and asked what the board was going to do about the high failure rate. They presented a detailed analysis of the problem, showing which courses had the highest rates of failure (ninth-grade algebra), but the board failed to act. Irma Parker recalls that during one conversation about the problem, the principal stated, "To be honest, we really don't know *how* to educate African

American kids." Given these responses, the twelve-member PCAD
Steering Committee worked tirelessly from December 19, 2000,
through the holidays, and by January 4, 2001, these parents unveiled
a document: "A Proposal: Plan of Action on Behalf of Underachieving Students in the Berkeley Unified School District." The
stated goal of the plan of action was:

> For intervention to be successful, it needs to be appropriate and
> intensive enough. Each succeeding intervention that fails increases
> the sense of hopelessness, frustration and anger. The interventions
> proposed here are designed to satisfy a very specific goal: Every ninth
> grade student will be given the support they need to complete the
> state and high school grade level requirements for ninth graders and
> be prepared to enter tenth grade [p. 9].

For students who failed a combination of two or more classes in
English, history, or math, the plan called for a radical intervention
program consisting of erasure of failing grades earned in the fall
semester and the creation of a small school-within-a-school for the
spring semester and summer school, with student-teacher ratios of
twelve-to-one, double-period English and algebra classes, and
required parent participation, among other features. In this way,
every student would have the opportunity to get back on track for
graduation.

Before going to the school board for a decision, PCAD took the
plan of action to the community at the Stone Soup Luncheon organized on the Martin Luther King holiday, January 15, 2001. Despite
having just a week to get the word out, more than eighty-five
people—including city councilpersons, current and past school
board members, the mayor's office, teachers, parents, the Berkeley
Black Firefighters Association, the NAACP, and others—turned
out in support. However, as might be expected, not everyone supported the plan, and the parents knew that winning school board
approval would be a struggle. School board vice president Shirley
Issel expressed a view that the proposed intervention was not necessarily the school's responsibility: "What the parents are asking for

is a confident assessment of academic, psychosocial and medical needs of the kids and to create an intervention to address the needs of students who are at-risk at a variety of levels. That's what parents are supposed to do [Mays, 2001, p. 1]."

However, by the time of the January 23, 2001, school board meeting, the parents' proposal had garnered overwhelming public support and had independently raised forty thousand dollars in contributions. Although one board member was adamantly opposed to the proposal, the plan received district funding to hire five new teachers. The money was enough to serve only 50 of the 250 students identified by PCAD. Nevertheless, the parents had accomplished what many thought was impossible: in just forty-five days, they had designed a concrete plan of action and secured board approval to open a full intervention program by January 30, 2001, the first day of the spring semester.

The students named the program REBOUND! as Irma Parker explains, "because they felt like in the game of basketball, if the ball goes up to the backboard and rebounds, you get a second chance at another shot. And so that's what they said that this program would do for them—educationally give them a second chance at improving themselves and becoming successful and being able to graduate from Berkeley High School." REBOUND! was set up as a full-day small learning community within the larger high school. An e-mail from a PCAD parent sent out in January 2001 to the Berkeley school community explained that the purpose of REBOUND! was to "help students who had not done well academically to begin engaging their many strengths in a caring environment where they are respected and supported, and where they are expected to succeed."

In yet another iteration of an inside-outside strategy, PCAD entered the school arena through REBOUND! working intensely with fifty students and parents. They demonstrated to the school and the district that:

- All students have the potential to learn and be successful in school.

- The racial achievement gap is neither inevitable nor impossible to remedy if there is sufficient political will.

- Parents care about and will take responsibility for their children's education.

REBOUND! proved to be an effective intervention. Nearly all of the students enrolled in the intensive second-chance courses passed and were back on track by the time they entered the tenth grade. The program also highlighted systemic but alterable conditions in Berkeley's K–12 public schools that reproduce large-scale failure, year after year, for hundreds of students of color. REBOUND! was more than a one-time intervention program: it was a call for systemic change, such that future ninth-grade classes would no longer have a need for such a drastic intervention.

In the following year, 2001–2002, PCAD led the effort to create a multiracial parent coalition and teacher support for small schools at BHS. They did so because they became convinced from their experience with REBOUND! and from their research at the school and review of the research literature on school reform that the large, impersonal high school environment contributed to widespread failure among students of color. They continued to put pressure on the school for change, and because they were parents, they carried a legitimacy that proved impossible to ignore. PCAD's commitment was to show the community that they were stepping up for their own children, and in a sense for all children. Much of what PCAD has accomplished since the REBOUND! program has followed what they call the "stone soup concept":

> We are not starting out with much. We have a vision of what we want for these struggling children, and we have ideas about how to achieve our vision. But we need all the sectors and individuals of our community who influence and care about our children to bring the resources and ideas they have and put them into the pot so that we can collectively nourish and educate these children [Parents of Children of African Descent, 2001, p. 3].

Latino Parents of BOCA Contribute to Change

In the Latino community, a similar organizing effort was beginning to take shape. In the fall of 2000, Father Crespin of St. Joseph the Worker Catholic Church, which has a strong presence in the Berkeley Latino community, began to gather concerned community members to address the issues that faced the Berkeley's Latino community. The first of several meetings of BOCA were held at St. Joseph's, a natural gathering point for the Latino community. The meetings were held in order to come to a consensus on the most pressing issue affecting students in the community. Of most concern was the state of Berkeley schools in general, and the experience (most often negative) that Latino students were having within these schools.

Although there were many problems at the middle school level and some at the elementary level, BOCA decided to focus on the high school due to the overwhelming issues: lack of safety and security, academic tracking of Latino students, and low teacher expectations, to name a few of the concerns parents cited. In particular, it had become clear that there were many problems with the way the English as a Second Language (ESL) program functioned. The majority of Latino students attending Berkeley High School were either currently enrolled or had been enrolled in the ESL program. Some had been enrolled in the program since kindergarten, and nothing was being done about the fact that the program was not succeeding in its basic goal of teaching these students to become fluent in English. Because of this apparent injustice or ineptitude, BOCA decided to focus its efforts on understanding what was happening in this program so that changes could be made.

All of the parents strongly supported programs that assist English learners, and the majority of parents agreed with the principles and goals of bilingual education. Yet the parents wanted to ensure that a program designed to teach students English would be used only for students who needed this service and that it would never be used as a method of tracking Latino students into low-level courses. BOCA began by interviewing key people involved in some capacity with the ESL program, including the superintendent of schools, the director of the ESL program, ESL teachers and students, and key members of the Latino community who were familiar with the program. The first interviews were conducted with members of the Diversity Project who had spent the previous year researching the ESL program. Their study found that:

- Students in the ESL program were physically isolated from the rest of the school due to the location of ESL classrooms.
- ESL students were not receiving adequate access to information about post-high school opportunities.
- Some Latino students, including some who were born in the United States, had spent their entire school lives in bilingual and ESL programs.
- The school district maintained no data on how many students exited the program, graduated from high school, or eventually went on to college.

(See Chapter One for a full discussion and analysis of the ESL program.)

After weeks of research and engaging more and more parents, BOCA held a community meeting at St. Joseph the Worker Church, attended by over three hundred community members. The meeting addressed the problems BOCA encountered within the ELL program and served as a forum to present demands for change to the superintendent, the ELL director, and two school board members, who were in attendance. BOCA began its June 11, 2002, meeting with this spoken invitation to these people in positions of power to work together in creating change:

> Many of our children are struggling. These same children whom we know to be bright, beautiful and full of potential are not fulfilling that potential. We realize that the cause for this is complex and its roots are found in the school, in the community, and especially in the larger society. But we are here tonight to ask the school community

to join with us in drawing a line; we refuse to accept anymore that our children's lack of success in school is considered "normal." We ask you to work with us in transforming Berkeley High School into a place that truly believes in the potential of each of its students and that is committed to realizing that potential.

Important changes began to occur as a result of BOCA's action: a new director of the ESL program was hired; the program was relocated to a central classroom building to address the issue of physical isolation; and most important, the school and the community became aware of the formation of a new parent group that would join forces with PCAD in demanding equitable education for all children.

The Coalition and Small Schools

Many parents in BOCA and PCAD have spent years individually confronting and engaging with the schools. One of the many achievements of the two groups is the creation of two distinct spaces for parents: one in the Latino community and another in the African American community. Although both groups were laboring to make Berkeley schools safe, productive, and empowering learning environments for all children, PCAD and BOCA worked independently of each other and in their own communities. Soon after PCAD's REBOUND! and BOCA's community action, an opportunity arose that would lead to the formation of a coalition between the two groups that would eventually focus on small schools reform for Berkeley High.

Some motion toward small learning communities and small schools had already begun. In the fall of 2000, Berkeley High School received federal funding to create an exploratory committee for small learning communities. The committee was formed to look at the possibilities of extending the existing school-within-a-school programs, which had been largely successful, to a schoolwide reform. Unfortunately, this initial committee was not representative of the whole Berkeley community. Noticeably absent were Berkeley High teachers, as well as parents and students of color who were the least well served by the high school and perhaps had the most to gain and the most ideas to offer to the restructuring effort. However, the exploratory committee missed an important opportunity to get actively involved with the most extensive small school effort of the time: REBOUND!

PCAD and the Diversity Project shared two main concerns about the movement toward small schools at Berkeley High:

- It was essential that any effort to reform BHS have a clear and explicit focus on equity.
- The effort must be led by those parents and students most affected by the inequities of the current structure of the high school.

By fall 2001, it had become clear that the exploratory committee had failed to gain traction or momentum and that parents of color through REBOUND! had been successful in leading a parallel movement that highlighted the need for small schools based on equity to address the achievement gap. In fall 2001, leadership made a voluntary transition from the existing small learning communities exploratory committee to a new parent coalition that stood for equity in the schools and for the education of all children. PCAD, BOCA, and parents who represented other communities of color whose voices are seldom heard, as well as parents of children with special needs, came together and formed the Coalition for Equity and Excellence in Our Schools to lead the ongoing effort to break BHS into small schools where students would no longer fall through the cracks.

The coalition set out to address the underlying reasons for systemic and long-standing problems at BHS and discover whether smaller schools could provide ways of eliminating the disparities in achievement among students of different races, minimizing campus violence and student alienation, and transforming the relationships between teacher and students, students and peers, school and community, administration and teachers, and administration and community. The coalition believed that small, autonomous schools of choice might provide the necessary preconditions and accountability to work toward more equitable outcomes for all students.

The coalition felt it was essential to collaboratively develop a small schools policy and at the same time educate teachers and parents to try to move toward this change. One of the first things it did was to organize a second Stone Soup Luncheon, Harvesting Our Strengths in the Search for Solutions, that called on the larger Berkeley community to learn about small schools and join the effort. As stated in the widely distributed Stone Soup II flyer:

> We hope to unite our community around restructuring our schools to educate all children. . . . Equity is essential to the stability of the whole. . . . Please come so that we may break bread together. As we unite and celebrate our strengths and the bounty of our land, let us remember the joys of our family and fellowship of our friends.

The luncheon proved successful in attracting many new community members. According to one parent activist, "Many strands of the community came together in the fall and hung our hats on the Small Schools Policy as a way to bring all-school reform that would once and for all bring the issues of educational equity to the center."

The coalition immediately began work on a policy that would outline its vision of small schools at Berkeley High. In order to create a plan that had the full support of teachers and students, who are central to any school reform, the coalition organized the Teacher Advisory Committee, which coordinated a campaign to interview all BHS teachers and counselors and organized a number of teacher and student focus groups. The teacher interviews culminated in a December 2001 presentation of the interview data to the entire staff, followed by a teachers' union-supervised secret ballot vote on the draft small schools policy, which called for the creation of several small, autonomous high schools to share the Berkeley High campus and contained specific provisions to ensure that the small schools would not be tracked or segregated in any way. In total, 164 teachers and counselors voted on the draft policy, with 51 percent voting in favor of the policy as written, 34 percent voting to pursue small schools in some other form, and just 16 percent voting for the status quo. This meant that 85 percent of teachers and counselors supported some vision of small schools.

With this support from staff and parents, the coalition took the policy to the Berkeley School Board. It is important to point out that the move toward small schools was initially a board-sanctioned idea for improving Berkeley High. The board had passed a resolution in July 2000 to explore the idea of small schools, and the district had sought and received the federal exploratory funding for small learning communities that became available in the wake of the Columbine High School massacre. However, when parents of color assumed leadership of the planning process, the administration and school board majority blocked any forward motion. The coalition found this unacceptable, as one member pointed out: "In light of the gross and persistent failure of the system to educate entire communities of children, as well as many individual children from communities who have traditionally been successful, a solution that proposes incremental change is unacceptable to us."

On December 19, 2001, the board held a special meeting to address the small schools policy, and the Teacher Advisory Committee presented the results of the vote. Later, during a portion of the meeting devoted to parents, a coalition leader testified:

> The situation in our schools is not right. We, parents of the Coalition for Equity and Excellence in Our Schools, are not going to take it anymore. It is no longer good enough for good and caring people to be simply good and caring. It is time for people to decide. In the face of the overwhelming evidence that documents the systemic segregation and discrimination against children of color in the Berkeley School District, what action is going to be taken? What line is going to be drawn?

Many people came out to support the plan. The boardroom was overflowing with teachers, students, and families. In addition, some who were adamantly opposed to the idea of breaking BHS into smaller schools also came out to support the preservation of the large high school structure that they believed allowed their own children to be successful. They did so even though it meant that large numbers of other people's children would continue to fail under the status quo arrangements at Berkeley High.

In the face of considerable pressure from the coalition, which was diverse but led primarily by African American and Latino parents, and pressure from the opposition, which consisted almost entirely of upper-middle-class white parents, the board chose to shut out the coalition. In fact, the board refused even to discuss the draft policy to which so many hundreds of people had contributed, sending the message that the small schools work was not the work of parents. The superintendent announced that she would consider pursuing the idea at a much later date, under her own leadership. The coalition, along with many community members, walked out on the meeting in protest that night after a coalition leader stood, turned her back on the board, and addressed the audience with the words of Frederick Douglass: "Power concedes nothing without demand."

Despite the stinging setback, much came out of the small schools effort and the formation of the coalition. Members of the Berkeley community who had historically been marginal and excluded from the decision-making process had come together around a common issue. Even after their defeat at the hands of the board, they continued to push the issue, and for that reason, the movement to create small, equitable schools remains alive at Berkeley High. PCAD and BOCA are active within their own communities and within Berkeley as a whole. The groups have taught us an important lesson: to make change, we must acknowledge and learn from our failures.

PCAD, BOCA, and the coalition remind us that transforming a school to produce greater equity in academic outcomes requires more than just good ideas. Ultimately, to change the structure of a school in a way that closes the achievement gap requires a change in power relations. If the parents of students who do the least well academically are disrespected and excluded from the governance process, it is highly unlikely that their children will be treated fairly and be provided the kind of education they deserve. The experience of groups like PCAD, BOCA, and the coalition also shows that deliberate action is needed to interrupt patterns of inequality. Their experiences demonstrate that simply working with the school or district cannot produce the change needed when educational and political leaders are unwilling to support their efforts. Parents have to become partners with each other to create demand for the type of transformational education they want to see for their children and must present an organized community, promoting a vision for equitable schools.

We close this chapter with commentary from parent leaders. Given how important parent empowerment and leadership was to the process initiated by the Diversity Project and carried on by PCAD, BOCA, and the Coalition for Equity and Excellence in Our Schools, we felt it was fitting to allow those who led the work to explain its significance in their own words.

Parent Voices

Behind the Scenes with Parent Outreach

Isabel M. Parra—BHS Parent, Diversity Project Member, BHS Staff

I have never seen such a turnout of parents as we had with the Diversity Project's Latino parent focus groups. Definitely, it was a lot of work. But I think that what made the difference was the personal contact with each parent, making them feel comfortable. It was the personal touch.

We started pulling the focus groups together six months before. I think the Latino culture and language made the difference. We needed to have something for our parents, we needed to make them feel important on that night, and having the focus groups in Spanish made a big difference.

For me, it was a plus working at the high school. I had access to the database and telephone numbers of Latino students, and I had been working in the community for many, many years. Through my job in the English as a Second Language Department, I was the first contact person at the high school when high school students from other countries came to Berkeley.

So in a way, I think that I had two advantages. One was to be staff at the high school, and the other one is that at some point in their life at the high school, immigrant families had a connection with me because I was the one who made sure that the kids were placed at the right levels, in the right English. And for the other Latino students, I've been involved in community issues. For those who didn't know me, it was a matter of having access to their telephone numbers and then making sure that we were making the personal contacts.

What we did is this. I got together with all the people in the Diversity Project who spoke Spanish, and we started having a big monthly dinner at a restaurant. Most of us were women. I read about how to put together focus groups, though I didn't have any experience. I knew we needed to start training people to lead the focus groups. We started with a focus group among ourselves to see how focus groups work, and from there, we just needed to add the other features that were missing.

We started contacting people three months before the date, and we called every single person—the mother, the father, sometimes even grandparents—and invited them. The first thing we needed to make sure to tell them was that the meeting would be conducted in Spanish, and that made a big difference. And we told them it was a meeting where they were going to have the opportunity to express their feelings, their anger, everything that they wanted to tell the district. This was their opportunity.

So we called three months before; then we called again a month before, then the week before. Then we came out with flyers; we made announcements at mass on Sundays in church. I also called some people from other parent organizers' phone lists to make sure everyone was making their calls and to confirm that people had been invited.

Parents were surprised that we were inviting them personally to a dinner where they were going to be able to speak in their own language and where people would listen to them. The school would never call them. If they were lucky, someone would send a written translation, but the personal contact was never there. I guess it is due to a lack of personnel—not enough money in the budget to hire someone to make the phone calls.

I was making phone calls the day of the focus group, but I never expected such a turnout. It was great. The ideas that came out of that night made you realize that the only thing that is different between Latino parents and any other parents is the language. It's not even the education; it's not even the social status. When it comes to things that matter with your kids, people don't stop. Then you can see that they are concerned about their kids' education and about their future, and it's just sometimes the language barrier and the means to communicate with the school that stand in their way. If given the chance, they will speak out.

Since the success of the Latino parent focus groups, I have used the same personal connection for other issues affecting Latino families in our schools. A good example is the dual-language immersion program that the district has at three elementary schools—Rosa Parks, LeConte, and Cragmont. But now the program is going to be in its fifth year, so kids are ready to go to middle school, and the parents were losing hope that they were going to be able to continue the dual-immersion curriculum into the middle school grades. So once again I got all the phone numbers, made the personal contact, talked to every family going to sixth grade, and the program is going to happen. It's going to start this year at Longfellow Middle School.

Nothing beats talking to people in their own language and really giving them the opportunity to express themselves.

Parents Learning from Parents

Julina Bastidas-Bonilla—Undergraduate Student Researcher, Diversity Project Member, BHS Parent

My experience on the Berkeley High School Diversity Project as mother/community organizer/undergraduate student researcher was perhaps one of the most valuable life learning experiences I have encountered. As a recent transfer student to UC Berkeley and mother of four, I had more than enough on my plate to consume every waking moment. I knew nothing of the Diversity Project as I sat reading and watching my middle school-aged daughter while she competed at one of her swim meets. As I held my undergraduate course reader up to shield me from the morning sun, I heard a quiet voice nearby. Here was this other mom with what appeared to be the same reader, smiling and pointing at the cover. Yes, this was definitely Berkeley, where everyone is a student. We scooted our chairs together and she began to "school" me about Berkeley High and of course the Diversity Project.

I entered the project as an undergraduate mother with a soon-to-be incoming Berkeley High freshman. What attracted me to this project was my curiosity about the behind-the-scenes mysteries of high school, a place that during my youth was unpleasant and unsafe, and eventually led to my premature departure. The Diversity Project seemed the perfect opportunity to do the "high school" thing again, but with a different twist that involved working with parents and students to help them figure out how to navigate this immense institution called Berkeley High.

The Diversity Project brought together a cross-section of parents, students, staff, administrators, and community members from various class and racial/ethnic backgrounds. This experience would profoundly increase my understanding of public education and the need for radical school reform.

Berkeley High in many respects is a rendition of my former high school—huge, impersonal, and not a place where parents felt welcome. As a matter of fact, a parent at school usually meant there was a problem. For most students of color today, this scenario is all too familiar and one that I strongly felt needed to change. In my countless conversations and interactions with Berkeley High parents, whether poor, black, Latino, Asian, or white, the message was clear: parents understood that the success of their children was dependent on access to resources. This is the difference between students who succeed and the disproportionate number of students of color who struggle or fail.

I began my journey on the Diversity Project in the fall of 1996. Our committee sought to take up the simple but arduous task of asking parents how they felt about their child's school experience and what they as parents needed from the school in order to help their children succeed. I refer to the "simple" in terms of creating wonderful ideas about how parents can become partners with schools. We were not a naive group. I believe we understood the pitfalls of parent involvement or exclusion due to cultural differences, including a host of systemic dysfunctions embedded in public schools. The issue at hand for us entailed learning how to ask the right questions, and the "arduous" task meant developing strategies of implementation and follow-through. Herein lies the problem: how to create nontraditional avenues of parent involvement so that you don't end up with a handful of overzealous moms, whacked out on coffee and cookies, who equate the word *equity* with giving up Advanced Placement courses.

The Diversity Project was all about challenging and changing the norms at Berkeley High, and we needed input from parents whose voices represented change. The most exciting part for me occurred when some of the parents joined the Diversity Project and created parent subcommittees. Through my work with the parents, I eventually became one of the coordinators of the Diversity Project's Parent Outreach Committee.

Through every aspect of my work on the Diversity Project— whether I was working with students, parents, staff, administrators, or graduate students—I walked away with a new perspective. Some of my most intense learning experiences took place during the many meetings I had with parents.

There was one meeting in particular with a group of mainly Latina mothers who were planning outreach strategies for an upcoming focus group, and I noticed that when I spoke, there was a peculiar silence. I wasn't sure how to interpret this strange feeling, but as it continued to occur at several other meetings, I had to take a step back to reassess what was taking place. I mentioned it to the co-coordinator, a Berkeley High School secretary and mother, who blew it off as nothing. However, I was concerned because our mission was about inclusion, collaboration, and equity. What I soon realized was that I was perceived as an outsider, mainly because I was from the "university" side of the project. What this really meant was that the element of class had surfaced, and it was incumbent on me to address this issue. The issue for me was, and continues to be, one of self-reflection and constant reevaluation of my work and of my interactions with others.

As an elementary school teacher today, I am constantly reevaluating my lesson plans and teaching methods, as well as my interactions with students, parents, and staff. I am committed to being a lifelong student where learning how to learn and build community are an integral part of my life. The Diversity Project will always be at the core of my thinking process as I move forward and encounter new challenges.

By Any Means Necessary

Michael D. Miller—Parent Activist and Executive Director of PCAD

An amazing journey has begun for a group of parents of different races. And given the time in history (the turn of the century/millennium), the place (the People's Republic of Berkeley), and the resources (the prestigious UC Berkeley just a stone's throw away, and median home prices, at this writing, well over a half-million dollars)—who would have thought that this journey would require such dedication and attention to an inadequate educational system for minority students? But such is the case.

In the fall of 2000, Parents of Children of African Descent (PCAD) burst on the scene and in a short time developed an intervention program for freshmen who were failing their first semester at Berkeley High School. That program, REBOUND!, was implemented at the beginning of the second semester of that school year. I use the term *burst* because the intensity, skill, and urgency displayed by this group was like no other. The status of our students at Berkeley High required nothing less.

Just about two years later, a member of the Diversity Project commented that the project had thought the results of their four-year study would be compelling enough to generate movement in our district. PCAD also thought the positive results and success of our intervention program, REBOUND!, would be compelling enough to create change in the Berkeley Unified School District. Yet we are still working very hard to realize change, while there are others who are working to keep things exactly as they are. The problems in Berkeley always seemed obvious to me: one high school in a town of 110,000 with a two-tiered system, a system that is now being referred to as apartheid. White and Asian students on the upper end were consistently doing very well. Black and Latino students were on the lower end, failing in high numbers, dropping out or being sent away to "alternative" schools. The following are academic performance index comparisons for Berkeley High School, based on standardized test scores, on a scale of 1,000:

1999–2000: whites, 901; blacks, 561
2000–2001: whites, 894; blacks, 516
2001–2002: whites, 881; blacks, 528

The battle for equality in education in the "Free Speech Capital of the World" rages on.

PCAD is still working to develop strategies for change in Berkeley. We meet, we talk, we develop broader coalitions, and yet there is a force that maintains the status quo. After two full years of committed community work, PCAD has hired an executive director; has applied for nonprofit status; is expanding methods of empowering parents and community members; will raise funds to support this work; will expand the student program AALL (African American and Latino Leadership) at Berkeley High School and beyond; will work in the middle and elementary schools; and will create a Web site, brochures, and other organizational materials for broader community and media exposure. PCAD has already begun to develop partnerships with local clergy, with the intent of providing support, services, information, and leadership training to members of those congregations. We will develop the capacity to go into neighborhoods and homes to spread the good news that as learning partners, the entire community can and should participate in the success of all students.

Our coalition work is focused on alliances with the Latino community. They too suffer from the inequities in Berkeley schools. Together and with other members of our community, we will identify school board candidates who will respond to the needs of the entire community, and not just select members. We also have been exploring taking all of this to the next level: the U.S. Department of Justice or the Office of Civil Rights. By any means necessary!

Who would have thought that in the year 2006, we would be fighting a civil rights battle in Berkeley, California?

For as Long as It Takes

Juana Villegas—Parent activist, Diversity Project member,
and a leader of BOCA

I've learned that sometimes you have to be a little rude. Let me explain by starting at the beginning.

First of all, I don't see any difference between my two periods at Berkeley High School with my older and younger children. In fact, in 2003, we see the same problems people had fifty years ago in times of racial segregation.

It started with Maria, my daughter. There was a white teacher who did not want to see students of color in honors classes. The very first day I enrolled her at Berkeley High, this teacher saw us at the door and he asked us, "Are you sure this is the right class for your daughter?" I replied, "If you are Mr. X, then this is the right class." I looked inside the room and saw twenty to twenty-five white kids; the only brown one was Maria. It was honors math. Then at back-to-school night, the same teacher asked me the same question: "Are you sure you are in the right class?"

Before the end of the first semester, Maria started to have trouble with this teacher, who kept telling her, "This is a really hard class for you," as if she was doing something wrong by being there. Maria's grades went down in math, and I felt something was wrong, so I went and stood in his classroom several times, and I saw that he ignored Maria's questions.

Even when we went to the counselor to see if she could be assigned to another teacher, the counselor asked, "Are you sure she is confident and capable enough to be in Honors Geometry?"

I found that going down to the school was the only way. Every day I asked questions, called by phone, but no one ever called me back. Even if I arrived early, I had to wait and wait. But I learned a lot from this experience: that you have to be even a little bit rude or nothing will happen. You have to have the attitude: "I have a question. You have the answer. I'm not leaving until I get my answer."

I started going to a lot of meetings. Even if I understood only 25 percent of what people said, I went to find out about the system. I went to the PTSA [Parent Teacher Student Association], the ESL program, the Bilingual District Advisory Committee, and Special Education. I found out that Special Ed was 75 percent African American, and they were unable to get out of this track because parents were in the dark about the mandates for quarterly reevaluation.

It was a bad experience to attend meetings where I asked a lot of questions but nobody could respond. For example, I asked why not have more counselors here, and the response was always about funding. But I know the money is there; it is just spent in different ways that do not necessarily benefit our kids.

We know what kids need. They need tutoring after school. UCO MESA [an academic support program for students from groups that are underrepresented in the University of California system] worked for us. Our parents and kids need to know about all the options and opportunities, but we have a hard time finding out, and the other parents don't share the information. So whenever I would find out about a program that might help our kids, I would tell *everyone* about it. I don't like the attitude of some parents: "The less you get, the better for us."

The Diversity Project was a big change because it had a lot of diversity—not white, white, white. We brown parents learned we were not the only ones having problems; Asians, African Americans also had problems. The only difference is that we weren't fighting together. We cannot do it by ourselves.

I'm so tired of hearing that the Latino community doesn't care about the education of our kids. We've mobilized for the board of education meetings and we filled the chambers. I got up to speak and asked them, "How many more parents do you want me to bring: Fifty? A hundred?" So that's what I did: the next time, we came in big numbers. We have to keep doing what it takes for as long as it takes to win justice for our children.

Breaking Through the Color Line in Sports

Vikki C. Davis—Parent Activist, PCAD

My son asked me in his freshman year if he could give up swimming to participate in football. I remember cringing at the thought of him playing football. He had played a little in middle school, but never full contact and never in pads. I remember him coming home tired and exhausted every day from practice. But once the season began, he was full of excitement and anticipation. After all, he had worked hard for weeks preparing for this day.

I remember his first game. There he was, number 73, standing on the sidelines. I sat watching, a proud mother waiting for her son to play. From that point on, I went to every single one of his games, watching and waiting to see my son play. I thought to myself how humiliating it must have felt for him and other players to work hard at every practice and not ever play. I was so glad when the football season ended.

I asked him if he would be interested in swimming again in the spring. I wasn't surprised at his response: he was not interested in swimming at all. We talked about other sports at Berkeley High. What I found interesting about his responses was that he referred to certain sports as "white" sports. I knew then that if I was going to get him interested in a sport other than football, I would have to get a group of his friends.

While at the Solano Stroll [a community street fair held in North Berkeley], we came across a booth for Berkeley High crew. They were passing out flyers for the recruiting picnic they were having in a few weeks. I started talking to other parents about crew. No one knew anything about this sport, only the rumors about the early morning practices. I talked my two boys into going to the picnic. I also had my sons each invite a friend. When we arrived at the picnic, no one greeted us. As a matter of fact, we were for the most part ignored. It felt as if we had invaded a private school event. I introduced myself to one of the coaches; he brushed me off. It was truly not a welcoming experience.

However, before leaving, I ran into a parent I knew from middle school. She shared her experiences with me. She talked about all the good things participating in crew had done for her son. She raved about what a wonderful experience her son was having. Finally, she then said how glad she was to see that my son was interested in rowing. She mentioned that the team needed to recruit more African American students. I knew that my son really wasn't interested in crew, but I wanted him to try something other than football this year.

So I got four of his friends together and suggested they give crew a chance. Their parents were all behind them trying another sport. My son and his best friend starting working out with the team. The two others committed once football season ended. It worked out because the season for crew really didn't start until the spring. For the first time in years, Berkeley High had five African American students participating in crew.

At the parent orientation, I was amazed how organized these parents were. You had to sign up to volunteer. Volunteer jobs could include, but were not limited to, buying food for the races, carpooling students, and hosting a pasta feed. If you didn't commit, you were required to pay an additional two hundred dollars per year. This was on top of the eight hundred-dollar annual dues. If you didn't sign up, someone signed you up. You were expected to participate! It was quite overwhelming at orientation. One other parent and I were the only two African Americans in the room. No one said very much to us. We could not believe what we had gotten ourselves and our children into.

One evening after practice, my son told me that one of the team members had asked my son why he didn't like him. My son's response was that he really didn't know this young man enough to form an opinion and asked him why he felt that way. This young man told my son it was because of his looks, or maybe I should say his hair. My son was wearing his hair in a large natural at the time. Another time that sticks out was when a teammate was jumped on in the men's locker room at school. After practice, a parent took our children (the four black guys) over to the hospital to visit him. I thanked the other parent for doing this, and I told her that I had planned on doing the very same thing. It's funny that we both felt that it was our responsibility to set an example and to show that not all black teen males were violent. You see, it was a black child who had randomly jumped this white kid.

By the end of the racing season, the children had really bonded. Some socialized outside crew. But it wasn't until the final race of the year that I felt welcome. My girlfriend and I had volunteered to be chaperones for the Southwestern Regional Championship that was held at Lake Natoma in Sacramento. The freshman team had come to know me, but the parents—well, that was a different story. But after that weekend, they pretty much knew who I was. I allowed the team to have fun, but I had rules they had to follow. I was clear about my expectations for the weekend. I made myself clear that there would be no gray areas, nor do I negotiate. I also made this clear to the parents during a dinner meeting. I believe that once the parents saw my interactions with their children and how their own children related to me, it opened a few doors to the parents.

The next year, I organized the Solano Stroll fund-raiser for the team. During the races that season, other parents and I talked about the challenges of having teenage boys. We began sharing our experiences at Berkeley High. I no longer felt as if I was invading a "private" public high school club, but that I was invited to be a part of a school team.

Si Se Puede : A Community Organizes for Change

Liz Fuentes—Elementary School Teacher, BOCA Activist and Parent

I have been a bilingual teacher in the Berkeley school system for the past eighteen years and have worked closely within the Latino community. Several years ago, our common concern for the situation of the children led to the formation of a community group, Berkeley Organizing Congregations for Action (BOCA). Many of us had been struggling for many years with educational issues in a sporadic, reactive way, but this was a coming together of the larger community to work for change.

We focused our concern on the English Language Learners (ELL) program at Berkeley High School. Many of the stories told by parents who attended the BOCA meetings were about the high school: worries about safety, access to classes and programs, and how difficult it was for their kids to continue on to college. Many of the parents themselves had not had the opportunity to go to school, and were working several jobs to support their children in doing what they had not been able to do. These mostly Spanish-speaking families told of many problems they and their children had in communicating with the high school.

We acquired a list of all the children in the high school's ELL program and sat together to go over the list. Many of the families had already spoken of their frustration. One response to the list was, "Oh this is a mistake, I know Miguelito, and he is perfectly fluent in English. . . . Julia, too, that is another mistake." But there was no mistake. Children born in this country and children fluent in English and who were here since kindergarten remained on the list of English learners. We also found that many students with learning disabilities were mistaken for students having language issues and were kept in the ELL program even though second-language learning was not their problem.

As a group, we decided to do some research. We first talked with people from the Diversity Project who had conducted a study of the ELL program during the previous year, and they shared their findings with us. We also contacted the people running the ELL program and teachers to discuss these children with them. We couldn't believe some of the responses we received. The head of the program told parents that it takes three generations to really learn a language, and that was why the child was still in the program! The parents were also told, "If you [the parent] take your child out of the ELL program, his or her failure is on you."

In the BOCA meetings, we compared stories and experiences, more people went to hear similar responses at the high school, and we discussed the findings from the Diversity Project and other sources. There were children in the ELL program who should not be there, and the children who needed to be there were not always getting what they needed in terms of access to programs and a future. Many families saw that the children were kept in the program for the needs of the program, not the children. Slowly, a plan evolved to challenge the way the program was run.

There was always a clear understanding that a well-run ELL program is essential for the students who need to learn English and that it was not the program as an idea that we were challenging, but the program as flawed reality. We saw this issue as a huge problem: these children were being deprived of access to the classes that would allow them to apply to the University of California and other colleges, and they were not aware of this until it was too late. Many students who were seniors wanted to go on to college but found that there was no time to take all the classes that they still needed. These kids were in a high school that was famous for its advanced and varied courses—more like a college than a high school—yet they were completely outside the loop. Their classes were off in a dark corner of the school, and they never ventured out to the rest of the academic world that was a few steps away. The ELL program was a kind of fiefdom that kept the children within its limits.

Parents and community organized around the ELL issue, and because of our insistence and concern, the program has begun to change: the children are no longer retained in the program beyond reason. The school changed the person in charge of the program, and the concept of the program now is to facilitate access to programs.

For me, this effort clarified the fragility of the educational process for many of our students. No matter how bright and capable they may be, no matter how much drive they and their families may have to succeed, the system is dead set against their success. Children who are so eager to learn when they are five or ten years old become the grim statistics of youth pushed out of school at age fifteen. Walls are placed everywhere, and the children and their families are constantly walking into them. In the midst of one of the "best" high schools in the area, many children were being marginalized and ignored. A young Latina graduate of Berkeley High spoke to that isolation when she told us that in all four years of attending the high school, no teacher ever called her by her name.

Each year now, as I send my fifth graders on to middle school and eventually to Berkeley High, it is with increased awareness of the obstacles they face and concern for their well-being. In spite of their enormous potential, their future is not clear.

Fighting for Educational Justice in the "Civil Rights Capital of the West"

Valerie B. Yerger—Parent Activist, PCAD

I am the mother of four African American children, all of whom have attended public schools in Berkeley, California. As a product of Berkeley and its schools, I was very happy when I first returned there to raise my children. However, over the years, I have come to witness that children of color have a more difficult time getting their needs met as students in the Berkeley schools than do their white counterparts. This awareness has led me to join other parents and community members to address this problem of educational disparity in our school district. Therefore, as a community activist and a founding member of Parents of Children of African Descent (PCAD), I advocate for educational equity on behalf of students of color within the Berkeley Unified School District. Professionally, I am a researcher investigating ways to eliminate health disparities. My experiences as a parent, community activist, and researcher all contribute to my perspective of Berkeley High School.

Through my eyes and heart, I have seen many social injustices imposed on communities of color, evident as disproportionate rates of poor health outcomes, violence, unemployment, homelessness, incarceration, and targeted marketing of tobacco and alcohol. Even further, I recognize the educational injustices that exist here in Berkeley, a place considered by many to be the "Civil Rights Capital of the West." These educational injustices are especially visible at BHS. For example, data collected over four years at BHS show that African American and Latino students are achieving at significantly lower academic levels than are their white and Asian schoolmates.

When my children were younger and attending elementary school, I was not so burdened with such concepts as the achievement gap, educational inequity, and academic tracking. At that time, I did not have conversations with other parents about how our children's academic journey in high school and college would be initially launched by how well they performed in their seventh-grade math class. Nor did the concept of the achievement gap take form for me until my oldest son entered high school, and I saw firsthand how black males in particular must struggle to maintain some sort of academic sanity. I have often wondered if my son's physical stature is threatening to his teachers, as he has brought home stories of how teachers appear hesitant to interact with him. Indeed, other parents of African American males indicate our sons are having similar experiences in the classroom.

It has not been easy for me to make appearances at BHS during school hours to periodically visit or volunteer in a classroom. I would imagine this is the case for other single parents who also must work full time. It is important for teachers and administrators to understand that parents are not always able to take time off from work to visit the school. I realize that my presence at the school acts as a reminder to teachers that my children are connected to someone who loves them. However, teachers must realize that I not only want the best for my children, but that I also expect teachers to be held accountable for what happens to my children in the classroom.

When a parent is unable to visit the school, teachers and administrators should not immediately judge that parent as being uninvolved. On the other hand, I have often heard parents disclose that though they may have the time to visit the BHS campus, they do not feel comfortable there, as they are not readily acknowledged or treated with respect by staff. This unfortunate situation can be intimidating for parents who wish to come to school to inquire about their children, and even more so if they have memories of negative experiences when they themselves were students.

It has been argued among some parents that providing academic and social support to those students in need of such services, especially during this time of the school district's fiscal crisis, will use up the district's limited resources. I do not know how parents, who understandably may want the best for their children, do not comprehend that children are adversely affected when they observe injustices being done to fellow students. I have heard white students talk about their experiences of being in segregated classes and isolated from students of color, many of whom were their friends in elementary and middle school. These white students know that many students of color are going into classes that do not prepare students for college. If they were to listen, white parents would hear the agony and frustration that their own children reveal, for example, in poetry slam sessions.

Just as educational injustices imposed on African American and Latino students affect white students, social injustices affect those not living in marginalized conditions. For example, health disparities, though disproportionately affecting communities of color, also burden white people. A crucial factor in eliminating these health disparities is to prepare students of color for higher education so that they can be trained as doctors, researchers, or policymakers who can appropriately address some of these social concerns. Students of color will be in a stronger position to continue on to higher education if they arrive at high school prepared and are then nurtured there for success.

6

SONGS OF EXPERIENCE

Student Reflections on Four Years at Berkeley High

Elena Silva

The Diversity Project's Student Outreach Committee began as an effort to involve Berkeley High students in the project's research and reform efforts. The idea for Student Outreach centered on two basic premises: that students are experts on their own experiences and should be directly included in the process of inquiry and reform at their school, and that students should be empowered to participate as leaders and partners in this process. The project's hope was that students, particularly those who were less successful and most marginalized within Berkeley High, would embrace the chance to express their concerns and critiques of the school and to organize and initiate change efforts, or, as one student wrote, "that frustrated grumbles will turn into screaming activism."[1]

In many ways, the Student Outreach Committee was an ambitious endeavor. Student participation in school-based activities at Berkeley High mirrored the larger problems of separation and inequity at the school. The 1996–97 Diversity Project study of extracurricular and cocurricular participation found patterns of racial separation among Berkeley High students, with few racially integrated activities, as well as an overrepresentation of white students as participants in mainstream academic/career activities, including Berkeley High's student newspaper, the *Jacket*, the school's literary magazine and yearbook, and the school's Student

Leadership class. Notably, the few academic activities that predominantly consisted of students of color centered on tutorial support services and work preparation, including Work Experience and the Homework Center, as well as smaller, alternative publications, including the English as a Second Language (ESL) yearbook, *In Living Cultures*, and the black student newspaper, *Ujamaa*. These disparities in participation among students added to the complicated effort of involving students in an adult-dominated and adult-driven research and reform process.

Engaging students in action research was an uncommon and unpracticed task at Berkeley High. Despite an abundance of student groups and activities at the school, few, if any, were focused on organizing students to participate in inquiry and change efforts. With the exception of the Diversity Project's emerging Student Outreach Committee and a separate youth organizing group, Youth Together, student leadership in school inquiry and planning was largely limited to the school spirit and student activity campaigns of the Leadership class or the isolated student representative on the school site council or school board.[2] "It's a vacuum, basically," explained one student from Student Outreach. "We're allowed to say whatever—total free speech—but it just sort of gets sucked up into nowhere. . . . Maybe like cyberspace, where it just swirls around and doesn't seem to end up anywhere."

This chapter focuses on the experiences of Berkeley High students who participated in Student Outreach and similar student-led efforts to critically examine and change their school. It begins by describing the Student Outreach Committee, highlighting both its achievements in researching and revealing the student perspective and its disappointments as it struggled to inform the school's formal reform agenda. Next, this chapter offers the voices of the students themselves as they reflect on four years at Berkeley High. Overall, this chapter offers a window into the lived experiences of students striving to be respected, connected, and supported in their efforts to define and shape themselves, their communities, and their school.

Student Outreach, 1997-2000

In the early weeks of the fall 1997 semester, the Student Outreach Committee was initially coordinated by a Chicano/Latino studies teacher, Julia González Luna; a Spanish and English as a Second Language teacher and UC Berkeley graduate student, Tamara Friedman; and a former Berkeley High student and UC Berkeley undergraduate, Vajra Watson. As a graduate student researcher for the Diversity Project, I joined the committee midsemester to support and document this emerging group of student researchers and activists. Over a three-year period, I became immersed in the students' efforts, observing and coordinating their attempts to understand and tackle some of Berkeley High's most pressing problems.

Targeting the involvement of students whose voices were most often silenced or excluded at Berkeley High and elsewhere (Fine, 1991), the coordinators recruited a group of predominantly black/African American and Latina/o students to join the committee. During its first year, this group met weekly to explore and address some of the most prominent problems of their school, including "segregation and tracking in the school and in classes," "unsupportive teachers and counselors," "not enough 'real' education," and, notably, "student voices that get shut down." Students described Berkeley High as both empowering and painfully discouraging to students of color:

> *Really* Berkeley High is a big mess for us who aren't "ideal" students. We don't fit the mold so that's too bad for us. *Ideally* Berkeley High would listen to what's up and pay attention to us.

> BHS empowers me by giving or posing opportunities for me to learn about my past, present, and future life. But BHS hinders me by not hearing my voice no matter how loud I scream. . . . If you are not in the elitist group, you are not heard. For those of us who are timid, shy, or ignorant of the opportunities, we fall through the cracks and are easily lost.

The students are not conscious of the control they could have over their education, especially nonwhite students, because it's not emphasized. So the administration is put in charge of a crucial decision-making process which holds a student's educational future in their hands. There's lots of talk and very little action.

As discouraging as some of the students' descriptions seemed, their discussions initiated a variety of exciting and dynamic projects aimed at researching and mobilizing the student body of Berkeley High and supporting the students who needed it most. Student Outreach planned and hosted an array of activities, including after-school and lunchtime forums to discuss a variety of issues with other students, visits to local schools to get a sense of how other schools were confronting similar problems, mentorship and support activities for incoming freshmen, a photo-documentary of the student experience at Berkeley High, and a series of video interviews with students about the school's plans for reform.

One of the most notable points to emerge from these efforts was a strong sense of disengagement and detachment among students, particularly from any school decision-making or reform efforts. Finding few opportunities and little encouragement for students to learn about and critically discuss their school experiences and their opinions about school practices and policies, Student Outreach was not surprised that students felt disconnected from the school's planning and reform. "Of course they don't care," explained one Student Outreach sophomore, "I mean, you only care about what you know, and they don't have any idea what the school's doing. . . . Of course they have nothing to say about it. Why should they?"

At the same time, Student Outreach found that students had strong opinions, significant concerns, and often powerful critiques of their school, yet possessed few strategies to express and articulate their ideas and interests in relation to the school. After a series of frustrating student organizing efforts, one student remarked,

It's easy to say students don't care . . . but you have to understand WHY students don't care. . . . The school is set up so that nothing would change if students went [to a meeting] and told their concerns. Everything is already decided and then brought to us . . . and students know that and they'll find other ways, you know, when something really pisses them off.

An exchange during one Student Outreach forum further illustrates the cynicism that develops among students who experience few avenues for expression. "If I don't like it, I'm just not goin' [to class]. Simple as that," one student stated. Another student asked a clarifying question, "You can't talk to your teacher?" while a third student called out from the back of the room, "And say what? What would he say to the teacher? 'Your class sucks!'?" The first student responded sarcastically, mocking the school's most recent attempt for more open communication: "Mmhmm. I'll go explain my problem on one of those 'comment cards'—that's what I'll do."

Hoping to insert the student perspective into the change plans of their school, the Student Outreach Committee was excited when, during its second year, it was invited to join the school's official strategic planning efforts. Encouraged by Berkeley High's newest principal, the group (now including students from the previous year as well as a dozen new students chosen by me, Julia, Vajra, and other Diversity Project teachers) agreed to review and respond to a draft strategic plan for schoolwide change at Berkeley High.[3] So began a period of several months during which the students met every Friday for several hours, either at UC Berkeley or in an available classroom, to read, assess, and revise the draft plan. They had been told that they would be included in a number of planning and decision-making meetings with school faculty and administration, and, in preparation, they developed a proposal outlining their position on reform issues.

Even with the invitation to participate and with the coordinated support from the Diversity Project, it was difficult for the students to simply slip into a planning process that was already well underway and certainly unprepared for the additional voices of students. Within the existing process, there was no time to consider how students might (or might not) fit into the process, and there was no mention that the process might be unfamiliar or disagreeable to students (or how to make it less so).

Entering the process largely unaware of and inexperienced with school planning and decision-making practices, the students faced a serious challenge in navigating the world of school decision making and reform. To the extent that this world was puzzling and alien to them, their burden included learning a new language and new behaviors to ensure that their voices would be heard.

The students would often pause to confer or question the meaning of various terms and expressions. "What does 'augmentation of instructional strategies' mean?" one student asked during a Friday afternoon meeting. As they pored over the draft plan for school improvement, a barrage of similar school management and reform-related questions framed the students' discussions: What does "restructuring" mean? What does it mean, technically, for classes to be "detracked"? How does "curriculum development" happen? At one point, these questions prompted me to bring the students copies of a recently published guide to the language of reform, *The Lingo*.[4] Even with this, it took tremendous patience for the students to sift through the planning document and determine which terms were worth discussing and which they could, as one student suggested, "skip over to save time." "Why can't we just speak English?" added another student as he tossed his copy of *The Lingo* back into the center of the table.

Inserting their voices into the adult-driven planning process proved to be equally frustrating for the students. Excluded from several early planning meetings, they felt left out and silenced in subsequent meetings that they attended. Even with the development of their own formal proposal, the students felt that their ideas were disregarded. After one meeting with teachers and administrators, a student responded: "They ignored us. . . . They weren't even prepared and they weren't willing to listen to us. . . . I coulda yelled the whole time and they wouldn'ta heard me. They already had a plan all thought up."

In fact, the more involved the students became in the school's official process, the more they came to recognize how limited their positions and voices were within the process. One student explained during one of our meetings: "They need us, like the principal said. But you know, they don't really need us. They don't really need our help. You think all those opinions are gonna matter when they sit down to do this thing? Nah. . . . They just need us to sit there and be Student A and Student B."

Notably, the character of the student committee had also changed by this point. After months of reading and reviewing a strategic plan, attending administrative meetings, and meeting to analyze next steps in reform participation, many students who had begun the process had dropped out of the committee, citing school-work, jobs, and family responsibilities as their reasons. Others directly expressed a disinterest in the school-related focus of Student Outreach activities. One student explained, "I just have my own priorities right now. They [Student Outreach] have some good ideas, but I'm not so much about empowering the school. I'm more about empowering myself and my people." As a black male, this student joined a number of other students of color, including immigrant students and students with limited English proficiency, in leaving Student Outreach.

Existing now as a much smaller group with the most participation from high-achieving, highly successful students at Berkeley High, the group was unable to mobilize the participation or represent the interests of students who were most negatively affected by the racial and class inequities at the school. One student later explained how certain student voices were privileged over others in the school's planning process: "Even when you bring students with different opinions to those arenas, they're the ones who get drowned out in the background anyways. . . . A student that has learned to . . . that has always known to talk a certain way will get heard."

Indeed, within the school's formal planning process, it seemed as though Student Outreach had twisted into a narrow version of its equity- and empowerment-based beginnings. As this planning process came to a close, a student concluded with disappointment, "The students who are getting things changed are all the students who are going to college anyway."

Recognizing that the group had dwindled in diversity and size and that even the remaining students felt discouraged by the school's process, those of us coordinating Student Outreach shifted its path once again in the following year, this time leaving the school's official reform agenda far behind. In this, its final year (1999–2000), Student Outreach focused on merging its efforts with those of other student groups in the hope of creating a larger, truly student-led movement. Combining Youth Together students and students from a variety of school clubs and organizations, notably those involving students of color—such as Hapa (a mixed-race student group), Raza (the Latina/o student group), and the Black Student Union), the students decided to call themselves Youth-N-Vision.

Meeting in the school's newly created Student Learning Center on Friday afternoons and, at times, during lunch, the group of a dozen to fifteen students planned and developed schoolwide forums on issues of inequity at Berkeley High and in their larger communities.[5] Combining Diversity Project research on Berkeley High statistics and Youth Together research on California's Proposition 21 (a juvenile crime ballot initiative that would try certain fourteen-year-olds as adults), the group was able to make a powerful variety of presentations to the students.

For the better part of a year, in fact, Youth-N-Vision seemed to be the beginning of a viable student activism movement at Berkeley High. Although outside the school's formal planning processes, the group had the potential to collectively represent voices of otherwise silenced or marginalized communities of students. Yet plans to continue the group's work fell victim to both the happy occasion of student graduation and the distressing circumstances of school change.

The seniors and informal leaders of Youth-N-Vision were leaving Berkeley High.

The codirectors of the Student Learning Center were also challenged by funding difficulties and cautionary remarks from the administration that the center might not survive its second year. Meanwhile, the Youth Together coordinator was moving on to a new job just as the Diversity Project was closing its official committee work at the school. Without adult support, space, and resources, Youth-N-Vision faced not only the difficulty of organizing and mobilizing for equity and diversity in their school, but also the well-established challenge of meeting these goals as students within an adult-centered institution.

Through their struggles to understand and represent the student experience, the Student Outreach and Youth-N-Vision students revealed much about the complexity of student life and student voice at Berkeley High. In their efforts to be heard and to participate in official and unofficial school change processes, the students also demonstrated how unpracticed and unprepared Berkeley High and its students are to engage in truly critical and collaborative processes of change.

For relevant and lasting reforms to occur at Berkeley High, particularly reforms that can accurately boast of collaborative practices and shared inquiry, it seems clear that this disconnect between its students and the institution must be bridged. Particularly in the diverse and often divided setting of Berkeley High, gaining an understanding of the variable and dynamic character of Berkeley High students is perhaps a first step.

The following section consists of essays written by seven Berkeley High graduates. All of these students participated either centrally or peripherally with the Diversity Project and willingly agreed to describe their experiences as students and as reformers of Berkeley High—in their own words, from their own perspectives. In their reflections, they recount their experiences of trying to find space and voice within traditionally adult-dominated change processes. Their stories are as different as these individuals, but together they offer a sense of what it is like to experience Berkeley High School as a student and as an emerging activist. In their combined essays, there is pain and pride and a call for much-needed change that is honest and deliberate and that unites rather than divides. They describe fear, embarrassment, anger, and uncertainty, yet they also describe the inspiration and fulfillment of finding a cause and a purpose that feels worthwhile and meaningful to them.

Student Voices: Reflections on Berkeley High

Finding the Power to Do What Is in Your Heart

Nabila Lee Lester

Being a student at Berkeley High School was the craziest decision I've ever made in my life. And when I say decision, I truly mean a decision, the kind that required little or no thought but felt right just the same. I had been raised in Harlem, New York, and later in Long Island, where I continually suffered from lack of self-knowledge. There was always a craving in me to exist in a place where I could truly be myself, even though I didn't know who "I" was. Yet there was also a resistance in me manifesting in my overenthusiasm for world philosophy and my love for argumentation. In the mix of that, I found myself one random evening flipping the pages of a Berkeley High catalogue while the snow fell on my Bay Shore lawn. Convinced immediately of my calling, I became overwhelmed with visions of a Japanese boyfriend and happier life. Upon assumption, I thought this place to be a heaven, some strange island where my blackness would no longer have to be mentioned in the sea of diversity.

My mother and I arrived in Cali having left a whole life behind. My first day of class finally came, and still my subconscious yelled, "Multiculturalism, Yeah"—and what a load of crap. Things proved to be the same as in Bay Shore as I walked into my calculus class and the same white faces gazed at me in confusion—motivated this time by surprise rather than irritation. And as the day continued, I began to understand Berkeley High in a course of classes—my Advanced Placement classes being all white and Asian and my core classes being thoroughly mixed. I guess this day could be renamed "the moment of clarity," for it became clear to me that there was no place on the planet that didn't suffer in one way or another from racism. From this moment on, I began to speak out at functions, and within a few weeks became the president of the African American Studies Department. Social resistance came to my doorstep and never went away.

Attempting change at Berkeley High is like trying to be a teacher in it. You are faced with all the problems of an urban center, made fully aware of the issues to the point of overarticulation, but provided with little or no support to change anything. In fact, you spend so much time discussing the problem that there was little time left to fix them.

So in light of the situation, I made an attempt from day one to hear things and change things. It first began with being the president of the African American Studies Department, a situation that warranted more expectations than given. We as a collective attempted to make students and faculty aware of the D and F rate, declining enrollment in the department, community issues, and black love. If you could name it, we had a forum about it. The level of involvement was astounding. Students mobilized enrollment and Black Knowledge days and supported faculty members within the classroom. However, people began to be weighed down with the complexities of issues, from the legacy of slavery to the D and F rate.

It was difficult trying to be young, do well in school, live life, and be a freedom fighter at the same time. Mostly it was the magnitude of issues that we attempted to understand and solve that made things seem so unattainable. We were in our small community trying to combat problems that have existed for hundreds of years, and only those who committed could not see these hopes were unrealistic. Furthermore, we did not possess the power to make large school changes. For instance, forums would happen to discuss the problem, but only twenty to fifty would be representing a school of over three thousand. Anything created in a bubble is bound to stay in a bubble.

If I could go back in time, I would realize that what we heard and said at forums in room H102 [the college-style African American Studies lecture hall] needed to be said in front of the entire school. Organization can work only if everyone affected is on the same page. Also I would realize that there isn't one way to do something. Finding people's strengths and appealing to their needs is very important so that everyone feels they have a part in change. Most important, student mobilization needs mentorship and leadership from teachers and parents. As brilliant and mature as students might be, they still need the direct leadership of elders who have tried to do the same thing. First, they need a person to help them set realistic goals and find resources. Then they need someone to help mediate and facilitate and help to keep everyone positive and hard working. After the leadership crew has developed those skills, the elder leadership can step back and allow students to regulate themselves. Having a center for such groups is also very important so that the student leaders feel connected to something, someone, and somewhere larger than themselves.

As far as my own experience at Berkeley High, I regret nothing. I think having the drive to see things for what they are and to take on the burden of social change requires courage and wisdom. I am personally very proud of what we accomplished as Diversity Project members and as activists. A lot has changed and will continue to change as a result. If I were to speak to freshmen today before they start on a similar journey, I would tell them that they have the power to do whatever is in their heart. They should know that it is not the result of change that they should focus on, but the process of change that is so amazing. What is today is never what will be tomorrow. That change is always possible if you choose to make it happen.

My Four Years on the Diversity Project

Joseph Christiano

I was thirteen years old going into ninth grade, but I did not look a day older than ten or eleven. My voice was still high-pitched enough to sound feminine, and I walked through the halls at five feet three inches wearing a cobalt blue Jansport backpack so large that it seemed capable of toppling me over. Everywhere I looked, I was surrounded by students who seemed to be twice my size. I remember someone telling me that students who look scared or vulnerable are more likely to get beaten up. So I walked to school scared that I looked vulnerable because of my size. This made me even more scared because I thought I *looked* scared. I remember dreading Spirit Week because I was told stories of freshmen being egged, jumped, or shoved into trash cans by upperclassmen. These stories were particularly frightening for me: due to my small size, I stood out from the crowd and constantly worried that I looked like an obvious freshman. This fear stuck with me throughout my first three years at Berkeley High, until I began to grow.

Whenever I walked through the halls or across campus, I made sure to be alert and aware of my surroundings. This meant that on the way to and from school, in between classes, and during lunch, I was jumpy and nervous, always on edge. My cautiousness paid off, and I never met any serious harm during my years at Berkeley High—although I did have many close calls and narrow escapes. I had everything from orange peels, eggs, water balloons, and rocks thrown at me, and I have seen bottles and even a watermelon thrown in other people's areas.

While Berkeley High's campus was a frightening place for me, I was able to find my niche inside the classroom. Under the protective eye of the teacher, I excelled because I felt safe and comfortable enough to be myself. But for many other students, classrooms seemed to be the worst part of Berkeley High. Inside classrooms, students are given tedious homework assignments. They are taught by awful teachers who can't cater to their needs. They are reprimanded when they act out because they are bored with the poorly designed lesson plans. And they do not feel comfortable, or even motivated, to participate in class. For me, however, I was more often than not interested in the subject at hand, and I never thought twice about asking a question or interacting with the teacher and fellow students.

I made the most of my friends in class, and they turned into a support system for me. Walking around with a friend or two in tow made Berkeley High a much less daunting place. I also found it easy to make friends and build confidence in myself by becoming a student liaison for the Diversity Project. As a student liaison, I met many other students, as well as Berkeley High teachers and staff. This gave me a sense of security and reassurance because I knew I could turn to any one of them if I ever encountered trouble. Making new friends was not the only reason I joined the Diversity Project. I was motivated by the prospect of getting paid and having a good extracurricular activity for college applications. In addition, I wanted to do something positive for Berkeley High.

When the Student Outreach Committee was formed, I became a member, in part because I truly wanted to give all students a voice but also out of a sense of obligation to the Diversity Project. Throughout my three years on the committee, I wondered what I could meaningfully contribute. I had everything going for me academically, and as a white male growing up with two middle-class parents who took an active role in my education, I did not share the same problems—lack of time, resources, and support—that affected my underachieving classmates, who tended to be African American and Chicano/Latino students from low-income families. Therefore, it was difficult for me to give constructive insight regarding many of the issues the committee intended to address.

I remember feeling out of place at some of the meetings because I was not sure what role I should play on the committee. I did not want to come off as preachy by explaining the habits of study that I used to ensure my success. At the same time, I felt frustrated because so much of my success depended on my life circumstances: not having any obligations or responsibilities outside school, while getting the support and motivation I needed at home. So during meetings, I tended to remain on the periphery and was guarded about anything I said.

In retrospect, I wish I had known more about the concept of being an ally and how I could have used my privileged position to work with and help support the underachieving students. But at the time I was not motivated enough to fight what I considered to be someone else's battle. I felt that the students who were suffering most should have been in charge and taken the lead. However, again in hindsight, I feel that I should have participated more in the process of working together to forge new ideas and solutions, using my experience as a successful student.

Despite having misgivings about my role on the committee, I remember feeling most comfortable when working on the strategic plan. I found it easy to collaborate and express my opinions, due to the well-organized meetings and small groups we worked in. Plus, we were able to accomplish our single specific goal: to review and make suggestions for the strategic plan. The only downside to this achievement was the disappointment that followed when we felt that our ideas were not implemented.

Although it was frustrating that our work on the strategic plan was never considered seriously and I struggled with where I fit in with the committee, my overall experience was profound. I learned how to work effectively with students, teachers, and parent volunteers. I also saw the difficulties of working within a bureaucracy. I was able to develop many friendly relationships with interesting people, and I felt the support one gets from working together with others for a common cause.

Looking back, I wish we had set aside more time for meetings, so we could have accomplished more. I regret that there was no single specific student leader who took charge of the group and inspired motivation in the other members. (It could have been anyone, even me.) Instead, most of the students on the committee seemed more comfortable with background roles, while letting others (mainly UC Berkeley students) prepare agendas and facilitate the meetings. Finally, I regret our lack of organization and perseverance, because we never seemed to follow through in carrying out our goals. But, all in all, being a member of the Student Outreach Committee was a valuable learning experience, and I am forever wiser because of it.

Born in America, Yet Foreign to the System

Jimmy Thong Tran

I didn't feel like the typical Asian American. From what I saw, there were two types of Asian Americans at Berkeley High: (1) Asian Americans who were apathetic about school and (2) Asian Americans who had already taken Algebra I before they got to Berkeley High.

It's funny how Asian Americans are stereotyped as both good or bad: good for being the good ol' model minority—model American citizens who abide by the laws, stop at Stop signs, score high on all the tests, achieving success despite all the hardships. Then there are the bad Asian Americans who are supposedly in triads, Asian gangs, driving stolen cars that do not stop for Stop signs, eat welfare incessantly, and hog up space in ESL classes. Two opposite ends of the spectrum, never in between.

I was in the lower percentiles of the SAT tests and I don't even drive. Hence, I was neither. Although my ZIP Code qualifies me for failure, my single child–single mother status motivates me to go against my ZIP Code's expectation. My mother isn't strict on me. She doesn't scrutinize my report cards. She seems to have enough confidence in me to trust my decisions. She has a silent expectation of me to succeed, which I try my best to listen to. Plus, she has too many other things going on in her life. Being an only child comes with a lot of pressure to succeed.

I was tracked into the regular college prep classes not out of the counselor's suggestions but out of my ignorance of the college process. I'm not trying to sound unappreciative of college prep classes; there are too many other high schools that do not have college prep classes. However, if a four-year college was to be given any consideration, college prep classes are just the bare minimum; hence I would be a bare minimum candidate, competing against the fully equipped, AP-class-taking, living-in-the-hills candidates. I just took all my classes, trying my best to get the best grades because my academic life has never tried to know anything lower than a 3.0. I was born in America, yet foreign to the system.

I never knew what an AP class was until I overheard my friends thinking about taking it. I honestly had no clue on what was involved in the college admission process until REACH! (UC Berkeley's Recruitment Retention Center) did a presentation at the Asian Pacific Student Union meeting. That day they presented got me thinking about my future. I also got frustrated over the fact that I had not known about all of it before. I had always been under the impression that as long as I maintained good grades in my classes, I would be able to get into any college. I can be naive.

AP classes, the SATs, the SAT II's, the extracurricular activities, the money it costs to apply were all factors taken into consideration. I had to get started. I didn't have time to be frustrated with a system where children with rich parents were privileged enough to hire private college counselors, able to afford the opportunity to attend meetings because they were instilled with the English language, while my mother works late night taking care of my little cousin for a couple dollars because her job just doesn't pay the bills, nor could it ever pay for quality English tutorials.

The one test that destroyed my confidence in my academic abilities was the algebra diagnostic test in seventh grade. It was the test that determined whether I would be placed in either Algebra I or prealgebra. My seventh-grade math teacher swore that the test would have no effect on us if we didn't pass it. In retrospect, I highly disagree. Yeah, algebra students had to wake up early, but damn, what that class was doing for their academic confidence and skills, what that class was doing to my academic confidence. I swear, every time I waited for Algebra I to get out, I saw friends come out of there, and I looked to them as the academic elite. I, who passed the GATE [gifted and talented] test after taking it two times, I, who was put into a special accelerated reading group in third grade, was taking prealgebra. I felt inadequate.

So when I was asked by peers why I chose not to get into the AP English class, I didn't tell them that I feel academically inadequate, I didn't tell them that I didn't feel that I would belong. I didn't tell them that it's because I didn't get into Algebra I in eighth grade. I didn't want to show friends that I was lacking in English composition and comprehension or not up to their level. I just tell them that I didn't want to, never truthfully justifying my reason: I was afraid.

Jump to senior year. I took community college classes because none of my friends would be there, and it would hopefully be just as challenging as any AP class at Berkeley High without the challenge of proving myself to my peers. I took Asian American history (which is also offered at Berkeley High) and a history of art. They turned out to be fairly easy, and what I really liked about them was that there was real diversity in those classes, not only in ethnicities but in age as well.

I was a senior in high school, and decisions had to be made. While I had my own future to figure out, Berkeley High had to figure out theirs as well. The Western Association of Schools and Colleges, the school accreditation board, was doing its evaluation of Berkeley High. We were granted a two-year accreditation, but were in danger of losing it altogether. Ms. Bled, the former college adviser, was forced out of her position because although she had the experience, she reportedly did not have the credentials that would "validate" that experience. We, the students of Berkeley High, were given a new college adviser. I was worried.

I am what senators, scholars, and so forth would call "economically disadvantaged," out of fear of not being labeled "PC." I call myself poor. Yes, college is possible for everyone—it is just a matter of knowing how to get that money that's there for the earning, deserving, taking, however you see it. Me, I am poor, and after all this crap, I felt I deserved what I have earned. I searched and applied to every scholarship I was eligible for. One really caught my eye: UC Berkeley's full-ride scholarship for "disadvantaged" students—$24,000 for four years. I managed to maintain good grades. My test scores, well, let's just say they're average. In terms of college admissions, I was "competitive." So I figured, why not apply to these scholarships because, really, there is no harm in applying. The value of the application is $24,000 alone. I was optimistic of the possibility.

I asked the college adviser about the scholarship. I don't remember what she said verbatim, and at the time, I was angrier at the fact that I had not known about this opportunity. But I definitely did not forget the last thing she had said: that there were students who were in more need of it than I was. That made me mad. She had never talked to me, one-on-one. She didn't know a thing about my personal circumstances, and yet she went on and made the assumption that I was less deserving. Does everyone have the Asian American model minority myth instilled in them? When it comes to the students and people, as cliché as this may sound, I find myself feeling the need to tell people over and over again: deal with people on an individual basis, and never make assumptions. I assumed people would know by now. Maybe I should stop making assumptions too.

I went on to earn a lot of scholarship money, along with getting into all the other colleges I applied to (hey, as an "economically disadvantaged" student, I like to brag about my accomplishments). I am now heavily involved in REACH! with hopes that I will inform people who are in like situations. I am an example of a "neither" Asian American student who has made it through the college process. College has been a bit hard because that inferiority complex has loomed over me a couple of times. The oppressive mentality is the only thing that hinders potential. (Well, that and discrimination.) Living by words of Tupac Shakur, I try my best to keep my "head up," walking around campus in my old tattered sandals (from high school). As my friend Mable says, "Wear poorness as a badge of how far you have gotten."

The People Most Affected Must Be Part of the Solution

Pranoumphone (Pam) Pradachith

One year after completing high school, I am faced with this enormous task of writing on the student experience at Berkeley High. How can I encapsulate the raw emotions and real experience of an average student who has survived a four-year journey through the battlefield of one of the most studied and debated public high schools in the country? Well, I begin with the simple answer that I cannot. One year later, I can say that the average student does not exist. I had a unique experience at BHS.

My journey through Berkeley High began before I was born. I am the product of a family scarred by the memory of war. I spent the first few years of my childhood in refugee camps in Thailand and then in the Philippines. Although I do not remember much, the wrinkles on my mother's hands and feet paint a clear story of my history. Under my father's strict demand of academic excellence, I saw my education as the only tool I had to build a road away from the faulty social and economic situation my family was in. This determination to be the one to save my family gave me a unique perspective toward my education. I was excited to start my freshman year at BHS. I was proud that my high school was the first in the country to voluntarily desegregate. I was excited about attending the only public high school in the country that has a black studies and Latino studies department. I came into BHS ready with a plan.

In my first year at Berkeley High, I started working at the East Bay Asian Youth Center as a member of their youth organizing team known as Youth Together (YT). In the wake of an outbreak of racial tension and violence in many Bay Area high schools in the early 1990s, Youth Together was developed with a vision that real solutions to the problems in our public high school would come only from young people themselves. The purpose of Youth Together was to identify the root causes of racial violence in our school and design a plan of action to address the problem.

Unlike the other YT sites, Berkeley High did not see racial violence as a major problem in our school. Rather, we identified that
our main concern was racial inequities. Berkeley High exists as two
separate schools. On one hand, students were graduating and going
on to continue their education at some of the top universities in the
country. On the other hand, students were failing out of Berkeley
High. The school was split between the students who have and the
students who have not. The students who had access to resources
such as technology, outside academic support, and financial security
did well and excelled. However, the students who lacked these basic
needs failed out at alarming rates. There was no support network set
up for students who needed the extra help. In a school of over three
thousand, it was easy for a student to get lost in the crowd or buried
under the bureaucracy.

This achievement gap was one of the main concerns of the
Western Association of Schools and Colleges when they visited
BHS. They ordered the school to create a plan of action in order to
address this issue. But how could a discussion about student
achievement and educational inequity happen without the voice of
the students? In any type of real change within a system, the voice
of the people who are directly affected must be part of the solution.

So rather than working with the school on their strategic plan
and joining the token student involvement committees BHS set up,
we developed our own plan to address the inequities at Berkeley
High. With a team of ten current students at Berkeley High and two
years of planning, we developed our own strategic plan, which we
titled the Equal Opportunity Project (EOP). EOP represented the
student voice. The brainstorming and planning for this program
happened completely independent of the school. Once the team finished the proposal, we started to question: How do we implement
this program? How does a group of students of color whose voice was
typically unheard and ignored at BHS convince the school board to
fund and find a space for a student center?

It was hard. We met with many board members and city people,
but the response was always the same: "We really admire your hard
work and dedication, but we just don't have the money in the

budget." There was no money to fund such a large program. However, while we were meeting with all these people, other people were discussing this same issue of inequity at the school. There was already a plan on the table for a Student Learning Center (SLC). We met with some of the folks planning the SLC and told them about our proposal for the EOP. We finally realized that we were not connected with the school site enough to have our proposal taken seriously, so we collaborated with the SLC and got many of our ideas implemented within the center.

I honestly believe that students know what they need the most. If they are able to use their voice and get what they want, then it adds so much to the culture. It's a personal thing that students take seriously because they worked for it, they were a part of building it. So they won't destroy it, but will work to protect and improve it. And that's why student voice is so important. Without the voice of students, schools serve no purpose. They are nothing but institutions where adults run and tell you what you need to know in order to continue this tradition of "we have master's degrees and we know what's best for you, so just shut up and deal with it."

Finding Myself

Jamie E. McMaryion

If I could go back and do high school all over again, the only thing I would probably change would be my academic status. I didn't do very well in my studies, but I managed to defeat the system by graduating anyway. But academics weren't the only problem. If I could have focused enough without outside distractions, I could have graduated top league. But the school needed me to fit in, and that held me back and caused a lot of emotional and mental problems. I felt the need to be accepted in every social group but was rejected most of the time.

Berkeley High is segregated by race and class. Matter of fact, it is so segregated that its broken-up parts are labeled. For instance, there are three major social and racially defined parts of Berkeley

High. First, there are the "slopes," where all the popular black kids who wore all the latest clothes (also known by my friends as the "Puffets") hung out. They never accepted anyone unless they could talk a lot of trash about people who didn't fit their criteria (me) and looked good through their eyes. I never fit the description. Then there were the Community Theater steps, otherwise known as the "senior steps." The senior steps were supposed to be for all seniors, no matter what size, shape, or color. Well, it didn't quite happen like that. They were all predominantly white—not the "cool Berkeley hippie" white, but the drive-BMW/Benz, live-in-the-hills white people. They were cool sometimes, but usually on specific terms—those who got straight A's, took all AP classes, and could pass for white (physically, meaning you almost looked white with the lightest skin, straightest long hair and greenish eyes, and economically, meaning your parents owned a house in the hills or drove one of the Ivy League cars). My application for their social club was rejected . . . despite affirmative action.

Near the G&H Building [all BHS buildings have letter names] was a wall of steps. That's where most of the Latino students hung out. They usually stayed to themselves and were usually nice to everyone. The only thing was they were all mostly in some kind of territorial war. So basically if you were okay with getting beat up on every other day, then you were in. I'm from Compton, California. I've done my share of living the hard life, and I really don't want to have to do it again.

I was a lost soul most of my first two years at Berkeley High. I didn't feel quite secure in the group of people I hung out with. There was always that little bit of insecurity lingering in the back of my mind. I never felt like I had the right clothes, lived in the right neighborhood, or drove the right car. My mom was a single parent of two teenagers, in and out of a job, and most of the time living off of the government. That was embarrassing.

I tried to find other outlets—things that forced me to not focus on all of the pain I was letting them cause me. I began to cut class to not have to face them. Then I began to experiment with smoking marijuana. It was a nice temporary escape, but it never really made it go away. It just made me permanently tired and irritated. Soon I became bored of not doing anything (plus the threat of possibly not graduating), so I began to write and take classes that better stimulated my intellect. I soon acquired a taste for politics and my culture, so I began to seek things that fulfilled that appetite. I got involved in more community-based activities, such as Students for Jericho. Although I despised Berkeley High at the time, I began working with the Diversity Project, which focused on trying to better the school (why should someone else have to go through what I went through?).

More politically and culturally focused programs and events began to grab my attention. I soon forgot about all the other problems that had haunted me before and instead began to love myself. I began to love myself for my dedication to my community and my new-found love for my culture. It also allowed me to let other people love me and allowed me to love other people. I also learned that it's not what people think of you, it's what you think of yourself. Instead of trying to be accepted by other people, I had to accept myself first. After awhile, I finally found a nice group of people who were willing to help me do so. It's been almost three years since I've been out of school, and I still am very good friends with them.

Fighting the Symptoms of a Larger Disease

Shabnam Piryaei

I walked through the cemented area littered with picnic tables, where once the B Building stood [before being gutted by an arson fire in April 2000]. Four years ago, this place seemed giant, and now I was staring through the remnants of the library, the principal's office, the entire ESL department. It's a strange feeling to suddenly feel disengaged from something you once felt so integrated into. And I say *something* and not *somewhere* because Berkeley High School isn't simply a location, it's a living system. It's a microcosm of the racial, political, economic, and social dynamics that thread the fabric of reality. And perhaps that's why it gets such a bad rap. The fourteen-year-olds entering that school are suddenly engulfed in one of the most raw organisms reflective of their anticipated reality. And reality is flourishing with imperfections.

It's bizarre to think that this system goes on after you've left and existed well before you were born. Here I was, walking the same route I'd walked multitudes of times before, and I couldn't recognize a single face or find any of my old teachers. It had been only a year and a half since I'd graduated, and yet I felt completely removed from this system that was once an integral part of my identity. Unexpectedly, I found myself tearing up with . . . nostalgia? How humiliating, I thought. I stood in the girls' bathroom alone, and suddenly realized how connected I felt with my experiences at Berkeley High.

I think I first saw a flyer for the Diversity Project in the Daily Bulletin, a page worth of announcements that were supposed, but often failed, to be read in class. Diversity was one of the key reasons that I left my high school in Pleasant Hill, California, after my freshman year. My parents immigrated with me from Iran after participating in the 1979 revolution, and at a generally apolitical and uniformly white College Park High School, I felt completely stifled. *Diversity* was the inviting term that lured me to that first meeting. From the beginning, the Diversity Project provided me with teachers, not like I'd ever experienced before. At these meetings I met kids my own age, or perhaps a few years older, who were accomplishing things in the community that I had only argued about. This was to be the beginning of my lesson on organizing, activism, and the barriers that accompany this struggle, a fight that is so poignant and difficult for high school youth.

It was during my junior year at Berkeley High, and my second year with the Diversity Project, that I learned my biggest lesson. It was the first time that I had been so marginalized and exploited. *So this is what it feels like,* I thought. Perhaps it was then that I felt the reality of my role in the movement and the role of my entire generation of youth. It was the first time that I felt so strongly the barriers against a change that my parents always taught me was necessary. And yet, who was I to complain? Yeah, I was an immigrant, and I definitely had my share of difficulties. My parents divorced just as I entered Berkeley High School, and our financial situation was always a tangible burden, but I had experienced the luxury of parents who have time and resources for their children. I had the luxury of falling on the higher-track classes in a school flourishing with the mirrored inequities of society.

The Diversity Project in its third year had become a more formal project, as representatives of the three-thousand-student population were "chosen" to give voice to the students of the school. It was well meaning, I'm sure. Clearly the blatant racial and academic disparities were viewed as problematic; however, this inequity within the school was analyzed as if in a vacuum. The disparity in the school was viewed only in the context of the school itself. The Diversity Project had essentially set out to solve the deeply sociologically ingrained problems of racism, stratification, and stigma without viewing them all as greater problems that couldn't be solved when isolated within the boundaries of a school, and couldn't be solved when students had only a fraction of the decision-making power, if any at all.

It was during this year that Berkeley High School was to be accredited, and suddenly we were essentially given tasks by the school administration, specifically the principal, and it was within this realm that we were free to exercise our creativity and leadership skills. It wasn't until after they stopped giving us tasks to fulfill, and in fact decided that the student portion of the Diversity Project would be eliminated, that we discovered other student organizations that had been tediously organizing against the unequal structure and had much more to show for it. These other organizations created their own youth-oriented agendas and had in fact been battling with the very administration that had constructed our programs.

Perhaps it was more difficult for the students of the Diversity Project to see through the administration's agenda, because so many of the teachers who we worked through were intensely motivated and understood the context of Berkeley High School's severe racial disparities. However, they were also simply another section of the project, and it wasn't until well into the year that I realized that for the administration, our task was mostly in our name.

And so now what? Was I disheartened at social change? Did I never again work within the sphere of a youth organization? Definitely not. If anything, Berkeley High prepared me for a reality that defines the existence of so many organizers and too many people of color at Berkeley High School. And through our own initiative, the student portion of the Diversity Project participated in a statewide youth conference on student voice, presented forums regarding social and political issues, and eventually created a solidarity group with other active student organizations on campus. Although Berkeley High School for me transcends just this experience, it's impossible to summarize my entire social system and all of the profound experiences within it. I do know that this complex system is going on well after we've left, as students and teachers continue to resist and organize to fight a socially ingrained symptom of a disease not unique to Berkeley High.

My Life on the Board of Education

Niles Xi'an Lichtenstein

In a school of three thousand students, Berkeley High offers the unique opportunity to develop individual political ideologies. The downside of having such an enormous academic and social environment is that there is often no place to give physical form to these ideas. In other words, the opinions and views of students are perpetually trapped beneath the surface waiting for some sort of break in the thick layer of apathy, anonymity, and structural complexity (that is, the web of administration and bureaucracy). I became involved in school reform campaigns from freshman year until the present. I first got involved with the Asian Pacific Islander Cultural festival. Although cultural events do not directly affect the resources of a school, they do create a culture and presence of understanding and organizing. They are key to any school reform effort. To understand the cultural context of our own lives allows us to bond together on more immediate and necessary platforms.

So I got involved with Youth Together freshman year and continued through to senior year. My three years of organizing with Youth Together was a good base, but I learned the most about student involvement and activity when I was on the board of education.

What did I learn? If you are part of the bureaucracy, then there are a lot fewer hoops to jump through in order to have access to resources or get a plan approved. Basically, I had more clout than ever before. If I wanted to call a meeting with someone, I did, and everyone arrived (on Berkeley time, of course). I was able to tap into all facets of the school, from the hills parents to the flats parents, and being diplomatic, I was able to learn about what their motives were, where they were aiming to gain resources, and what they were going to use them for.

I also had the advantage of being approached by people. People all over were more than willing to share their views and ideas, and we know everyone in Berkeley has them. The years before, as just a student organizer, I would have to track people down and ask them about their views, ideas, whether this idea would work, and so on. As a board rep, people, principals, district staff, teachers, parents, and students offered that information freely.

At times this radical change upset me, because it told me that what youth have to say isn't as relevant to adults unless that youth is given an official title. This was a major difference. The funny part is that the insight of youth probably had the most relevance in all the situations that I was confronted with at board meetings. The example I like to use most happened when I had just joined the board. Over the summer, the district hired a consultant, and most likely paid him pretty well. After examining the school, he issued an official report summing up his recommendations. After reading it, I laughed. It was ironic that they paid him money to tell them everything I, or any other student, could have told them if they had asked.

I also learned the importance of good organizing techniques and how to compile a presentation with appropriate voice and sufficient information. In other words, students weren't listened to because most of their presentations were based on purely subjective opinion. What people want to hear is "expert opinion" and facts. Unfortunately, students have limited access to these so-called experts and the general resources needed to back a powerful presentation. My theory is if you give kids who are interested in reforming the school even $100,000 and give them access to resources, they could produce an excellent program, whether it is mentoring, tutoring, or something else. Not only is student insight so vital to a good program, but students also have incredible public relations skills. Have you ever been to a BHS party that was announced just that afternoon? By night, three hundred people are trying to crowd into a house.

All the programs I've seen go through the high school lack the student buy-in necessary. The district and community are too scared to push students; we hold them to such a low standard sometimes that we miss out on so much potential. I still am a diehard advocate of a community service requirement that would force students into a four-year, rollover-mentoring program. So students need an outlet, they need respect, they need resources, they need to be pushed or given the accountability, and they need leaders.

Leaders are something we lack at Berkeley High. Our principal is always in the shadows. People don't even know the face of the principal and have very little contact with him (a lot of them thought he was a security guard). Don't get me wrong, he is doing a good job and has a lot on his plate, but we need leaders. We need a head of leadership who will inspire students. We need good teachers who don't leave after a few years. Students have no examples to follow. The Civil Rights Movement has the glimmer of a ghost in the history of Berkeley High. Legend only shines so bright, and though we are dealing with some of the same problems as thirty years ago, the problems aren't as in our face. Students aren't taught how to organize, and the structural enormity frightens students who have no previous experience in dealing with authority.

Just as another observation, all the programs at Berkeley High are instituted too fast. They hit the ground running, yet the programs lack the endurance to keep up the pace necessary to survive.

Among students and staff, organization and planning are often the crippling point.

The profile of most student organizers are kids who are going to college. A lot of times these kids don't suffer from the problems that they are organizing around, and so that flame, that passion that is needed to amend these problems, isn't there. It is always ironic that the ones who need the most help don't have the push or the resources to organize, and those who do possess the time or resources often see organizing as a chapter in their lives and lack the internal motivation.

As the student board member, I couldn't represent everyone. The most important lesson I wish I had learned earlier was don't worry about image (I saw a lot of egos get in the way of things in the district), don't feel like you have to take on everything, just focus on one idea to help the school and let that be your personal project, and organize with all your heart. Like they say, it is better to do one thing really well than a bunch of things not so well. Berkeley High is tired of things done not so well.

I always say Berkeley High cannot be seen as an institution to correct; it needs to be seen as a being to nurture—a being that reflects students who are all anxious to learn and do well—they are just waiting for an environment that is anxious to teach them. There is so much potential at this school, but we need to feel like a community first, before we organize together. Often groups get together on the sole basis of an idea to organize around. It is good to have a platform, but don't forget the humans who are doing the work. Humans should get to know each other well before they take on a project. We have the perfect pieces for community; we are just looking for the proper places for those pieces to create that common unity.

Conclusion

"*Get Involved!*" was the opening statement on one of the Student Outreach recruitment flyers. Yet involving Berkeley High students in equity-based research and change was a challenge in a number of ways and for a variety of reasons. First, Berkeley High students are a diverse and dynamic population that cannot be understood or represented as a single, monolithic body with a common experience and perspective. Moreover, within a culture of racial and class-based separation and inequity, "the" student voice of Berkeley High is often characterized by the experiences and perspectives of those who are most engaged and successful, predominantly white and middle-class students. This not only discourages the involvement of students of color, immigrant students, and poorer students, but also perpetuates the privilege of certain students and certain student interests. Also, with few avenues and resources for students to consider their own agency and to learn about how schools change, mobilizing and energizing students to participate as change agents proved to be difficult. In fact, some of the most powerful lessons the students learned were less about change and more about how schools manage to stay the same (Silva, 2002).

Still, within Student Outreach and similar student inquiry and organizing efforts, students also learned to value their voices and opinions and to use them to advocate for themselves and their peers. In demanding a seat at the planning table, they challenged the conventional notion that students are passive receptors of education and that only the finest few can rise to the powerful echelons of decision making. These students demanded not only to be heard, but to be acknowledged as active and creative members of the school community. Set within the context of equity-based efforts, these students not only came to understand the meaning and significance of having a voice and asserting their own agency, but also came to recognize the tremendous gaps in voice and agency that they could not fill.

The essays in this chapter are primarily by students who represent a certain level of academic and social success at Berkeley High. These are the students who are still in contact with me and with other members of the Diversity Project. Yet they are also diverse in many ways and offer a glimpse of student life at Berkeley High. They express frustration with the school's efforts and their own attempts to understand and negotiate student diversity. Jimmy and Jamie poignantly describe their struggles to define and validate their racial and class identities, simultaneously trying to fit in and resist being stereotyped. As Jamie finds herself rejected from various social circles, without "the right" clothes, hair, or attitude, Jimmy resists falling into one of the two prevalent Asian American type-casts at Berkeley High, instead defining himself as "neither." Nabila writes of a similar journey, as she responds to "a craving in me to exist in a place where I could truly be myself, even though I didn't know who 'I' was."

Nabila continues by giving us a sense of how complicated adolescent student life can be: "It was difficult trying to be young, do well in school, live life, and be a freedom fighter at the same time." And yet this web of identity, responsibility, and purpose is also what the students express as important and meaningful to them. Shabnam remarks on the profound realization that she is part of something much bigger than herself, a "complex system . . . that goes on after you've left, and existed well before you were born." She goes on to explain the significance of learning lessons on "organizing, activism, and the barriers that accompany this struggle," a struggle that students recognize as difficult but also valuable and necessary.

Joey describes his process of negotiating a voice and carving out a space for himself within the Student Outreach group. It is a difficult process, he admits, but one that taught him many lessons about bureaucracy, change, and the compelling support of "working together with others for a common cause." Ultimately it is this kind of challenging and common purpose that the students seem to seek, although opportunities for such are neither frequent nor widespread. How could more students experience this in their schools? Niles offers a straightforward recipe for Berkeley High: "Students need an outlet, they need respect, they need resources, they need to be pushed or given the accountability, and they need leaders." Added to this is the encouragement and incentive for students to care about their school, and the space, both cultural and structural, for students to participate. Pam poses a simple question to suggest that the inclusion of students in school change would benefit the institution as much as the students. "How could a discussion about student achievement and educational inequity happen without the voice of the students?" she asks, and then continues: "In any type of real change within a system, the voice of the people who are directly affected must be a part of the solution."

These students' essays demonstrate how complex and diverse student experience can be at Berkeley High. Yet their words demand attention not only to their own experiences as Berkeley High students, but also to the perspectives of students who are missing from this chapter. Indeed, attention to who is served and who is ignored, who is heard and who is silenced is one of the primary lessons to be learned from these students and the Student Outreach experience. As researchers, teachers, and students, we must remind ourselves that it is simple only in theory to extend power to the least powerful, to give voice to those who feel silenced, and to provoke the participation of those closest to dropping out altogether.

Particularly at a school struggling to overcome a tradition of racial and class inequality and division, more is needed than a philosophical commitment to democratic decision making and student participation. A school must do more than preach platitudes about the importance of student involvement and youth voice. It must go further, even, than creating opportunities for students to melt into the traditional model of adult-generated, adult-driven reforms. If Berkeley High wants all of its students to engage and achieve in school, it will have to build a structure and a culture that fosters the voice and participation of all of its students. While it is clear that students at BHS can and do contribute to Berkeley High's problems, it is equally important to acknowledge that the activity and voice of students can also have an impact on the school in positive ways. They need not only adults and peers to model positive behavior and relationships, but also the opportunities and encouragement to develop these behaviors and relationships within school.

Notes

1. From a poem written by Niles Xi'an Lichtenstein, published in "Conscious Seed," a special insert of Berkeley High's student newspaper, 1999.

2. Youth Together, a collaboration of five community-based organizations working in five high schools in the Bay Area to reduce racial conflict and violence, had recently organized a diverse group of Berkeley High students to lead a youth-driven school change campaign at Berkeley High. Youth Together and Student Outreach had similar goals and some parallel efforts, and during the 1999–2000 school year, they combined efforts to form a collective student group called Youth-N-Vision. The students writing pieces for this chapter participated in Student Outreach, Youth Together, and/or a combination of the two groups. The Leadership class occasionally tried to inform school improvement efforts, at one point drafting a proposal to improve schoolwide communication. Yet with the responsibility of planning and hosting major student events (homecoming, prom, graduation) and the reputation that this was the type of work Leadership engaged in, these efforts were limited and mostly short-lived.

3. Berkeley High had been receiving significant criticism for its failures to address persistent inequities and its inability or unwillingness to involve all stakeholders, including students, in the planning and change process. Inviting Student Outreach into the process ensured a certain level of student participation in the process.

4. Developed and published as a part of the Annenberg Challenge, *The Lingo* is a short introduction to school reform vocabulary. Written by Kathleen Cushman, it includes clear and easy definitions to such terms as "cycle of inquiry," "authentic assessment," and "stakeholders." For a copy, see http://www.annenberg institute.org/Challenge/pubs/Lingo/LINGO/contents.html.

5. The Student Learning Center was developed from a proposal by Youth Together students, several BHS teachers, as well as support from the Diversity Project.

Conclusion

LESSONS LEARNED

The Limits and Possibilities of Using Research to Counter Racial Inequality

Pedro A. Noguera

The Diversity Project undertook its work with the explicit goal of using research to initiate a reform process that would begin to close the achievement gap between students of color and affluent white students and that would lead to greater equity at Berkeley High School. But long before the project came to a formal end, it had become clear that our efforts would not bring about the decisive results we had hoped for. This is not because we failed to work hard enough or because we gave up too soon. It is not even an admission that such changes are impossible. Rather, the inability of our concerted efforts to produce lasting changes at Berkeley High School that would raise minority student achievement, reduce disparities in student performance and outcomes, and create a more equitable school structure and culture is due to the weakness of the theory of change that guided our work (Connell, 1995) and our failure to anticipate the ways in which certain features of the school would make change difficult to bring about.

From the outset, we understood that research and the presentation of findings would not be sufficient to prompt changes at the school. For years, data showing wide disparities in the academic performance of white students and students of color were available and widely discussed at the school. While our research succeeded in identifying the factors that contributed to the disparities and in keeping the issue at the center of the school community's attention for a sustained period of time, the basic patterns and issues we identified were by no means new or unfamiliar. The project's research illuminated how seemingly neutral structures at the school reproduced patterns of inequality, and it showed what kinds of changes were needed to ameliorate these inequities, but it could not and did not succeed in bringing about the changes. Perhaps most important, the project's research has been used as a tool by African American and Latino parents from Parents of Children of African Descent (PCAD) and Berkeley Organizing Congregations for Action (BOCA) to ensure that efforts to promote equity at the school are not abandoned.

It is also true that others outside Berkeley who share our concerns about racial inequality in education and who are engaged in similar efforts have been able to make use of the research we produced. Eight dissertations have been written on various aspects of the project's research, and there have been numerous papers written and presentations made at local, regional, and national conferences. In fact, we decided to write this book about the project's work in the hope that others might learn from it and be moved to apply some of the lessons learned to enhance the effectiveness of their own work. Despite all of this, we are compelled to acknowledge that the Diversity Project was always more than a research initiative, because it was undertaken to prompt organizing for change and reform. For this reason, we humbly acknowledge that we did not accomplish what we set out to do.

What went wrong? Was there some crucial flaw in our thinking and planning that might explain this failure? More important, could we have approached the work differently and thereby achieved more promising results?

The simple answer to these questions is yes, but the crucial flaw was not what many radical academics might regard as a failure to understand the source of educational inequality. Several scholars (Bowles and Gintis, 1976; Willis, 1981; Anyon, 1997; Rothstein, 2004) have argued that the reproduction of inequality in schools is merely a manifestation of a larger process at work in society. According to this view, school reforms that lead to greater equity are impossible to achieve until efforts to address social inequality in the larger society are undertaken. The capitalist economy of the United States operates on the premise of inequality between classes and groups; there will always be far more workers than owners and far more people who are poor than rich. Proponents of this perspective contend that the educational system serves as a means to rationalize and justify these social arrangements, as in the belief that the poor are poor because they did poorly in school and have not "earned" the right to obtain greater status and wealth (Bowles and Gintis, 1976). Under the cover of a pseudo-meritocracy—a system in which status is determined by effort and merit—education is used to make the inequality that is intrinsic within a capitalist system appear natural and warranted.

In additional, unlike many other democratic capitalist nations that have well-developed social welfare systems, poor people in the United States often lack basic services (such as health care, child care, or housing assistance), and the degree of inequality in American society is greater (Danzinger and Gottschalk, 1993). Poor children, many of whom are children of color, are disproportionately enrolled in schools that have access to fewer resources (both human and material), and because many of their basic needs are not met, the two conditions contribute to lower academic performance. Richard Rothstein, author of *Class and Schools* (2004), makes this argument in particularly compelling terms: "The influence of social class characteristics is probably so powerful that schools cannot overcome it, no matter how well trained are their teachers and no matter how well designed are their instructional programs and climates" (p. 6).

While it is hard to argue with the points raised by Rothstein and others, we take issue with his pessimism related to possibilities for school change or the likelihood that education can be used to counter inequality. The Diversity Project undertook its work because we genuinely believed that it is possible to create a school

that is more equitable—a place where race and class do not determine or predict academic outcomes.

Our optimism is not rooted in some naive notion that Berkeley
is a special place—more just and fair than others—or that collective will and effort alone can counter the larger forces of inequality
in society. Rather, it is based on the concrete experience of knowing
students who have come from disadvantaged circumstances but
who have managed to excel academically and beat the odds. It also
comes from working with teachers who are so talented and committed that they manage to find ways to enable their students to
achieve well beyond the expectations that others hold for them
based on their race and class. Finally, our optimism is based on the
knowledge that a small but significant and growing number of
schools have found ways to successfully educate low-income students of color, and their existence serves as yet another source of
proof that something can be done to bring about change, even
without the broader and more fundamental reforms in society that
are certainly needed.

Nonetheless, despite the optimism that led us to believe that
Berkeley High School could be a place where racial disparities
in achievement could be reduced through school change, we did not
achieve our goals at the school. Wide disparities in academic performance remain, and the school is still polarized, racially divided, and
fundamentally unequal. In the remaining pages of this book, I will
discuss two unforeseen obstacles that thwarted our efforts and also
identify the flaws in our strategy. I do so in the hope that others will
learn from our mistakes and find ways to avoid them in the future.

Organizational Dysfunction and Lack of Leadership

From 1996 to 2002, five different principals or coprincipals served
as the leaders of Berkeley High School (during 2001–2002, the
school was led by two coprincipals). With each change in leadership, the school experienced a change in direction, a new set of

priorities, and a disruption in its efforts to address equity issues. All of the leaders expressed support for the work and goals of the Diversity Project, but the transition from one leader to another was always accompanied by changes in key personnel and the adoption of a new plan for the school. While changes in leadership are common to many schools, the frequency of changes in leadership at BHS was a sign of larger underlying problems in the school itself.

One of these underlying problems was staff morale, which during the years we worked at BHS was very low and has been a problem at the school for many years. The reasons for low morale varied, but several obvious factors undoubtedly contributed to the problem. For example, many basic operations at the school, from copy machines to rest rooms, did not work on a regular basis. Graffiti covered the walls in several parts of the school, and from 1996 on, major portions of the physical plant were under construction. During the 1998–2000 academic years, dozens of fires were reported at the school, one of them so severe that the central administration building was destroyed (Maran, 2000; Wing, 2002). Although the culprit was never discovered, there was widespread speculation that the arsonist was a school employee, since some of the fires were started in areas of the school to which students could not gain access.

Amid so much turmoil and upheaval, it was difficult to keep the school focused on efforts to address equity. With many of the staff concerned about the basic operation of the school, maintaining efforts to address achievement at the school was difficult.

In addition to all of these problems, BHS is a large school with over three thousand students, and during the years we worked there, its enrollment climbed steadily at a time when less classroom space was available due to construction and the big fire. Discipline problems such as class cutting, fights, and numerous conflicts between students and teachers, described in detail in Chapter Three, added to the sense of chaos that often prevailed. On several occasions, we were forced to realize that efforts to promote equity and achievement had to take a back seat to the effort to establish calm and order.

The Diversity Project was aware that instability in leadership posed a major obstacle to the changes we hoped to bring about, and at various times we sought to assist the school's leadership in addressing the larger organizational issues. However, these efforts to provide support and to work collaboratively with the leadership created another problem: we became overly identified with the leadership of the school. In a school where teachers and administrators were often at odds, this became a substantial obstacle to our work.

Conflict versus Collaboration in the School Reform Process

From the start, the Diversity Project sought to blur the lines that typically separate researchers from those who are the subjects of their research. We did this to avoid some of the suspicion and distrust that often characterizes relations between researchers and schools, and because we hoped it would lead to greater willingness to support the findings generated from the research. To accomplish this, teachers, administrators, students, parents, and other staff were consciously included in every aspect of our work. After the first year, the project was led by one university researcher (myself); one BHS administrator and former teacher, James Williams; and in year 3, teacher LaShawn Routé-Chatmon became a third codirector. In addition, five teachers served on the core team of the project, and they each received one period of release time so that they could participate fully in the work. Through this type of collaborative leadership structure, we hoped to increase the likelihood of soliciting the participation from the school staff in our work and decrease the sense that they were being studied by university-based researchers.

Our approach largely succeeded. Over the four years, scores of teachers collaborated in the project on research teams, participated in workshops, opened their classroom doors to project members who were shadowing students, brought their classes to participate in the project's class of 2000 Internet survey, and attended seminars and professional development workshops that we sponsored.

However, our approach created another set of unanticipated problems. The theory of change guiding our work was based on the naive assumption that when school staff, district leaders, and the broader community were made aware of the ways in which the school was shortchanging certain students by denying them educational opportunities, they would be willing to support changes to make the school more equitable. As we showed in Chapter Five in the discussion and analysis of our efforts to organize parents, it took us awhile to realize that good intentions could not be assumed.

In retrospect, it is surprising that we did not anticipate more opposition to our efforts. Though blatantly inequitable, the status quo at BHS had long served the interests of affluent white students. The reason that 12 percent of the class of 2000 students entering BHS in the ninth grade came from private middle schools is that the high school offered these students an education that was as good as, or even better than, that of many private schools in the area. With numerous honors and Advanced Placement courses, a rich array of electives (including German, Latin, computer science, and outstanding visual and performing arts), and extracurricular activities (including crew, fencing, jazz band, and an award-winning student newspaper), BHS had an established reputation as a school that offered an enriched learning environment and supported academic excellence. That over half the students at the school were not well served had for years been overshadowed by the excellent service the school provided to its most privileged students.

For the parents of students who had been successful at BHS, the Diversity Project's efforts to close the achievement gap by initiating reforms that would expand educational opportunities for students of color were perceived by some as threatening. During the first few years of our work, our efforts drew little opposition. One active parent leader did voice opposition to the Parent Resource Center we helped to establish in the fall of 1999, saying, "I don't need a center; all I need is someone to pick up a phone when I call." But active opposition to the recommendations we issued for changes at the school did not emerge until the last two years of the project's work, when groups like Parents of Children of African Descent (PCAD) and the predominantly Latino Berkeley Organizing Congregations for Action (BOCA) began organizing for major organizational changes, such as the conversion of the large high school into small, autonomous, equitable schools sharing the campus. It was at this stage when recommendations for change were being considered that the imbalance in power between low-income parents of color and affluent white parents became more apparent.

Among BHS staff, opposition to our efforts was muted for most of the first four years. It was not until we began putting forward recommendations for change that required those who taught honors courses to open them up to students of color that some teachers began to actively oppose our work. While the politically correct culture of Berkeley made it difficult for these individuals to state openly that they did not want these students in their classes, they were able to couch their opposition to some of our recommendations as a defense of academic excellence and high standards.

For example, after our first year of research, we showed teachers how ninth-grade math placement influenced the experience of students at BHS and ultimately had great bearing on college eligibility and admissions, as described in Chapter One. Our data showed that African American students, particularly those who came from outside the school district (Oakland and Richmond), were being channeled disproportionately into low-tracked Math A (prealgebra) courses without any assessment of their skills and that these students were overwhelmingly experiencing failure. Our data showed that students who failed the first semester of ninth-grade math (in the fall of 1996, over 50 percent of the students who took Math A failed the course) were highly unlikely to complete the math course sequence needed to be eligible for admission to California state universities.

Although no one disputed the data, considerable opposition was generated over the recommendation that prealgebra be eliminated or offered in the summer for incoming ninth graders who were perceived as needing more preparation. We recommended that the lower-level course be eliminated and that all entering ninth-grade students be enrolled in algebra with academic supports, or, if they were ready, placed into a higher-level math course. We also recommended that the school double the number of math and science courses that students were required to take in order to graduate, so that graduation requirements would match the state universities' entrance requirements. At the time of our research, BHS students were required to complete two years of math and two years of science before graduating. We recommended that the requirement be raised to four years of each subject to match the University of California and California State University admissions requirement.

Both recommendations met fierce opposition from math teachers, even from some whom we thought were sympathetic to our efforts to promote equity at the school. Some seemed to be genuinely concerned that placing students with weak skills in more rigorous courses would be setting students up for failure. Others seemed more bothered that they would have to teach low-achieving ninth-grade students at all. For many teachers, Math A was regarded as an undesirable course because African American ninth graders were regarded as immature and more disruptive than other students. For this reason, Math A courses were typically assigned to the newest and least experienced teachers, while veteran teachers were assigned the higher-level math courses. By expanding access to algebra, a larger number of veteran teachers would have to teach ninth graders. Again, opponents of the recommendation to expand access did not come out and say that they did not want to teach these students. Instead, they framed their opposition as concern for the well-being of students who were likely to fail, even as we pointed out that they were failing already.

This example and several others like it revealed the limitations of using collaboration as a means to reform BHS. To be fair, our desire to collaborate and minimize conflict was in part strategic. We understood that forcing the staff to implement reforms through a top-down approach was unlikely to lead to success. We hoped that our research would effectively make the case that change was needed, and once teachers understood how students were being shortchanged, they would support efforts to change practices and policies that contributed to failure. In many cases, but not always, this strategy worked, and eventually we came to the realization that if the educators would not embrace equity, we would have to find ways to force the issue, even if that meant generating conflict. We came to this realization because we understood that ultimately, issues pertaining to equity in education are a form of educational rights and social justice, and not a matter of professional prerogative.

Recommendations for Change

At the end of each year, the Diversity Project made recommendations to the high school community. Some of these, such as the creation of a center for parents and the development of a strategic plan, were adopted right away. However, it was in June 2000 that the Diversity Project presented its most important findings and final recommendations to the Berkeley School Board and to the high school community. Interestingly, the school board unanimously endorsed the report's findings and made a verbal commitment to continue to work for equity at Berkeley High. Some of the project's recommendations, such as the expansion of the Student Learning Center, were implemented during the following year. However, many recommendations were ignored or only partially implemented, while others continued to serve as organizing issues that were taken up by staff, parents, or students in years to come.

Although many of these policies were not adopted, we present them here in the hope that some of them may be applicable to other high schools and school districts. The recommendations represent a combination of ideas intended to alter policy and practice to further broader goals of educational equity. Following is a selection of recommendations that arise out of the chapters of this book.

Take Steps to Close the Education Gap

- Eliminate curriculum choices that permit, and often encourage, some students to leave high school unprepared for college or without the skills and credentials to secure living-wage jobs (Wing, 2003). For example, many students chose to fill their schedules with easy classes that carried high school graduation credit (such as proctoring, PE, art), but left no room in their schedules for classes required for university admission or for classes that would teach them to think critically, write well, plan projects, or solve mathematical problems as required for good jobs in this age of communications and technology.

- Adopt a mentor program to provide advisers and advocates inside and outside school for students in need.

- Align high school graduation requirements with UC and CSU admissions requirements, so that a greater number of Berkeley High graduates are prepared for college and for well-paying work (Wing, 2003).

- Adopt an advisory system to provide more students, especially ninth graders, with greater access to adult advice about course selection, study skills, and plans after graduation. Adopt a specially designed freshman advisory system in the ninth-grade core to reduce alienation and the large number of ninth-grade students who get lost and fall behind academically. This will require teachers to be trained to serve as advisers in extended homeroom periods. Use the existing small number of guidance counselors to provide training for teachers on counseling.

- Ensure that effective and highly qualified teachers are assigned to teach students who are most in need, including in remedial, English Language Learner, and Special Education courses. This also includes ninth-grade courses and entry-level math courses.

- Provide opportunities for individual attention and acceleration for students who are behind so that they can catch up with graduation and college entrance requirements. Tutorial programs that make use of college students and adult volunteers can provide these services.

- Support the development of smaller schools or schools-within-schools to create a more personalized learning environment. Each of these smaller learning communities should reflect the race and class makeup of the school and provide a rigorous and academically enriched curriculum for all students.

- Develop a system for collecting and analyzing discipline data in order to institute early intervention to support students and teachers who are frequently involved in incidents that require disciplinary measures.

- Establish needs assessment procedures in on-campus suspension (OCS) that identify students' academic needs and underlying learning, social, or emotional issues that may be related to behavioral problems. OCS could then link these students to appropriate services.

- Conduct ongoing, substantive professional development and team building for school safety officers, teachers, administrators, and school staff to improve understanding of the relationship among achievement, discipline, race, and gender.

- Provide ongoing professional development for teachers in the area of cross-cultural teaching, culturally relevant pedagogy, and the use of culturally relevant materials in the curriculum.

- Involve BHS faculty who possess expertise in multicultural education in the design and implementation of schoolwide professional development services.

- Encourage and create opportunities for on-site sharing of best teaching practices and strategies in teaching, through hands-on workshops or structured peer observation.

- Administration must provide instructional support and useful and meaningful feedback to teachers on how to improve their teaching in order to close the achievement gap in their own classrooms.

Work Toward Sustained Involvement of Marginalized Parents

- School administration should provide deliberate and concise communication about the ways parents can be involved in the high school. This should include explicit advice on how to support their students' academic needs and future goals after graduation.
- School leadership should establish a clear system for gathering input, feedback, and suggestions from a broad base of parents on how to improve the school and make it more responsive to the needs of their students.
- The entire high school community should support the creation of a new, inclusive parent organization focused on the pressing issues of access to the best-quality teachers and curriculum and to equity in student achievement outcomes.

Enhance Student Learning and Participation

- Find ways to include meaningful student input in all school reforms.
- Support bridge programs for middle school students and families. This should include an orientation program for entering first-year students and families and a formal process for induction of new students into the school.
- Support the involvement of community-based organizations and individuals in developing and guiding college and career days, mentorships, and more comprehensive service-learning within and beyond the school walls.
- Develop and strengthen networks of academic and personal support for students, including personalized smaller learning communities, expansion of the Student Learning Center, and other affirming learning spaces with positive adult leadership.

Unfinished Business: The Struggle Continues

Although the Diversity Project formally came to an end in June 2002, the effort to close the achievement gap and advance educational equity at Berkeley High School continues. As we pointed out in the Introduction, in 1999 Berkeley joined a national consortium, Minority Student Achievement Network (MSAN), in an effort to learn from and garner support from school districts with similar demographic characteristics. The fifteen school districts that founded MSAN have supported research, similar to that carried out by the Diversity Project, to understand the factors that contribute to disparities in student achievement. Although MSAN has not been particularly effective at achieving its ambitious goals, its willingness to treat the achievement gap as its central goal has helped to keep national attention on the issue. We hope that Berkeley will remain involved in these types of national initiatives related to race and equity because a great deal can be learned from the experience of similar schools throughout the United States.

There are other reasons to remain optimistic about efforts to support educational equity in Berkeley. The City of Berkeley remains deeply committed to supporting public education by generating community resources for schools at a time when a devastating fiscal crisis in California has resulted in deep cuts in funding for education. The mayor of Berkeley has supported efforts to enlist the private sector in efforts to support students in need in the form of tutoring, health services, and counseling, and the Berkeley Public Education Foundation continues to generate donations to support teachers and recruits volunteers to support the schools.

These initiatives are genuine and serve as yet another indication that Berkeley's progressive values are more than merely platitudes to an ill-defined ideology. While such measures do not level the playing field in education or reduce the degree of racial inequality in the schools, they do provide tangible benefits to all students. Moreover, many of Berkeley's initiatives target the needs of the most disadvantaged children, and that too must be recognized as an authentic sign of commitment to social justice.

Still, Berkeley is not the beacon of hope we imagined it could be when we started our work in 1996. In many respects, it is a lot like the rest of America: deeply divided over issues related to race and class and fundamentally unequal. Yet because there continue to be many teachers and staff, parents, students, and community activists who persist in the belief that Berkeley can and should be a special place that manages to move beyond America's quagmire with regard to race, the basis for hope remains, and for that we all have good reason to feel optimistic about the future.

EPILOGUE: Finishing School

Jabari Mahiri

I am originally from the flatlands of Chicago, and one of the first things I discovered while riding my bicycle in the Berkeley hills was the phenomenon of "false tops." After miles of climbing, I would think I could see the summit, only to realize when I got there that the road merely curved and continued to ascend.

Encounters with false tops also characterized a kind of bicycling that we saw (through extensive research) and sought to change (through numerous projects) in the practices and policies of schooling at Berkeley High. Over time, this institution's development and maintenance of at least two distinct experiences of schooling amounted to widely divergent pathways and cycles of school participation for students, parents, and even teachers. Dual systems for cycling students and others through the schoolplace were key vehicles of the stark disparities in equity and achievement that the Diversity Project research intricately documented and revealed. For some of its students, Berkeley High acted as a kind of finishing school, while for others it posed severe challenges to the very act of finishing school. A widely varying quality of life and learning is typical in bimodal schools like Berkeley High that provide one trajectory of access and academic challenge for affluent, largely white students and quite another for less affluent students, who in this case are predominantly African American and Latino.

Obviously aspects of these disparities reside in the socioeconomic geography of the hills and flats that are similarly contrasted in the North and South sections of Berkeley. Yet as our research repeatedly showed, profound disparities also resided in the structures and cultures of schooling—manifested in the complex interplay of race, ethnicity, and gender, as well as socioeconomic factors.

Cycling in the Berkeley hills yields a dramatic view. While ascending, you can clearly see various sections of the city and how they join and divide. You can see the proximity of Berkeley High to the University of California at Berkeley. At certain turns, you are able to see just how far you have come, and perhaps how far you have to go. The Diversity Project tried to provide the school and community with a similar vantage point. Its comprehensive research gave the school a panoramic view of itself and, like one definition of panorama, a view that continued to unfold and expand.

The Class of 2000 Study formed the centerpiece of this evolving view by providing an increasingly detailed picture of the variety of student experiences from ninth through twelfth grades. This study made explicit the array of factors that contributed to racialized disparities in student achievement. It first identified who the students in the class of 2000 were with respect to racial and ethnic diversity, socioeconomic status, public or private feeder schools, and academic achievement levels as they entered the high school as ninth graders. Next, using annual electronic surveys as well as case studies of a representative sample of the students, it delineated the nature of their varying experiences in the school and how these experiences covaried with achievement, graduation, and dropping out. Importantly, after analyzing the data across four years, this study determined that the patterns of achievement were highly correlated with the specific academic tracks students were placed on in ninth grade and that these patterns grew more distinct over time.

Beginning at the end of the first year of the project, numerous presentations of class of 2000 data and other Diversity Project research findings were made to a variety of stakeholders: the school's staff, the school board, student and parent groups, city leaders, and the university community. These presentations often included students, teachers, and parents speaking out and representing their particular perspectives on the issues of equity and achievement addressed in the research. It should be emphasized that a fundamental tenet of the Diversity Project's research and out-reach activities was to effect high levels of collaboration between people from the school, the university, and the larger community.

The Diversity Project did not want to simply be "in" the school but "of" the school. This tenet was reflected in the project's earliest forms of organization, where the original steering committee (the Core Team) was composed equally of teachers in the school and rep-resentatives from the university, and the Extended Team for research and outreach activities was composed mainly of high school staff, students, and parents who reflected the diversity of the school, in addition to a few graduate students and one or two professors.

The Diversity Project's Parent and Student Outreach commit-tees contributed substantively to principal Theresa Saunders's strategic plan that was adopted for implementation in the 1999–2000 school year. Early on, however, the project's participants began to see how numerous immediate concerns and daily emer-gencies often diverted attention away from attempts at productive change. One of the more interesting concerns in this regard was the short shelf life of principals. During the six years of the project's involvement in the school, principal turnover was a frequent occurrence. From Larry Lee (1996–98), to Theresa Saunders (1998–2000), to Frank Lynch (2000–01), to coprincipals Mary Ann Valles and Laura Leventer (2001–03), new principals arrived every couple of years.

Numerous other factors addressed throughout the book (like the alarming number of fires between 1998 and 2000) contributed to a context for schooling in which instability was the norm. These chaotic conditions affected every student, but the effects were uneven across student groups in that the high-achievement groups were still able to thrive academically, despite the adversities.

Central strategies and beliefs of the Diversity Project also were being tested in their own trials by fire. The core belief was that the project could, in fact, help create contexts and conditions for sys-temic change to close the gaps in equity and achievement. In the words of Pedro Noguera, "We have committed ourselves to setting a context and implementing a process whereby change is imminent and irreversible." The other side of this coin was inscribed with the belief that systematic research was essential to progressive school reform. The hope was that the project's research would have the effect of holding up a mirror to the school to provide an undistorted view of the practices and problems connected to student and school success and failure. If the reality of schooling could be accurately reflected, it was thought, then this reality could eventually be changed.

The transformative value of making highly visible the divergent realities of life and learning in the school proved to be one of the false tops encountered by the project. Some stakeholders looked into the mirrors that the research provided, yet were unable or unwilling to use these views of the school's problems to effect more equitable outcomes. For example, the project's final report in June 2000 presented comprehensive baseline data that the school could use to accurately assess its progress toward increasing achievement for all of its students. The school, however, never really used these data to either stimulate or systematically evaluate any work toward rising above these baselines. Among other things, the 2000 report showed the extreme differences in the frequency and intensity of its discipline procedures for African American students, particularly in comparison to other student groups. It also illustrated direct connections between teaching and learning and discipline, and made specific recommendations for changes in discipline policies and procedures, as well as in the processes and perspectives for teacher professional development with respect to better serving low-achieving students.

The project's belief that research and recommendations would be viable in helping the school change conditions that contributed to student failure did not adequately address how intricately these problems were embedded in the structures and cultures of the school. The problems of student failure not only had complex historical roots; there also were specific interests being served by their perpetuation. For example, parents and some teachers of high-achieving students resisted recommendations to place the most effective teachers and additional resources in classes for students who were furthest behind and wanted to limit detracked, heterogeneous classes to the ninth-grade English/history core only.

Clearly, more equitable change required going beyond the research findings to finding effective ways of changing the interests and perceptions of administrators, teachers, students, and parents who had benefited from the maintenance of the status quo. After its first year of work, then, the project began several capacity-building projects in tangent with its research initiatives. Two outreach committees—one for parents and one for students—were established in 1997, and considerable energy was put into outreach efforts to help effect lasting change. Perhaps most significant, these efforts were realized in a Parent Resource Center at the school, which in turn contributed to ongoing, grassroots parent organizations and movements led by parents of color.

In the project's fifth year, these initiatives evolved during the project's transition from codirectors Pedro Noguera, James Williams, and LaShawn Routé-Chatmon, to a structure where I became a codirector with veteran teacher Dana Moran and graduate student Anne Okahara. The large Extended Team phased out, and a new, small Core Team became the main organizational unit that included two more teachers and five more graduate students. Three of these teachers and graduate students had been integral participants in the Diversity Project since its inception, and all demonstrated deep commitment to working toward equity at Berkeley High School.

The ultimate objective was for the project's work to be sustained by various stakeholders in the school—a kind of passing of the torch. Perhaps the realization of this objective was most apparent in the ongoing work of Parents of Children of African Descent (PCAD), the most authentically parent-driven movement for whole school reform around issues of equity and achievement that I have seen in my work as an educator. Led by African American parents, it used Diversity Project data as well as its own research to forcefully challenge the high school and the entire district to develop ways to effectively change some of its structures and culture of inequality. PCAD supplemented this challenge with its own original strategies and agendas for implementing programs to help bring about systemic change toward greater equity and higher achievement for all Berkeley High School students. Two of these programs were the REBOUND! small school program in spring and summer 2001 to help students who were failing at the end of their first semester of ninth grade to catch up in their grades and school credits, and their leadership in a movement to break up this large high school into a series of more equitable and personalized small schools sharing the Berkeley High campus.

The Diversity Project participated in the Small Schools Exploratory Committee and helped conduct the teacher interviews in conjunction with the Teacher Advisory Committee to inform and help generate faculty, parent, and administrator consensus for restructuring the school into a network of autonomous small schools. Although this effort garnered widespread support from staff and community, it met with resistance, and the plan was never implemented. However, in 2003, the superintendent, district, and Berkeley High took a step toward restructuring by joining the Bay Area Coalition for Equitable Schools network with a commitment to transform half of the high school into small schools-within-a-school by the fall of 2005. In September 2003, the Berkeley School District Board unanimously approved Communication Arts and Sciences as the first of several small schools-within-a-school. Serving approximately 350 students, it reflects the diversity of the larger school and emphasizes a personalized, project-based curriculum with a social justice focus. In September 2004, Community Partnerships Academy became the second small school program, built on the strengths and legacy of the Computer Academy, a long-standing small learning community at Berkeley High. In fall 2005, two more small schools programs began: AHA! (Arts and Humanities Academy, with a focus on integrating academics with visual and performing arts) and the School of Social Justice and Ecology.

Key to the future of Berkeley High is the extent to which these changes in structure can facilitate productive changes in the entire school's culture of teaching and learning with respect to its most underperforming and underserved students.

Conditions for change have been made imminent, but they clearly are not irreversible. This is why the work at Berkeley High is unfinished business. This book (along with several doctoral dissertations) documents the school and the community's vital ascension toward a summit of equity and high achievement for all of its students, along with all the false tops along the way.

References

Adger, C. T., Snow, C., and Christian, D. (eds.). *What Teachers Need to Know About Language*. New York: Delta Systems Company, 2002.

Anyon, J. *Ghetto Schooling: A Political Economy of Urban Educational Reform*. New York: Teachers College Press, 1997.

Ayers, W., Dohrn, B., and Ayers, R. *Zero Tolerance: Resisting the Drive for Punishment in Our Schools*. New York: New Press, 2001.

Berkeley High School Diversity Project. *Berkeley High School Diversity Project: Project Report*. Berkeley, Calif.: BHS Diversity Project, June 1999.

Bernstein, M. "Suburban Schools Feeling the Pressure from NCLB." *Westbury Times*, Mar. 18, 2003, p. 1.

Bourdieu, P. "Cultural Reproduction and Social Reproduction." In J. Karabel and A. H. Halsey (eds.), *Power and Ideology Education*. New York: Oxford University Press, 1977.

Bourdieu, P., and Passeron, J. *Reproduction in Education, Society, and Culture*. Thousand Oaks, Calif.: Sage, 1977.

Bourdieu, P., and Wacquant, L.J.D. *An Invitation to Reflexive Sociology*. Chicago: University of Chicago Press, 1992.

Bowles, S., and Gintis, H. *Schooling in Capitalist America: Educational Reform and the Contradictions of Economic Life*. New York: Basic Books, 1976.

Children Now. *California Report Card 2004*. publications.childrennow.org/publications/invest/reportcard_2004.cfm, 2004.

Coleman, J. "Social Capital and the Creation of Human Capital." *American Journal of Sociology*, 1988, 94, S95–S120.

Coleman, J. S., and others. *Equality of Educational Opportunity*. Washington, D.C.: U.S. Government Printing Office, 1966.

Connell, R. W. *Masculinities: Knowledge, Power and Social Change*. Berkeley: University of California Press, 1995.

Currie, E. *Confronting Crime: An American Challenge*. New York: Pantheon Books, 1985.

Danzinger, S., and Gottschalk, P. *Uneven Tides: Rising Inequality in America*. New York: Russell Sage Foundation, 1993.

Davidson, A. L. *Making and Molding Identity in Schools: Student Narratives on Race, Gender, and Academic Engagement*. Albany, N.Y.: SUNY Press, 1996.

Dewey, J. *The School and Society*. Chicago: University of Chicago Press, 1995. (Originally published in 1900)

Eckert, P. *Jocks and Burnouts: Social Categories and Identity in the High School*. New York: Teachers College Press, 1989.

Elmore, R., Abelmann, C. H., and Fuhrman, S. H. "The New Accountability in State Education Reform: From Process to Performance." In H. F. Ladd (ed.), *Holding Schools Accountable: Performance-Based Reform in Education*. Washington, D.C.: Brookings Institution, 1996.

Epstein, J. "A Response." *Teachers College Record*, 1993, *94*, 710–717.

Epstein, J. L., and Hollifield, J. H. "Title I and School-Family-Community Partnerships: Using Research to Realize the Potential." *Journal of Education for Students Placed at Risk*, 1996, *1*(3), 263–278.

Erickson, F. "Transformation and School Success: The Politics and Culture of Educational Achievement." *Anthropology and Education Quarterly*, 1987, *18*(4), 335–356.

Farkas, G. "The Black-White Test Score Gap." *Contexts*, Apr. 1, 2004, pp. 12–19.

Ferguson, A. A. *Bad Boys: Public Schools in the Making of Black Masculinity*. Ann Arbor: University of Michigan Press, 2000.

Fine, M. "(Ap)parent Involvement: Reflections on Parents, Power and Urban Schools." *Teachers College Record*, 1993, *94*(4), 26–43.

Fine, M., Weis, L., Pruitt, L. P., and Burns, A. *Off White: Readings in Power, Privilege, and Resistance*. New York: Routledge, 1997.

Finley, M.K.V. "Teachers and Tracking in a Comprehensive High School." *Sociology of Education*, 1984, *57*, 233–243.

Fordham, S. *Blacked Out: Dilemmas of Race, Identity, and Success at Capital High*. Chicago: University of Chicago Press, 1996.

Gans, H. J. *People, Plans and Policies*. New York: Columbia University Press, 1993.

Gee, J. P., Hull, G. A., and Lankshear, C. *The New Work Order: Behind the Language of the New Capitalism*. Boulder, Colo.: Westview Press, 1996.

Goodman, W. "School Integration Falls Short of Ideal." *New York Times*, Oct. 17, 1994, p. A24.

Gordon, E. W., Bridglall, B. L., and Meroe, A. S. *Supplementary Education: The Hidden Curriculum of High Academic Achievement*. New York: Roman Littlefield, 2005.

Gordon, R., Piana, L. D., and Keleher, T. *Facing the Consequences: An Examination of Racial Discrimination in U.S. Public Schools*. Oakland, Calif.: Applied Research Center, 2000.

Greenhouse, L. "The Supreme Court: The Justices, Context and the Court." *New York Times*, June 25, 2003, p. A1.

Gregory, A., and Mosely, P. "The Discipline Gap: Teachers' Views on the Overrepresentation of African American Students in the Discipline System." *Equity and Excellence in Education*, 2004, *37*(1), 18–30.

Harklau, L. "'Jumping Tracks': How Language-Minority Students Negotiate Evaluations of Ability." *Anthropology and Education Quarterly*, 1994, *25*(3), 347–363.

Hilliard, A. *The Maroon Within Us: Selected Essays on African American Community Socialization*. Baltimore: Black Classic Press, 1995.

Holland, A., and Thomas, A. "Participation in Extracurricular Activities in Secondary School: What Is Known, What Needs to Be Known." *Review of Educational Research*, 1987, *57*(4), 437–466.

Jencks, C., and Phillips, M. *The Black-White Test Score Gap*. Washington, D.C.: Brookings Institution, 1998.

Kirp, D. L. *Just Schools: The Idea of Racial Equality in American Education*. Berkeley: University of California Press, 1982.

Kohn, A. "Only for My Kid: How Privileged Parents Undermine School Reform." *Phi Delta Kappan*, 1998, *79*(8), 569–577.

Ladson-Billings, G. *The Dreamkeepers: Successful Teachers of African American Children*. San Francisco: Jossey-Bass, 1994.

Lareau, A. *Home Advantage: Social Class and Parental Intervention in Elementary Education*. Bristol, Pa.: Falmer Press, 1989.

Lareau, A. "Social Class and the Daily Lives of Children: A Study from the United States." *Childhood*, 2000, *7*(2), 155–171.

Lee, S. J. *Unraveling the "Model Minority" Stereotype: Listening to Asian American Youth*. New York: Teachers College Press, 1996.

Lemann, N. *The Big Test: The Secret History of the American Meritocracy*. New York: Farrar, Straus, and Giroux, 1999.

Lucas, S. R. *Tracking Inequality: Stratification and Mobility in American High Schools*. New York: Teachers College Press, 1999.

Lucas, T., Henze, R., and Donato, R. "Promoting the Success of Latino Language-Minority Students: An Exploratory Study of Six High Schools." *Harvard Educational Review*, 1990, *60*(3), 315–340.

Maran, M. *Class Dismissed: A Year in the Life of an American High School: A Glimpse into the Heart of a Nation*. New York: St. Martin's Press, 2000.

Mays, J. "Parents Urge Action on Achievement Gap." *Berkeley Daily Planet*, Jan. 19, 2001.

McCready, L. T. "Queerying the Marginalization of Black Male Students in an Urban High School." Unpublished doctoral dissertation, University of California, Berkeley, 2002.

McDonald, J. P. *Teaching: Making Sense of an Uncertain Craft*. New York: Teachers College Press, 1992.

Mehan, H., Hubbard, L., and Villanueva, I. "Forming Academic Identities: Accommodation Without Assimilation Among Involuntary Minorities." *Anthropology and Education Quarterly*, 1994, *25*(2), 91–117.

Miller, S. L. *An American Imperative: Accelerating Minority Educational Advancement*. New Haven, Conn.: Yale University Press, 1995.

Moran, D., McCready, L., and Okahara, A. "Mesosystemic Reflections on the Reproduction of Racial Inequality at Berkeley High School." Paper presented at the Annual Meeting of the American Educational Research Association, New Orleans, La., Apr. 2000.

Mosely, P. M. "The Gap in Black: How Black Teachers Experience Racial Disparity in Student Achievement." Unpublished doctoral dissertation, University of California, Berkeley, 2003.

Moses, R. P., and Cobb, C. E., Jr. "Quality Education Is a Civil Rights Issue." *Harvard Education Letter*, 2001.

Nathan, H., and Scott, S. (eds.). *Experiment and Change in Berkeley*. Berkeley, Calif.: Institute of Governmental Studies, 1978.

National Coalition of Advocates for Students. *New Voices, Immigrant Voices in U.S. Public Schools*. Boston: National Coalition of Advocates for Students, 1988.

Noguera, P. A. "Ties That Bind, Forces That Divide: Berkeley High School and the Challenge of Integration." *University of San Francisco Law Review*, 1995, *29*(3), 719–740.

Noguera, P. A. "The Role of Research in Challenging Racial Inequality in Education: An Analysis of a School/Community Based Effort to Reform an Integrated Urban Public High School." Paper presented at the annual meeting of the American Educational Research Association, Montreal, Canada, Apr. 1999.

Noguera, P. A. *City Schools and the American Dream*. New York: Teachers College Press, 2003.

Nygreen, K. "Educating for Democracy and Democratizing Research: Critical Pedagogy and Consciousness at an Urban Alternative High School." Unpublished doctoral dissertation, University of California, Berkeley, 2005.

Oakes, J. *Keeping Track: How Schools Structure Inequality*. New Haven, Conn.: Yale University Press, 1985.

Oakes, J., Wells, A. S., Jones, M., and Datnow, A. "Detracking: The Social Construction of Ability, Cultural Politics, and Resistance to Reform." *Teachers College Record*, 1997, 98(3), 482–510.

Olsen, L. *Made in America: Immigrant Students in Our Public Schools*. New York: New Press, 1997.

Olsen, L. "Learning English and Learning America: Immigrants in the Center of a Storm." *Theory into Practice*, 2000, 39(4), 196–202.

Orfield, G., and Eaton, S. E. *Dismantling Desegregation: The Quiet Reversal of Brown v. Board of Education*. New York: New Press, 1996.

Orfield, G., and Kurlaender, M. *Diversity Challenged: Evidence on the Impact of Affirmative Action*. Cambridge, Mass.: Harvard Education Publishing Group, 2001.

Parents of Children of African Descent. "A Proposal: Plan for Action on Behalf of Underachieving Students in the Berkeley Unified School District." Berkeley, Calif.: Parents of Children of African Descent, Jan. 4, 2001.

Perry, T., Steele, C., and Hilliard, A. G. III. *Young, Gifted, and Black: Promoting High Achievement Among African American Students*. Boston: Beacon Press, 2004.

Phelan, P., Davidson, A. L., and Yu, H. C. *Adolescents' Worlds: Negotiating Family, Peers, and School*. New York: Teachers College Press, 1998.

Platt, A. "'The Triumph of Benevolence': The Origins of the Juvenile Justice System in the United States." In R. Quinney (ed.), *Criminal Justice in America: A Critical Understanding*. Boston: Little, Brown, 1974.

Powell, A. G., Farrar, E., and Cohen, D. K. *The Shopping Mall High School: Winners and Losers in the Educational Marketplace*. Boston: Houghton Mifflin, 1985.

Rothstein, R. *Class and Schools: Using Social, Economic and Educational Reform to Close the Black-White Achievement Gap*. New York: Teachers College Press, 2004.

Sadker, M., and Sadker, D. *Failing at Fairness: How Our Schools Cheat Girls*. New York: Touchstone Press, 1994.

Shirley, D. *Community Organizing for Urban School Reform*. Austin: University of Texas Press, 1997.

Silva, E. "The Broken Mic: Student Voice in Urban School Reform." Unpublished doctoral dissertation, University of California, Berkeley, 2002.

Skolnick, J. H., and Dilulio, J. J., Jr. "Wild Pitch: 'Three Strikes and You're Out' and Other Bad Calls on Crime." In J. H. Skolnick and E. Currie (eds.), *Crisis in America's Institutions*. (11th ed.) Needham Heights, Mass.: Allyn & Bacon, 2000.

Stanton-Salazar, R. "A Social Capital Framework for Understanding the Socialization of Racial Minority Children and Youths." *Harvard Educational Review*, 1997, 67(1), 1–40.

Stanton-Salazar, R. D. *Manufacturing Hope and Despair: The School and Kin Support Networks of Mexican American Youth*. New York: Teachers College Press, 2001.

Talbert, J. *Teacher Tracking: Exacerbating Inequalities in the High School*. Stanford, Calif.: Center for the Research on the Context of Secondary Teaching, Stanford University, 1990.

University of California Office of the President. *1998–99 U.C. Reference Guide for Counselors*. Oakland: University of California Office of the President, 1998.

Valdés, G. *Con Respeto: Bridging the Distances Between Culturally Diverse Families and Schools: An Ethnographic Portrait*. New York: Teachers College Press, 1996.

Valenzuela, A. *Subtractive Schooling: U.S.-Mexican Youth and the Politics of Caring*. Albany, N.Y.: SUNY Press, 1999.

Wacquant, L. "Negative Social Capital: State Breakdown and Social Destitution in America's Urban Core." *Netherlands Journal of Housing and the Built Environment*, 1998, *13*(1), 25–40.

Wells, A. S., and Oakes, J. "Potential Pitfalls of Systemic Reform: Early Lessons from Research on Detracking." *Sociology of Education*, 1996, 135–143.

Wells, A. S., and Serna, I. "The Politics of Culture: Understanding Local Political Resistance to Detracking in Racially Mixed Schools." *Harvard Educational Review*, 1996, *66*(1), 93–118.

Willis, P. E. *Learning to Labor: How Working Class Kids Get Working Class Jobs*. New York: Columbia University Press, 1981.

Wilson, W. J. *The Truly Disadvantaged: The Inner City, the Underclass, and Public Policy*. Chicago: University of Chicago Press, 1989.

Wing, J. Y. "An Uneven Playing Field: Behind the Racial Disparities in Student Achievement at an Integrated Urban High School." Unpublished doctoral dissertation, University of California, Berkeley, 2002.

Wing, J. Y. "Closing the Racial Achievement Gap in Diverse California High Schools." Los Angeles: UC ACCORD, 2003.

Wolters, R. *The Burden of Brown: Thirty Years of School Desegregation*. Knoxville: University of Tennessee Press, 1984.

Index

The Trouble With Black Boys

And Other Reflections on Race, Equity, and the Future of Public Education

By: **PEDRO A. NOGUERA**

ISBN 978-0-7879-8874-6
Hardcover | 352 pp.

"Pedro Noguera has provided here an accessible account of the role race plays in the continuing disenfranchisement of students of color. These essays challenge educators to look at what we <u>can</u> do in schools rather than focus on factors out of our control. Once again Pedro Noguera has cut to the quick with his cogent analyses, research-based findings, and personal stories to change our minds and open our hearts to possibilities."
  –**Lisa Delpit**, executive director for the Center for Urban Education and Innovation, Florida International University

Race will continue to be a source of controversy and conflict in American society for many years to come. We cannot simply wish away the existence of race or racism, but we can take steps to lessen the ways in which the categories trap and confine us. *The Trouble With Black Boys* is a brutally honest—yet ultimately hopeful—book in which Pedro Noguera examines the many facets of race in schools and society and reveals what it will take to improve outcomes for all students.

One of the nation's most important voices on the subject of equity and social justice in education, Noguera examines the link between racial identity and school-related behavior, the significance of race in the racial achievement gap, and the educational future of Latino immigrants. He discusses the role of leaders in restoring public faith in education, recommends investing in the social capital of students and their parents, and ultimately proposes how to reclaim the promise of public education. From achievement gaps to immigration, Noguera offers a rich and compelling picture of a complex issue that affects all of us.

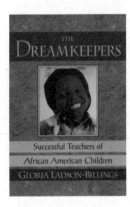

The Dreamkeepers

Successful Teachers of
African American Children

By: **GLORIA LADSON-BILLINGS**

ISBN 978-0-7879-0338-1
Paperback | 208 pp.

"Education, like electricity, needs a conduit, a teacher, through which to transmit its power— i.e., the discovery and continuity of information, knowledge, wisdom, experience, and culture. Through the stories and experiences of eight successful teacher-transmitters, **The Dreamkeepers** *keeps hope alive for educating young African Americans."*
  —**Reverend Jesse L. Jackson**, president and founder, National Rainbow Coalition

Quality education remains an elusive dream for most African American children. Historically, they have been denied schooling, subject to separate and unequal education, and forced into unsafe, unhealthy, substandard schools.

In *The Dreamkeepers*, Gloria Ladson-Billings explores the positive signs for the future. Who are the successful teachers of African American students? What do they do? And how can we learn from them? Written in three voices—that of an African American scholar and researcher, an African American teacher, and an African American parent and active community member, this book is a mixture of scholarship and storytelling. The author's portraits of eight exemplary teachers who differ in personal style and methods but share an approach to teaching that affirms and strengthens cultural identity are inspiring and full of hope.

Gloria Ladson-Billings is a professor of education at the University of Wisconsin, Madison. She has served on the faculties of Santa Clara University and Stanford University and spent over ten years working as a teacher and consultant in the Philadelphia public school system.

Powerful Learning
What We Know About Teaching for Understanding

By: **Linda Darling-Hammond, Brigid Barron, P. David Pearson, Alan H. Schoenfeld, Elizabeth K. Stage, Timothy D. Zimmerman, Gina Cervetti, Jennifer Tilson**

Foreword by Milton Chen

ISBN 978-0-470-27667-9
Paperback | 288 pp.

What type of teaching produces *powerful learning*?

In *Powerful Learning*, bestselling author Linda Darling-Hammond and an impressive list of co-authors offer a clear, comprehensive, and engaging exploration of the most effective classroom practices. They describe what is known about effective teaching and learning in the areas of reading / literacy, mathematics, and science, and provide a practical review of teaching strategies that generate meaningful K–12 student understanding both within the classroom walls and beyond. Rich stories, as well as online videos of innovative classrooms and schools, show how students who are taught well are able to think critically, employ flexible problem-solving, and apply learned skills and knowledge to new situations.

Sponsored by the **George Lucas Education Foundation** (GLEF), a nonprofit foundation dedicated to gathering and disseminating information on K-12 teaching and learning in the Digital Age.

Linda Darling-Hammond is the Charles E. Ducommon Professor of Education at Stanford University, where she serves as co-director of the School Redesign Network and the Stanford Education Leadership Institute. Among her nearly 300 publications are the award-winning books *The Right to Learn, Teaching as the Learning Profession, Preparing Teachers for a Changing World,* and *Powerful Teacher Education.*

Learning from Latino Teachers

By: **GILDA L. OCHOA**

ISBN 978-0-7879-8777-0
Hardcover | 288 pp.

"By having Latina/o teachers' perspectives at the center of this book, Ochoa offers a distinct view on the current state of education. This book is a must read for everyone who is in or cares about education and the future of this country."
—**Alicia Velazquez**, Early Academic Outreach Program at the University of California, Riverside

After decades of struggle, inequalities in schools for Latina/o students persist. They attend more segregated schools than they did thirty years ago, they are vastly underrepresented in honors and advanced placement courses, and over forty percent do not complete high school.

Learning from Latino Teachers offers insightful stories and powerful visions in the movement for equitable schools. Based on Gilda Ochoa's in-depth interviews with Latina/o teachers who have a range of teaching experience in schools with significant Latina/o immigrant populations, this book offers a unique insider's perspective on the educational challenges facing Latinas/os. The teachers' stories provide valuable insights gained from their experiences — coming up through the K-12 system as students and then becoming part of the same system as teachers.

In addition to the interviews with teachers, the book includes the voices of students, family members, and other school officials. The narratives and strategies for changes found in *Learning from Latino Teachers* provoke introspection, reflection, and action that will speak to all those who have questioned our current educational system.

Gilda L. Ochoa is associate professor of sociology and Chicana/o studies at Pomona College, where she teaches courses on education, Latinas/os in the United States, and the sociology of race/ethnicity, class, and gender.

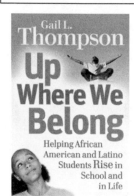

Up Where We Belong

Helping African American and Latino Students Rise in School and in Life

By: **GAIL L. THOMPSON**

ISBN 978-0-7879-9597-3
Hardcover | 352 pp.

"Gail Thompson is an important voice in the struggle to achieve equal educational outcomes for children of color. Her passionate commitment to our children and families springs forth from these pages. This book is filled with valuable information and solutions. It is 'must reading' for all educators."

—**Janice E. Hale**, professor of early childhood education, Wayne State University; author, *Learning While Black*

What will it take to get all students—even the most disenfranchised—engaged in school and motivated to learn and achieve?

In *Up Where We Belong*, Gail Thompson used information from candid questionnaires and focus groups to discover a huge gap in perception between how teachers and students view their school experience. The book explores this disparity, and uncovers some of the reasons for students' low achievement, apathy, and frustration. Most important, she offers vital lessons for transforming schools—especially for underachieving kids and students of color.

Throughout the book Thompson passionately discusses the controversial aspects of race relations in school. From the negative perception of black boys to well-meaning but misguided attempts to honor diversity through ethnic history activities, Thompson shows how every little thing matters. While this may sound alarming at first, it also means that all teachers, parents, and school leaders have it within their power to improve student achievement by reflecting on their own perceptions and developing practices and policies that really motivate students to connect with learning.

Gail L. Thompson is associate professor of education at Claremont Graduate University and a respected speaker, workshop presenter, and consultant. Her research has focused on beliefs and perceptions about African-American students. She is the author of *Through Ebony Eyes: What Teachers Need to Know But Are Afraid to Ask About African American Students* and *What African American Parents Want to Know.*

Change Leadership

A Practical Guide to Transforming Our Schools

By: TONY WAGNER,
ROBERT KEGAN, LISA LASKOW LAHEY,
RICHARD W. LEMONS, JUDE GARNIER,
DEBORAH HELSING, ANNIE HOWELL,
HARRIETTE THURBER RASMUSSEN

Foreword by Tom Vander Ark

ISBN 978-0-7879-7755-9
Paperback | 296 pp.

"Change Leadership is a truly wonderful and brilliant book. The ideas are powerful, deep, comprehensive, and grounded with tools to turn them into transformative action. A rare book that captures both the awful difficulty of causing change and a way to do it."

—**Michael Fullan**, former dean, Ontario Institute for Studies in Education, University of Toronto; author, *Leading in a Culture of Change*

The Change Leadership Group at the Harvard School of Education has, through its work with educators, developed a thoughtful approach to the transformation of schools in the face of increasing demands for accountability.

Modeled after the Harvard Change Leadership Group's nationally acclaimed "learning gyms," *Change Leadership* is a vital resource that pulls together the best of the information available on organizational and individual transformation and provides a personal training regime for change leaders. This book provides a framework to analyze the task of school change along with exercises, concepts, and tools that guide educators through their role as agents of much-needed system-wide change in schools.

Tony Wagner is co-director of the Change Leadership Group (CLG) at the Harvard Graduate School of Education. He is also Education Chair of the Harvard Seminar on Redesigning American High Schools. He consults widely with schools, districts, and foundations around the country and internationally and is Senior Advisor to the Bill & Melinda Gates Foundation. Wagner is the author of *Making the Grade* and *How Schools Change*.